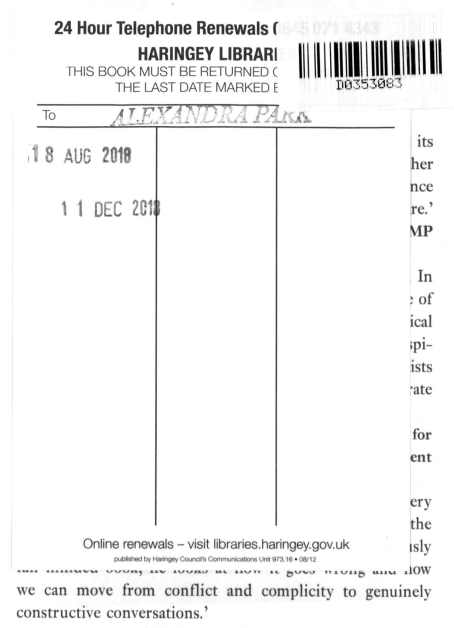
its
her
nce
re.'
MP

In
e of
ical
spi-
ists
rate

for
ent

ery
the
usly

...............minded book, he looks at how it goes wrong and how
we can move from conflict and complicity to genuinely
constructive conversations.'

Nick Spencer, Research Director at Theos

'Without doubt, we need a better conversation about faith in
public life. This clear and accessible book provides an engaging
account of some of the key issues. I recommend it warmly.'

**Grace Davie, Professor Emeritus in the Sociology of
Religion at the University of Exeter, UK**

'Both Christians and Atheists are often guilty of wilfully misunderstanding each other. Krish Kandiah's brilliant book urges both sides to begin a proper conversation. His insightful analysis of the way we caricature each other is combined with a grace-filled approach to seeing the best in each other.'

Justin Brierley, Presenter of Premier Christian Radio's 'Unbelievable?' radio show and podcast

'With humour, humility, and charity, Krish Kandiah calls us to a better conversation around faith and unbelief. Our society desperately needs such a conversation, and this book might provoke it. I pray and hope that it is widely and seriously read.'

Dr Steve Holmes, Senior Lecturer in Systematic Theology, University of St Andrews UK

'Krish offers a set of lenses that helps us all see more clearly how to negotiate our way in a complex, faith-shaped world with wisdom and grace. Thoughtfully and provocatively, he invites us to consider commonly held beliefs around Christianity and Atheism through a framework that will help us in our relationships, serve the common good, and protect religious liberty.'

Tracy Cotterell, Managing Director, London Institute for Contemporary Christianity

'This book is a welcome contribution to the challenging of preconceptions and stereotypes on both sides of the argument. In essence, it teaches us to look for the best in those with whom we disagree, and the world needs to take that on board today more than ever.'

The Rev'd Canon Dr James Walters, Chaplain & Senior Lecturer in Practice, Director of the LSE Faith Centre

'Can we really value what others value? Krish thinks so, and encourages us to be generous in our understanding of people who believe differently to ourselves. This book is a welcome challenge to complacency on all sides.'

Katie Harrison, ComRes Faith Research Centre

'A great antidote to the current tide of opinion that religion is to blame for the world's ills. I like the thesis that Christians and Atheists have more in common than they realise. We should dream as Luther King did that a day will come when we are at peace.'

Rt Hon. Caroline Spelman MP

'The author of this remarkable book was born into an affectionate family whose religion was Hinduism, but he converted to Christianity. This experience has given him an urge to help our society to develop a way of discussing differences in what we hold to be true in a way that is respectful to one another and encourages freedom of speech.'

Lord Mackay of Clashfern

'Faith and religious literacy really matter in all areas of public life. Krish very helpfully lays out why this matters for all people, regardless of their particular faith (or no faith). The whole book is grounded in actual experience working at every level of society. Required reading now for all engaging in developing a better public life together.'

Bishop Paul Butler, Bishop of Durham

'*Faitheism* demonstrates what happens when those with deep differences don't talk at each other or past each other, but rather to each other. A winsome model in Christian civility.'

Dr Dan Strange, College Director, Oak Hill College

'At a time of great ignorance about religious faith, can those with and without faith still live harmoniously together? This illuminating and readable book tries to promote communication and mutual understanding, instead of blank hostility.'

Professor Roger Trigg, Senior Research Fellow,
Ian Ramsey Centre, University of Oxford

'*Faitheism* is both serious and lively, and deeply and movingly personal. My first thought was to recommend it for students, but then I realised the rest of us could also profit from reading it. Do so!'

Michael Ruse, Professor of Philosophy,
Florida State University

'Dr Kandiah tries to prod us into radical commitments toward acting out our Christianity for the greater good.'

Jerry Pattengale, Professor at
Indiana Wesleyan University

'We need to find a way to live together properly, not alongside each other in uncomfortable suspicion. I hope this book makes both sides think very deeply and realise, as they turn the pages, that they are not in fact different sides, but neighbours.'

Isabel Hardman, Assistant Editor, *The Spectator*

FAITHEISM

**Why Christians and Atheists
have more in common than
you think**

KRISH KANDIAH

HODDER &
STOUGHTON

First published in Great Britain in 2018 by Hodder & Stoughton
An Hachette UK company

1

A CIP catalogue record for this title is available from the British Library

ISBN 978 1 473 64894 4
eBook ISBN 978 1 473 64895 1

Typeset by Palimpsest Book Production Limited, Falkirk, Stirlingshire
Printed and bound in Great Britain by Clays Ltd, Elcograf S.p.A.

Hodder & Stoughton policy is to use papers that are natural,
renewable and recyclable products and made from wood grown in
sustainable forests. The logging and manufacturing processes are expected
to conform to the environmental regulations of the country of origin.

Contents

Introduction

It ended with a vial of poison, a dagger and two young people lying dead. Four hundred years later, the tragic conclusion of *Romeo and Juliet* cast its cautionary shadow over two more young people. Two people, also from very different backgrounds, yet helplessly in love.

My fiancée and I had found a quiet spot in Shakespeare's hometown where we could sit by the river, watch the swans glide past, and plan our future life together as husband and wife. Naturally, we wanted a happier ending than the bard had offered.

Our conversation that day worked through our differences one by one. My family were immigrants from Asia; hers could trace their British ancestry back through the generations to the resettlement of the French Huguenots in the seventeenth century. Mine were nominal Hindu; hers were committed Christians. I had grown up in a bustling liberal city in the south of England; my in-laws-to-be lived in a sleepy mid-shire village. Said in-laws both had postgraduate qualifications and earned their salaries in education; my parents were paid weekly – often in cash. And then there was the fact that I was brown – and she was white.

Some family members warned us very clearly that our relationship would never work. Were they right? Or could we prove them wrong, overcome the differences and build a marriage that would last? We began to dig down into the questions they had raised, and many more of our own. Before we left Stratford that day we stopped by a second-hand bookshop and bought a small dusty hardback copy of Shakespeare's most tragic of tales. Twenty-some years of marriage later our little red copy of *Romeo and Juliet* still stands on our bookshelf to remind us of those questions, that conversation, and our resolve to make the relationship work even when we didn't have all the answers.

As the curtain falls on the final and heart-rending scene of *Romeo and Juliet*, the audience are left thinking: 'What if . . .?' What if Juliet had been better at communicating her plan of faked death? What if Romeo had spent more time making sure he understood the plan? What if they had been able to talk things through with their parents? What if the enmity between these two great families could have been resolved sooner? What if, instead of focusing on their differences, people had recognised what they had in common? What if their common attributes – same language, same age, same hometown, same economic backgrounds, same skin tone – united them rather than differentiated them? What if conflict and tragedy could be avoided and the misunderstandings and miscommunications that generate them could be resolved?

It is this last question that has given this tale of two star-crossed lovers resonance way beyond the time of Shakespeare and the city limits of Verona. *Romeo and Juliet*, despite its tragic storyline, has been Shakespeare's most popular play for centuries because we all know a little of the terrible cost of conflict. We all have people in our lives who live and think in very different ways to us. We all experience something of the pain and damage misunderstandings cause us and those we love. The relational breakdown is painful at a micro scale. But our world is also reaping the whirlwind of relational breakdown at a macro scale. When we look at the overall picture of global conflict, we have to ask ourselves: *what if there is a better way to handle our differences?*

Recently I have watched two politicians, from different ends of the political spectrum, being told on a national television news broadcast that their faith was not acceptable in public life. The interviewer forcibly suggested that what they believed about God and the world should be kept personal and private, as those beliefs would negatively influence their ability to govern fairly. Imagine someone telling a politician that their skin colour, their gender or their sexual orientation might negatively influence their ability to do their jobs. Thank goodness that our culture now recognises such assertions for the prejudice and ignorance they are. But when it comes to issues of faith, we often do not recognise the biases that still exist. It is time to figure out how to become a genuinely inclusive society on all fronts – including that related to faith or no-faith.

Faith and Atheism[1] seem diametrically opposed to one another; they are definitely not what anyone would call a match made in heaven. Like the fictional Capulet–Montague feud, there is a whole history and heritage of conflict, misunderstanding and even violence between devotees of the two groups, as well as a trail of victims left in their wake. Believers and Atheists are not supposed to get on. And yet, in marriages and homes and streets and workplaces and communities across the world, there are those from both camps who are avidly trying to build deep and meaningful relationships across the divide. Maybe it is time to sit down by the river, metaphorically speaking, and talk through our differences openly and constructively. Might it be possible to raise the questions, and seek out ways to build positive and strong relationships with those around us? Could honest and authentic conversation lead to us not only believing the best about each other, but also believing the best for ourselves?

But what if you identify with neither group? Think about the audience at a *Romeo and Juliet* play. None of them are Capulets or Montagues. However, despite not belonging to either house, they are drawn into the story, they identify with the protagonists, understand something of the conflict, feel something of the pain, and empathise with Romeo and Juliet as they seek reconciliation. Similarly, those of us reluctant to be identified with Christians or Atheists are not excluded from the conversation. In fact, you may have a unique perspective to bring to the table.

According to the Pew Research Center,[2] one of the fastest-growing religious group in the world are called 'nones'. They are the second-largest 'religious group' in North America and much of Europe. They are a diverse collection of people, that includes agnostics and Atheists as well as those who have an eclectic mix of spiritual and religious beliefs but don't identify with any particular faith group. They are caught in the middle of the public war of words between Christians and Atheists. If this group describes you, then this book may help you not only to understand the viewpoints of the committed Christians and Atheists in your personal and professional life but also to uncover how their worldviews are intrinsically linked to your own.

There is perhaps an opportunity here, not only to forge a new relationship with those we have traditionally been in conflict with, not only to check our beliefs and values through rigorous field-testing, but also to achieve something even more significant. In the past twenty years there have been huge leaps forward in the way society regards people of different race. There has also been huge progress in the gender-equality debate. What if now we can apply the lessons we have learned in accepting and valuing those of differing cultures to those coming from very different faith positions?

In our divided world, how can those with and without faith and everyone in between learn to get along? More than that, how can we live well together? In our 'faitheist' world, significantly shaped by both the spiritual and the secular, is there, in fact, more that unites us than divides us? Can we not only make peace with each other, but also help make peace for each other? Can we discover principles that could help people with all sorts of different beliefs and values find a way to relate and live well together?

Maybe you are an Atheist and you have a colleague at work who is a Christian. Or vice versa. Although officially you both speak the same language, perhaps you have noticed that you seem to talk at cross-purposes on a whole range of issues. Offhand comments and opinions pique or rile you. What if these differences could make your relationship not more awkward, but more authentic? What if these differences, instead of making your workplace less friendly and less productive, could actually enhance your working environment and bring better collaboration? What if these differences could strengthen instead of undermine your own beliefs?

Maybe you are a Christian and your spouse is an Atheist. Or vice versa. You love each other deeply but you avoid talking about anything faith-related because it always seems to stir up controversy. So a vital part of your life and identity and values goes unshared between the two of you. What if there is a way not only to acknowledge these differences, but also to enjoy robust discussion, find meaningful common ground and strengthen the relationship? What if more authentic discussion can produce a more authentic faith and a more authentic marriage, and even a more authentic home that truly is welcoming to all?

Maybe you are uncertain. Perhaps you consider yourself spiritual but not religious, or you are simply undecided. You know Christians and you know Atheists, but you are unwilling to join either camp. The war of words between committed Christians and ardent Atheists puts you off getting involved. You may feel you have found the sweet spot, or you may feel you are wandering aimlessly around a dangerous no man's land. So, what if there is peace to be made, or truth to be found, or common ground to own?

Aiming to be accessible to all, *Faitheism* assumes little or no understanding of either Christianity or Atheism. This book is organised into short chapters that demonstrate a simple method of communication and understanding relating to some crucial areas of life together. By tackling head on the traditional areas of greatest conflict, we can see most clearly the advantages of a new conversation for everyone. The skills and principles that are explored in these ten chapters are applicable in a myriad of complex and contentious issues that are beyond the scope of this book.

The Conversation Matrix

Faitheism is based on the best thinking in the new area of 'faith literacy', a field that is helping to build bridges in an age of increasing polarisation in society. In an engaging manner, this book will challenge us to find a deeper understanding of our own worldview, build better relationships and create more productive collaborations with people who do not share our view of life, faith and the universe.

I have spent a lot of my time in professional and public discourse facilitating and mediating conversations between Atheists and Christians and people of other faiths, and find that time and again I come across similar challenges and controversies. *Faitheism* offers a framework for secular and sacred interaction that is much needed at a time of great political, economic, and cultural division and confusion in the world.

As a member of the Standing Committee for Religion and Ethics at the BBC, I have witnessed the struggle broadcasters face as they seek to represent the breadth of society – trying to offer programmes with religious content, but without offending people who claim no or different religious affiliations.

In my work with social workers, I have seen that although they recognise that people from faith communities often make very motivated, committed and supported carers, they also need to safeguard children against any form of proselytisation, radicalisation or other forms of spiritual abuse.

I have worked with journalists who, despite no formal faith training, face the challenge on a daily basis of sensitively covering global news stories involving people from faith contexts.

I have worked with teachers who are struggling to teach about faith as part of the National Curriculum to an increasingly diverse cohort of students.

I have worked with aid and development charities who are faced with the challenge of seeking to help lift some of the world's poorest people out of poverty and yet wanting to honour and respect their religious backgrounds, values and dignity.

I have worked with the Home Office as the charity I founded seeks to provide carers for thousands of unaccompanied refugee children who are fleeing religious persecution and violence, and whose beliefs need to be protected once they come to the UK.

Many politicians face conflicting pressures from those who are suspicious of faith and the harm it could do, and those who are motivated by their faith to do good and build a caring society.

I work with medical professionals who frequently come across a huge range of practical, social and ethical dilemmas when it comes to treating people of different faiths.

In the consultation and facilitation I have led around faith, conflict and literacy, it is clear that a new framework is needed to enable professionals across the board to promote constructive collaboration and defuse situations that could otherwise escalate into significant conflict. But help is just as badly needed for many of us in our everyday lives.

Our family regularly welcomes foster children from Muslim, Hindu, Christian and Atheist backgrounds into our home, and we are often faced with the personal challenge of how to make each one of them feel welcome, and how to take seriously all of their needs, whether emotional, physical, social, cultural – or spiritual.

Those of us who offer comfort to a grieving relative or who discuss current affairs across the garden fence may well benefit from thinking through some of the personal, relational and cultural challenges and benefits of faith literacy.

Couples who span the Atheist–Christian divide may benefit from richer and healthier communication.

Facing up to this challenge could help us appreciate the life-choices our children or grandchildren may be making.

Faith literacy will help us when, in our book club debates or amid our running group banter, questions of life, the universe and everything suddenly catch us off guard.

It will help us keep the courage of our convictions without losing our friends – or our jobs – in the process.

Equality and diversity training is important, but it is not

without difficulty when it comes to faith. For that matter, both halves of the term 'faith literacy' are disputed. Most obviously, for some the term 'faith' relates to irrational and unjustified belief, while for others it means warranted, committed belief. Faith, for some, means a low-level thing, to do with tradition and cultural family background, while for others it represents a 24/7 devotion that impacts on everything they do. For some, the word 'faith' represents a radical cause to unite behind and effect positive change in society; for others, it is inseparable from radicalisation that brings aggression and violence that seeks to damage society. We will look at the nature and origins of personal belief commitments more closely in Chapter 1, and the outworkings of those commitments in subsequent chapters. For now, it is worth noting that even using the term faith can be provocative and misleading.

But not only is the term 'faith' contested, the term 'literacy' also carries a spectrum of inference. Literacy relates primarily to the ability to read or write, but in recent years the term has come to take on a wider remit. When we speak of 'computer literacy', 'media literacy' or 'political literacy', we mean the ability to understand, interpret and act competently within these differing spheres of understanding. For example, we all recognise the information revolution that has taken place since the invention of the Internet. While I would not expect someone who was deemed computer literate to know everything about everything when it comes to this information revolution, I would expect a certain level of competency in using electronics: managing communication between different devices, or recognising and understanding messages on different social media platforms. We live in a world where the majority of the population adhere to or affiliate with some form of religion. We live in a culture where faith has played a pivotal role in shaping our art, literature, music, laws and politics. Being faith literate does not mean knowing every chapter of the Bible and every *sura* of the Qur'an, but it does mean being able to recognise the ways that faith impacts the people we interact with day to day and being aware of when our own beliefs and assumptions might prejudice the way we relate to them.

When I was at school, it was normal for me to be called 'Paki' or to be told to 'go back home'. I got used to being asked if my mother had left me out in the sun for too long or forgotten to get the shower fixed. Although this kind of language was normal both inside the classroom and outside on the school playground and football pitch, I cannot remember a single occasion when a teacher intervened. One teacher told me in front of the whole class that the reason I was so bad at swimming was because I was brown. No teacher would get away with that nowadays: racially offensive language and prejudice is taken very seriously in our schools today. What happened? How did this change take place? We became aware of our racial bias, we became race literate. Something of the same revolution needs to take place when it comes to our understanding of faith and Atheism.

I have had the opportunity to help a wide range of medical professionals, academics and social workers work through these issues, and have developed a model that can be broadly helpful as a starting point.

The model I have called the 'Conversation Matrix' recognises that understanding of others relies fundamentally on good communication. This goes back to the Romeo and Juliet dilemma: if only they had been able to communicate better what they were doing (and why and when and how), the tragedy could have been averted. In today's world our conversation is more multi-modal than ever. The means and the media of communication are increasing, with different modes of etiquette in different environments and platforms; and the complexities of social diversity add an extra dimension. Good communication across contextual divides is vital. When it comes to conversations between those who believe and those who don't, this matrix can help us see where traditionally we have gone wrong and where, potentially, we can change and improve the way we interact.

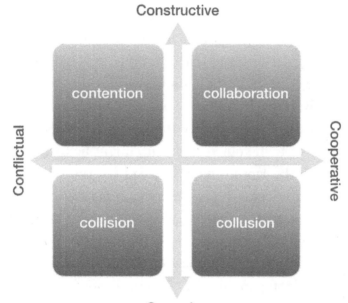

The four quadrants in the diagram above offer four different modes of conversation: collision, collusion, contention and collaboration. When it comes to interaction between Christians and Atheists, there are plenty of examples of all four of the above modes in historical and contemporary practice, as we will see. As we determine to find ways to improve our conversations, each chapter will demonstrate ways to move them towards the constructive and cooperative ends of the scale. I am not suggesting that there is no room for conflict, as I believe that occasionally conflict can be useful. But when conflict has been the predominant basis of interaction between Christians and Atheists, it is surely time to shift our focus onto alternative, mutually enriching models of conversation.

Let me use an everyday example of how the quadrants of this Conversation Matrix can help us analyse interactions. Imagine I discover my teenage son has broken the laptop I bought him for his birthday. I am sure you can picture the scene. I accuse him of being negligent or clumsy or of downloading risky software. He claims it is not his fault and accuses me of jumping to conclusions. I begin pressing buttons in a bid to reboot it. He tells me I am making the problem worse and he will sort it out himself. This is *collision*. Our conversation is terse and difficult. Our relationship, like the laptop, is broken.

One way of fixing our relationship might be to avoid talking about fixing the laptop ourselves, and instead to think of an alternative way forward. If we were to report the laptop to the insurance company as stolen, then eventually the computer could be replaced at minimal cost. This is *collusion*. The relationship is more important than anything else, and the problem – the broken laptop in this case – can be dealt with in a dishonest or dismissive way in order to protect that relationship.

Another member of the family refuses to let us compromise our integrity on this occasion and challenges us to sit down again and talk about fixing the laptop. We want to find a solution but our ideas are very different. I want to phone a friend. My son wants to consult YouTube. I want to restore it to factory settings. He wants to rewire the motherboard. Although we have very different approaches, there is at least a basic agreement that there could be a way forward that would result in fixing the laptop, even though it remains broken for the time being. This is *contention*. We present our disagreements and opinions, perhaps even quite forcibly, while still protecting some level of the relationship by listening to the options and working towards an agreed common goal.

The optimum way forward, *collaboration*, is when we put all our ideas on the table without recourse to fighting, and slowly and systematically work together until we find and agree on a solution. After a few days, with various phone-calls and lots of googling, not to mention a trip to the local hardware store and considerable perseverance, we have a result. The laptop is fully functioning again. Not only that: my relationship with my son has been strengthened as we have spent time problem-solving in a constructive, meaningful way. We look back and laugh together at the mistakes we made and the blows we almost came to. And we celebrate our achievement all the more, because of the time and effort that went into it.

This simple example can help us see how there are choices in the ways we communicate that can lead to radically different outcomes. We cannot assume there is no difference between Christian and Atheist approaches to life. But we do not have to stop being true to our core convictions in order to find a way to talk and work together. There will be times when we will collide, but collision does not have to be the end of the story.

Instead of a broken laptop, imagine the problem to hand is a nuisance neighbour who needs dealing with, a funeral that needs planning, a vote that needs casting, a child that needs disciplining, a complex ethical decision that needs making. In each case the Christian and the Atheist viewpoints could be set to collide. I am not suggesting those involved sit down and contemplate the four quadrants before they proceed. This framework is not supposed to constrain or in any way manip-ulate conversation. However, an awareness of alternative approaches to interaction may enable us to better engage with people we know and love. It can help us to check our own standpoint more honestly, relate to one another more deeply, and work together more constructively.

Before we look at some examples of how these interactions could work in practice, using some provocative examples, there are seven core assumptions that I want to flag up before we begin.

1. It is worth trying to move from conflict to cooperation in our conversations

Life is complicated enough without unnecessary conflict. Most of us long for better relationships – at work and at home. I have worked in contexts where there is unresolved conflict, and it is toxic not just to personal well-being, but to productivity as well. Many of us will know the pain of conflict in family relationships. Our national news is full of events that arise from political and socio-economic conflicts. On a global scale many people are quick to blame religion as the cause of war and conflict, but, as we will see, this may be to misunderstand how religion functions, as well as the role of secular ideologies. If we can find ways to promote cooperation we have a better chance of resolving misunderstanding and conflict, and making the world we live in a better place.

2. It is worth trying to be more constructive and less corrosive in our conversations

Facing such pressing issues as global poverty, climate change, the AIDS epidemic and the refugee crisis, corrosive attitudes like cynicism, criticism and complaint are a luxury for the self-absorbed. These attitudes rarely lead to activism. In fact, they usually exacerbate the problem. They instil guilt and resentment, and make solutions hard to find, and even harder genuinely to work towards.

Sometimes we need to acknowledge when corrosive attitudes have brought unconscious bias into our perceptions, conversations and dealings with others. So many of the problems in our world could be resolved if only we were able to swallow our criticisms and complaints and choose to be more constructive in our conversations. One thing this book is not going to provide is knockdown arguments for or against Christianity or Atheism – but it will seek to blow up some of the prejudices and caricatures on both sides that prevent constructive conversations from taking place.

3. Neither Atheism nor Christianity are going away

The global Christian population is on the increase. According to the best study of its kind, somewhere in the region of 2.4 billion people claim some kind of Christian allegiance, making it by far and away the world's largest faith, claiming over 30 per cent of the global population.[3] According to the same study,[4] there are around 136.4 million Atheists in the world, which is about 1.8 per cent of the global population. This dataset counts as Atheists those who specifically marked it on the relevant survey.

Meanwhile, other studies in North America and Western Europe have revealed a growing number of what sociologists are calling 'Nones'[5] – those who tick the 'none' box in surveys and polls about religion – many (though of course not all) of whom would also identify as Atheist, but who may resist the very idea of religion as a worthy area of self-definition. The millennial generation are particularly highly represented among the Nones in the West, and some countries claim that up to 25 per cent of their population should be counted collectively as Agnostic, Atheist or 'None'. An Agnostic refers to someone who neither believes nor disbelieves in the existence of God – practically and etymologically this is the 'Don't Know' category. The term Atheism, though, derives from the Greek, in which 'a' means without and 'theos' means god. Michael Martin, editor of *The Cambridge Companion to Atheism*, goes on to distinguish between two types of Atheism: positive Atheism, which refers to someone who believes that there is no God or gods, while negative Atheism refers to those who do not have a belief in God, effectively the Nones.[6] For the purpose of this book we will generally use broad definitions for both Christians and Atheists, although at times we may need to differentiate groups within the sectors.

Although their global number is relatively small, Atheists have a significant influence on the global media, and in academia internationally. Rather than seeking to deny either the prevalence or significance of Atheism or Atheists, it is important for Christians to recognise and respect them as a growing group with high levels of influence. Similarly, it is important for Atheists to recognise the global and growing Christian population.[7] Irrespective of the numbers, Christians and Atheists are both often considered minority groups in the UK, and so it is important not only to acknowledge both groups, but also to protect freedom of speech and conscience and religious liberties in the two communities.

4. We are better together but we don't have to pretend to be the same

There are many wonderful benefits of living in a pluralist and multicultural society. It is one of the defining features of a modern democracy that as a society we make space for people with different views, customs, languages and beliefs. Indeed, a commitment to protecting the human rights of all members of society irrespective of race, gender, sexuality and religion is a fundamental building block of progressive thought. Most of my friends and colleagues, Atheist and Christian alike, hold these values in high regard.

Hence, I believe that finding a meaningful way for Christians and Atheists to do more than just tolerate each other's existence but find positive ways to live, love and work together is vital for the flourishing of our society. Nonetheless, the differences between Christians and Atheists cannot be ignored. The very fact that Christians define themselves as followers of Jesus Christ, whom they believe to be God, while Atheists assert that a core part of their identity is centred upon the non-existence of God, makes it hard to imagine two more diametrically opposed positions. Yet it is my contention that most Atheists and most Christians have more areas of shared vision and values than one might expect. Christians would understand this to come from what theologians call 'common grace', while Atheists may articulate this in terms of a shared humanity. Either way, despite our differences, there is much to commend a society where both groups can be valued and work constructively together.

5. Atheists and Christians alike have a rationale to work at mutual respect and understanding

Many Atheists express their values in terms of humanism – a belief in the dignity and value of all human beings.[8] Christians also believe in the dignity and value of all human beings, based on their belief that each person is made in the image of God. For both Atheists and Christians, these different rationales establish common core values which provide a robust justification for freedom of religion, freedom of conscience and mutual respect, care and tolerance. Sadly, just as it is true that it is easy to point to examples of Atheists who have lived in ways diametrically opposed to these humanist ideals, it is also easy to find examples of so-called Christians who have failed to live consistently with their beliefs about the universality of the image of God in our fellow human beings. But, as we shall see, exceptions do not prove the rule. Following the train of thought of both humanistic Atheism and confessional Christianity leads to a well-grounded expectation that both groups should have strong motivation to work at more constructive and cooperative approaches to engagement with one another.

6. Atheists and Christians have the right and freedom to convert

Respecting the twin values of freedom of conscience and freedom of religion means that both Christians and Atheists can allow the other the right to hold firmly to the convictions they choose and also acknowledge that a change of convictions is permissible. Within robust and respectful conversation between two people of opposing views, there is always the chance that an argument can conclude in the realisation that one's own views may be misplaced. If there is no room for conversion then there is no true freedom of religion: the ability to change beliefs is included in the very notion of freedom. Therefore, in a free society, it must be acceptable for Atheists to become Christians, and for Christians to become Atheists. In fact, one could argue that 'conversions' should be seen as an indicator of a free and cosmopolitan society. Freedom of religion and of conscience cannot mean avoiding conversation on core beliefs, as this would deprive the other person of the ability to make an informed decision based on the totality of the evidence available. Respecting our freedom, however, means that conversation rather than compulsion allows the space and choice to change.

7. We always seek to believe the best

The conviction that all human persons are worthy of dignity and respect, coupled with the conviction that freedom to make an informed decision results from conversation on issues of core beliefs, leads to what I hold to be the central core of all conversation – 'believing the best'. Believing the best *for ourselves* means that we remain humble and teachable in our personal search for the truth. Believing the best *about another* means we continue to treat others with respect, whatever their beliefs, opinions and reasoning. Believing the best about a *subject of conversation* means there is freedom given to both sides to search out the most coherent, relevant and trustworthy belief system, based on evidence, values and other considerations. There may be persuasion, but never pressure. There may be mission, but never manipulation. There may be conversation, but never compulsion. There may be disagreement, but never disrespect.

In a bid to genuinely and meaningfully understand our own views as well as those held by our colleagues and spouses, our neighbours and friends, we will tackle some difficult subjects in this book. Each chapter will begin by myth-busting, taking on a commonly held stereotype of the Christian/Atheist debate. As is so often the case, the stereotypes are far from the whole truth. We will have to undo false premises and expose corrosive attitudes on both sides of the debate. As we deconstruct the hostilities and challenge unhelpful preconceptions, we can begin to work towards finding constructive ways forward – personally, relationally and culturally – over issues as diverse as morality and mortality, sexuality and science, ethics, charity and the supernatural.

Wherever you are starting from, would you come with me as we seek a more collaborative 'Faitheism' approach? Two particular memories come to my mind as we move forward.

The first is when, as an undergraduate student and the leader of a large and active Christian student group on campus, I became increasingly convinced that an essential part of my faith should include showing the compassion of God to those who are most in need in the world. My unlikely ally in this regard was an Atheist friend whose strong commitment to social change overrode any qualms he may have had about publicly associating with me and the Christian student group. We teamed up and ran a campaign on campus that included an Amnesty International letter-writing programme, a Christian ethical clothing initiative and a boycott of some UK banks that had, at the time, distinctly unethical practices. We were united in a common cause, and I will never forget walking side by side, rolling an eight-foot-high inflatable globe around campus for the sake of that cause, the two of us wearing T-shirts with messages that flatly contradicted each other.

Second, a few years later, as a new homeowner eager to meet my new neighbours, I remember knocking on a door only to be greeted by a rebuff. My smile, my introductory greeting and my offer of a coffee all fell flat. The guy next door looked at me with outright suspicion. And, to be fair, that caution was not necessarily misplaced. After all, it is true I was secretly hoping the guy would welcome me in with open arms and ask for my help in discovering the meaning of life. A few weeks later, though, my car was playing up, and as I poked around optimistically under the bonnet with a spanner, who should wander over but the world's most unfriendly neighbour, toolbox in hand. In five years of living next door to the guy, we never had one face-to-face conversation. But through side-by-side collaboration over various projects, we forged a strong friendship where anything could be discussed. We later became dads within weeks of each other – and as we parented our daughters together, we both had our perceptions about the meaning of life subtly changed.

That inflatable globe and the misfiring engine taught me a lesson that lies at the heart of this book: diverse core values, deep conversation and dynamic collaboration – whichever order they come in – can ultimately bring harmony, and when they do, there is so much to be gained.

Chapter 1

Christians are weird / Atheists are normal

Collision

The homeless man shuffled back a few centimetres into the shop doorway as it began to rain, but he was soon disturbed by a passer-by who asked if he could point him in the direction of Burger King. The passer-by had just come out of a long business meeting, and was taken a little by surprise when the homeless guy left all his worldly possessions right there and accompanied him to the eatery in question. The two men chatted as they walked, and when they arrived at Burger King, the businessman bought dinner for both of them. They were there for about an hour, talking and waiting for the rain to stop. During conversation, the businessman happened to mention that he didn't believe in God. The homeless man's response took him by surprise: 'You are much too nice to be an Atheist.'

A public servant explained to me that they had a problem with recruitment. The issue was that there were a lot of Christians who showed an interest in joining the caring professions, but not so many Atheists. 'It's a shame,' she explained, 'because we don't have a problem with Atheists. Christians, however, are socially deviant and so we "red flag" them in the review process.' Just a week earlier I had been at a Westminster event where a similar sentiment was expressed. A professional psychologist commented that if a patient mentioned God during a counselling session, this could very well result in a referral for psychiatric assessment. My Chemistry professor had warned me about this twenty years before. He believed that faith and science could not mix, and so when he overheard me talking about church in a long laboratory session, he turned to me and said: 'You are much too smart to be a Christian.'

There was a time, not so long ago, when it was socially deviant to be an Atheist, and socially acceptable to be a Christian. There was a time when Christians were deemed to be the smart ones, and Atheists were considered to be in need of a head examination. But there has been a switch, just in the past couple of decades. There is now a new normal and a new weird.

This switch has happened before. There have been huge shifts in public opinion towards and against Christianity and Atheism over the centuries. Strangely enough, the first Christians were described as Atheists. That was the label given to them because they rejected the traditional gods of the time. They didn't have any physical images of God, and they didn't have any temples. This led the Christian thinker Justin Martyr to write in the early second century:

We admit that in respect of such supposed gods as those (i.e. the gods of ancient Greece and Rome) we are atheists: but not in regard to the most true God, the Father of righteousness and moderation and the other virtues, the God who is without a trace of evil. Him we worship and adore, and his Son, who came from him and taught us of these things . . . These we worship with reason and truth.[1]

Christianity started as a minority faith, whose claims that Jesus was the long-awaited Messiah that Judaism predicted, were not only rejected by the Jewish authorities, but were also anathema to the Roman ruling power that had invaded Israel at the time.

Christians gained a public reputation for vice and immorality. They were accused of cannibalism because they had been over-heard talking about 'eating the body of Christ' when they took part in Holy Communion, when bread is eaten to represent and celebrate God's love shown in allowing Jesus to die for the sins of the world. Christians were also accused of sexual devi-ancy because they referred to other members of the Church as 'brothers and sisters', and husbands and wives were misun-derstood to be incestuously related.

Christianity was also seen as politically seditious, as it was believed to challenge the rule of the Roman Empire, and it upset the influence of the Jewish ruling elites. That was why Christians were beheaded, crucified, and savaged by wild beasts as entertainment at the Colosseum. Famously, the Emperor Nero blamed Christians for a fire in Rome in AD 64, and if this was when a new phase of persecution started, it only ended with the passing of the Edict of Milan in AD 313, which allowed for the toleration of Christianity. About a hundred years after that edict, under the reign of Emperor Theodosius I, Christianity became the official religion of the Roman Empire, and other religions and pagan practices were suppressed. It seems that what had been a persecuted minority then became complicit in a new persecution, paving the way for Christianity to remain the dominant religion in the Western world for over one a half thousand years.

Atheism, too, has a mixed history. During ancient times philosophers such as Plato argued that Atheism was inherently dangerous, because it undermined the God-ordained rule of the monarch.[2] Plato, in his writing on law, was very vocal in his opposition to Atheism, believing it was a cause of vice and immorality.[3] Much later, in the thirteenth century, Thomas Aquinas argued for the inherent immorality of Atheists because they were seen to have no moral framework, and therefore, he said, were dangerous to society as a result.[4] Then, in the eighteenth century, the philosopher Thomas More described a utopia in which religious tolerance would extend to all residents except those who 'did not believe in God or the immortality of the soul'.[5]

One of the most infamous instances of legal discrimination against an Atheist in the UK was in the nineteenth century when Charles Bradlaugh, one of the founders of the National Secular Society, was excluded from the British Parliament for refusing to swear allegiance on the Bible. He was forcibly expelled from the House numerous times, fined for voting illegally, and once even imprisoned in the Tower of London. Eventually, after he was re-elected for the fourth time, the Speaker of the House agreed to offer him his right to affirm, rather than swear allegiance on the Bible.

Up until recently, it has been far easier in terms of social acceptability to call oneself a Christian than an Atheist. The legal system, the educational system, the political system, the social holidays and community or parish life all catered predominantly for those who went to church on Sundays and conformed to religiously derived social norms.

But times are changing, and it is far more acceptable now to be an Atheist than perhaps ever before. It would certainly – and rightly – create a constitutional crisis if someone were to be expelled from Parliament for being an Atheist today. Yet, recently, a Christian Member of Parliament famously felt discriminated against because of his faith. Liberal Democrat leader Tim Farron expressed in his resignation speech his experience as a practising Christian in public life:

> The consequences of the focus on my faith is that I have found myself torn between living as a faithful Christian and serving as a political leader . . . To be a political leader – especially of a progressive, liberal party in 2017 – and to live as a committed Christian, to hold faithfully to the Bible's teaching, has felt impossible for me.[6]

Farron here reacted – in pretty polite terms – to social pressure against his beliefs that would have been unheard of a generation or two ago. Although there remains a large degree of Christian privilege in the West, due to the religious freedoms built into the law in Western democracies, and although we know very little of persecution compared to the abuses that are taking place under military dictatorships and other unjust regimes elsewhere in the world, there is nevertheless a developing undercurrent of suspicion, even antagonism, towards Christians. In politics, media and our social system, there appears to be what we might call 'unconscious' or 'implicit' bias when it comes to relating with faith groups in general, and Christians in particular.

Most people recognise the existence of bias in their lives. For example, socially we tend to find it easier to associate with people who are similar to us in age, interests, culture and background. We have come to expect a degree of bias in our news sources, as media outlets often betray their political allegiances in their reporting. We have always had bias in our political system, where an unusually high percentage of our political class have been educated in exclusive schools and at elite universities. Sadly, we must recognise that elitism, racism, sexism, favouritism – and the spin that goes with them – are still a part of our society.

Over recent years, though, there has been a growing awareness that not all of our biases are explicit or conscious. Unconscious bias describes the negative associations we hold, which, even though they are outside of our awareness, have a significant influence on our outlook and actions. Some argue that unconscious bias is far more prevalent than conscious prejudice, and, strangely, it can often be the opposite of our conscious values. In other words, people who consider themselves fair, equitable and kind may nevertheless respond in a negative way at a gut level to other people because of differences in ethnicity, sexuality, gender or ability. Indeed, according to the wide body of literature in this area we can sometimes show bias even to groups that we identify ourselves with. It has been noted, for example, that highly regarded female academics may discriminate against their female colleagues. This could come out in a lack of public acknowledgement for their work, or more subtly, in whether or not they recommend them for awards or promotions.[7]

The implicit associations we have can be very difficult to override, even when we come to recognise them to be wrong, as they are so deeply woven into our psyche.[8] Christians are beginning to recognise both conscious and unconscious bias against them, but it was not that long ago that the shoe was on the other foot. Atheists have long been seen as socially deviant, and in some contexts this is still the case. For example, it is illegal to be an Atheist in some Islamic countries, and even in Western cultures, Atheists argue they can still feel marginalised and excluded. There remain seven states in America whose constitutions include a religious test, which would, in theory, prohibit Atheists from taking public office.

Despite our so-called progressive and tolerant society, sadly there are still many areas of public life where there is an implicit bias against all sorts of people, including those from ethnic minorities, women, couples who don't have children, people from working-class backgrounds, people with disabilities, those from the LGBT community, as well as those who call themselves Christians, Atheists, secularists, humanists or agnostics.

At school I was called sambo, nig nog, Paki and wog. I knew I had a lot of nationalities covered in my ethnic make-up, but never once did anyone manage to correctly identify my Malaysian-Indian-Sri Lankan-Irish ancestry. I was also, even as a child, mildly aware of the difference between conscious bias and unconscious bias. While other kids' parents were kind to me in the playground, they stopped short of inviting me to their children's parties. I often wondered if my dad was laid off work because of his skin colour or if my mum was given the most demeaning tasks to perform at work because of her ethnicity. Although my neighbours freely accepted us, enjoyed our hospitality, and reciprocated generously, nonetheless I sometimes overheard anti-immigrant rhetoric. If they realised, they may have said something like 'Present company excluded', or 'But you're different – we know you.' What sounded like – and was meant as – a compliment, still grated against me, even from a young age, because of an irreconcilable sense of the hypocrisy shown.

On one occasion a friend's dad took me to London to a computer fair. It was a much-appreciated gesture for a computer-mad twelve-year-old, and I had a fantastic day with his son, discovering all the latest gadgetry. But at the end of the day I got too close to a car speeding through the car park, and my bag full of freebies brushed the car's door. The driver slammed on his brakes, got out of his car and began shouting racist abuse at me. As I looked to my friend's father to rescue me from this mad-eyed stranger, he walked away, saying he didn't know me. He would have claimed not to be racist, there was plenty of evidence (not least my being there that day) to show that he wasn't racist, and yet his decision not to stand up for me betrayed an underlying collusion with racist attitudes that perhaps he was unaware of himself. It was a long and silent journey home.

I am personally grateful for the huge steps forward Western societies have made to recognise xenophobic and racist language and attitudes, although there is still a long way to go in tackling bias and prejudice in all its forms. In recent years most business and public sector environments have invested in specific training to help challenge both conscious and unconscious bias in the areas of race, gender and sexuality. But implicit bias due to someone's faith background has not been widely studied or challenged. It would seem to be the next logical extension of the quest for equality, especially as faith is already in theory a protected category according to the Equalities Act. Public services and authorities are legally required to 'eliminate discrimination, harassment, victimisation'. They are also supposed to 'advance equality of opportunity between persons who share a relevant protected characteristic' and to 'foster good relations between persons who share a relevant protected characteristic and persons who do not share it'.[9]

In other words, neither Christians nor Atheists are supposed to be discriminated against. And yet, both groups can put a case forward for feeling marginalised – and often they point the finger at one another.

On the training days I run for public servants I ask delegates what they associate with three different groups of people. The first is 'Christian', the second 'Muslim' and the third 'Atheist'.

Everyone in the room is university educated. Everyone has been through a rigorous selection process, and they have all received extensive training on inclusion and diversity. Nevertheless, group feedback shows that the overwhelming majority of the words associated with Christians are negative: 'Bible-basher', 'intolerant', 'bigot', 'homophobic' are just a few. Sadly, the words associated with Muslims are worse: 'jihadi', 'terrorist', 'suicide bomber'. The words associated with Atheists as a group were far more positive: 'discerning', 'thoughtful' and 'rational'. This is by no means a scientific study at this stage, just the fruit of a substantial number of workshops. But from these in-practice experiences and from anecdotal evidence, the prevailing climate has changed. Atheism is becoming more socially acceptable, respectable and even aspirational. Christianity, on the other hand, is increasingly understood to be socially deviant and suspect. There has been a switch. Christians are the new weird. Atheists are the new normal.

Collusion

Despite the implicit bias that many Atheists have towards Christians and Christians have towards Atheists, there is more collusion going on when it comes to Christianity and Atheism than you might think. Let me put it provocatively:

> Many Atheists live like Christians, yet they claim not to believe in God.
>   Many Christians live like Atheists, yet they claim to believe in God.[10]

There is often a disconnect between confession and behaviour, from both sides of the fence, that may well have something to do with unconscious bias, association and social acceptance.

Perhaps you have seen the political surveys that come up on social media platforms, where you are led through a number of questions exploring your views on particular policies and then told which party you have most affinity with. Despite their upbringing and heritage and even personal identification with a particular party, many people's views end up being closer in practice to a party that they would never have considered voting for. It can be similar for our ideological views. Whatever we may call ourselves, whatever we may say we believe or don't believe, a broader or deeper survey of our life values may throw up some interesting conclusions. Some Atheists live lives that are more consistent with the moral and ideological framework provided by the Christian faith than with their own atheistic assumptions. Some people who call themselves Christians will actually have more in common with Atheists than they may like to think, and may live more consistently with Atheist convictions than with Christian beliefs. We shall see this illustrated on several occasions during the course of this book.

At one level this crossover is understandable. If you grew up in London and then moved to Lagos as a teenager, you might still speak with an English accent, even in your forties. Similarly, there is no doubt that Western civilisations have been shaped and formed significantly by the Christian faith. Theo Hobson argues that many of the most treasured aspects of secular humanism owe their origins to the impact of Christianity on the moral imagination of the West.[11] So, as Western cultures transition from a majority Christian population to one where confessing Christians are in a minority, it is not surprising that there is a time lag in the transition from one moral framework to another. This would account for some Atheists having subconsciously adopted a Christian-based moral outlook.

Equally, because the cultural artefacts that are being generated by contemporary Western media, such as movies, popular music, news reports and advertisements, have a predominantly secular humanist outlook, it is not surprising that Christians who are immersed in this culture may subconsciously adhere to an atheistic mindset.

This mingling of mindsets can be both beneficial and beguiling. Because Christians and Atheists occupy the same cultural space, watch the same movies, read the same books, follow the same evening news, listen to the same radio stations and inherit so many common cultural assumptions through the shared stories we tell about history and life, there are many cultural bridges. These allow us to converse, get along well with one another on the day-to-day level, which is all very beneficial to a cohesive society. Even without realising it, we end up borrowing from and blending with each other's belief systems. As human beings, we beg, borrow and steal from all sorts of sources as we seek to make sense of the world. This is beguiling, in good and bad ways. Our minds synthesise the different threads of information that we are exposed to. Often at a subconscious level we try to knit together ideas, impressions, emotions and images that we are exposed to through our senses, our imagination, our families, our media consumption and our personal history. It becomes very difficult to extract one thread from another. Those who self-identify as Christians and Atheists often take a more conscious approach to their core beliefs. Both Christians and Atheists are likely to attempt to be consistent in what they say they believe about the world, and how they live. For those of us who call ourselves Christians or Atheists, our beliefs are an essential part of our identity – that should be self-evident, by the fact that we want to be known as such. And so when, in the name of human rights and tolerance,

Christians are told not to bring their beliefs into work, it is not unlike being invited into your own home and told not to join in the family meal. The idea of a tolerant, welcoming public space is one that owes its origin story to values promoted over the centuries by Christianity, so to then exclude Christians from participating in that society is particularly vexing for them. Similarly, when Christians try to encourage others to consider converting to their faith, but live according to the same principles as their Atheist neighbours, the suggestion of moral superiority is galling for Atheists. It can feel to the Atheist like someone borrowing your lawnmower and then trying to get you to buy it back off them when they are done with it.

Most of the time the collusion of blended worldviews effectively allows Christians and Atheists to live together fine. But there are serious limitations, and when we come up against those limitations, the flimsy bridges we have built cannot stand the pressure. The sharing of ideas between Christians and Atheists may sound positive, but what if it is less like sharing, and more like plagiarism? When put to the test, those views and values that we have copied from our philosophical counterpoints just don't add up.

Contention

Despite the collusion between many Christians and Atheists in borrowing from each other without recognition or attribution; despite the collision in perception due to both conscious and unconscious bias against one another; there is still a place for a gracious yet robust form of contention. In fact, it is precisely because of the collusion – the complexity and the improvised nature of the relationship – that this contention is so urgently required in our nation.

Some Atheists argue, as we will see in Chapter 2, that Atheism is not a philosophy or a position or even a belief system. Because Atheism is based on fact, they might say, there is no inbuilt prejudice or rhetoric or unconscious bias. For many Atheists, they may feel that there is no axe to grind, no alternative agenda, no undertow of opinion, no ulterior motive when they speak about the basis or importance or future of Atheism. In other words: Atheism is right and normal. Christianity is not.

There are some important things to recognise in this attitude. First, even if we can argue that Atheism has only one tenet, namely that 'God does not exist', this is still a propositional statement about the nature and make-up of the universe. It is a metaphysical statement, as it makes an overarching declaration about the entire physical universe. It is a speculative and theo-retical statement, as there is no definitive proof that God does not exist. In other words, it cannot be demonstrated to be objective or 'based on fact', and we must acknowledge at least the possibility of personal bias in the declaration. More about this in the next chapter.

Second, most things we assert or believe about the universe are connected to other beliefs. Imagine I told you that I believe that the *Apollo* astronauts had never truly landed on the moon. You naturally respond to that statement with, 'Why do you believe that?' How I answer your question will betray the frame-work that I am using to approach the world. I could reply that I believe all history is illusory and that our lives are being played out a little like that of Truman Burbank's from the movie *The Truman Show*. Or I could reply that I have been abducted by aliens and taken to the moon and it is really made of cheese, so the astronauts must have landed on another rock in the galaxy by mistake. Or I could reply that the event was fabricated as propaganda to assert the superiority of the USA to the Soviet

Union. Whichever answer I give, you can pretty soon begin to pin down the conceptual, political and moral framework I am using to interpret the world we live in.

In the same way, to believe in God or not to believe in God is not a single isolated belief that can be easily extracted from every other belief we have. When we amend our outlook on the world, either by removing or adding our belief in God, it is more like removing or adding a colour from a photo. If you have ever used digital editing software on a computer, you know that it is possible to alter the colour palette that makes up a photo. If you remove blue from the picture, this does not just affect the blue parts of the image like the sky; it has a knock-on effect on every other colour in the photograph. The whole image takes on a vastly different hue. In the same way, adding or removing God from our view of the world has a number of knock-on consequences. As the writer and Oxford academic C.S. Lewis famously put it, 'I believe in Christianity as I believe that the Sun has risen: not only because I see it, but because by it I see everything else.'[12] The Christian faith informs everything that Christians see and do in the world.

Imagine two identical houses. They stand side by side in the street. One day a storm lashes through the town and one of the houses crumbles into a pile of debris, while the other house comes through unscathed. It turns out that the foundations of the houses were quite different. One had a well-built solid foundation, and the other one did not. It may have just been a small difference, unnoticeable to anyone who walked past, but it was not an inconsequential difference. This illustration was told by Jesus to explain the impact that belief in God has on someone's life.[13] Christians and Atheists have foundationally different views about the world, views that are not inconsequential. Remove or replace the foundation and there will be huge knock-on consequences.

When it is asserted that Atheism is normal, and that faith should be removed or distanced from public life, it is not the simple request that it purports to be; instead, it is tantamount to asking Christians to remove the foundation of their life. Because Christians derive their understanding of meaning, purpose, morality, wisdom, hope and personal worth from their God-centred perspective, removing their faith turns their whole world upside down. What reason have they got now to get up in the morning, to strive to do their best at work, to be compassionate to those they relate to, to organise their priorities, to obey the law, to take care of their spouse and children?

Not only that, but when it is asserted that Atheism is normal and that faith should be removed from public life, then the foundations on which we have built those things that we treasure most about our society begin to crumble. Friedrich Nietzsche understood this point well when he wrote his famous, perhaps semi-autobiographical, parable of the madman who rushes into the town square enquiring after the whereabouts of God. The villagers explain that God is dead – together they have murdered him. But then the madman realises the wider implications:

But how did we do this? How could we drink up the sea? Who gave us the sponge to wipe away the entire horizon? What were we doing when we unchained this earth from its sun? Whither is it moving now? Whither are we moving? Away from all suns? Are we not plunging continually? Backward, sideward, forward, in all directions? Is there still any up or down? Are we not straying, as through an infinite nothing? Do we not feel the breath of empty space? Has it not become colder? Is not night continually closing in on us? Do we not need to light lanterns in the morning? Do we hear nothing as yet of the noise of the gravediggers who are burying God? Do we smell nothing as yet of the divine decomposition? Gods, too, decompose. God is dead. God remains dead. And we have killed him.[14]

In Nietzsche's poetic language he explores something of the borrowed intellectual, moral and spiritual capital that belief in the existence of God provides for us. He suggests that we have not yet faced up to the harsh realities of life after God as he continues his parable with the words:

'I have come too early,' he said then; 'my time is not yet. This tremendous event is still on its way, still wandering; it has not yet reached the ears of men. Lightning and thunder require time; the light of the stars requires time; deeds, though done, still require time to be seen and heard. This deed is still more distant from them than most distant stars – *and yet they have done it themselves.*'[15]

A century after Nietzsche's death, we are still only beginning to see the implications of what it means to live life as if God is dead. If we ever fully experience it, then perhaps we will be able to claim that Atheism is truly normal. Just as there is a time lag between moving to a new country and one's accent changing, so there is a time lag between the removal of the foundation and the collapse of the building. We have not yet fully realised what it means for Atheism to take centre-stage or the implications of the changes that are afoot.

If Atheism is – albeit slowly – becoming the new normal, then by extension, faith and, in our society, Christianity in particular, is becoming the new weird or abnormal. It is a strange and uncomfortable experience for us Christians in the West to be labelled as socially deviant. Of course, it is a label that is difficult for anyone to wear. Most of us have an inbuilt desire and drive to fit in, not stand out. A classic psychological experiment developed by Solomon Asch in the 1950s tested social conformity by asking participants which of three lines was the longest. The answer was obvious, and yet the first seven people consistently picked the wrong line. They were in on the whole ruse and chose the wrong answer to the question deliberately, having been instructed to do so. In the initial experiment, about a third of genuine participants followed the lead of the seven stooges and also gave the wrong answer. The power of conformity is very hard to resist: it makes you disbelieve your own eyes, doubt what you thought you knew to be true, put aside your own opinions and take on another's without question.[16] Whether Atheism or Christianity is the accepted norm, how many of us trust our independent thinking? This is a particular challenge facing Christians today. Will they continue to speak out for what they believe to be true when more and more voices are saying the opposite?

This is not a new challenge, however. Right from its inception, Christianity has involved seeing the world in a way that is radically different from the majority. Jesus' values and views caused conflict with the ruling majority back in the first century. Jesus spoke to women, when that was considered taboo. He welcomed the children, who were supposed to be neither seen nor heard. He included the excluded, touched the untouchables, criticised the religious leaders, preached repentance and forgiveness, challenged the political structures and social mores, and claimed an exclusive offer of eternal life.

Jesus was upfront not only about the fact that this style of counter-cultural living would be expected of his followers, but also about the difficulties it would involve. He said that being a Christian would be like living as sheep among wolves, would involve taking up one's cross – being socially excluded, persecuted, even killed. Christians were always supposed to be weird, strange, counter-cultural.

Writing in the second century, an early church leader explained what this looked like:

> They live in their own countries, but only as aliens. They have a share in everything as citizens, and endure everything as foreigners. Every foreign land is their fatherland, and yet for them every fatherland is a foreign land. They marry, like everyone else, and they beget children, but they do not cast out their offspring . . . They busy themselves on earth, but their citizenship is in heaven. They obey the established laws, but in their own lives they go far beyond what the laws require. They love all men, and by all men are persecuted. They are unknown, and still they are condemned; they are put to death, and yet they are brought to life. They are poor, and yet they make many rich; they are completely destitute, and yet they enjoy complete abundance. They are dishonoured, and in their very dishonour are glorified; they are defamed, and are vindicated. They are reviled, and yet they bless; when they are affronted, they still pay due respect. When they do good, they are punished as evildoers; undergoing punishment, they rejoice because they are brought to life.[17]

Something happened to Christianity when it became a mass cultural phenomenon. It lost something of its radical cutting edge. Compromises were made. Over time a thin veneer of

Christian observance became the norm in place of the radical generosity and courageous self-sacrifice that Jesus modelled. Christianity became a religion, rather than a movement of people driven by their relationship with God and intent on making a positive difference to the world. Counter-cultural Christians became cultural Christians, nominalism overtook radicalism, the weird became the normal. This is not to under-play the many positive contributions that the Christian worldview has made to Western civilisation – but it might not be such a bad thing if Christianity reclaimed its true identity as being socially deviant.

Even within the long era when cultural Christianity has arguably outweighed true faith as the predominant expression, there have been some notable exceptions of Christians who stood out from the crowd and spoke out against social norms. William Wilberforce is one example whose outspoken views against the transatlantic slave trade got him into so much trouble. During the Second World War, Dietrich Bonhoeffer refused to conform to the Nazi Party's strictures on the Church, speaking up valiantly against Hitler, and he was even involved in a plot to kill the Führer. He ended up imprisoned and executed for his faith. Corrie ten Boom was motivated by her Christian faith to hide Jews from the Nazis in her cellar. She was betrayed, imprisoned, bereaved of her sister in prison and yet still offered forgiveness to her captors and persecutors. Martin Luther King headed up the non-violent civil rights movement in the USA that fought for racial equality; he was a Baptist church minister whose Christian faith was the primary motivating force in his life. He led a mass movement of peaceful protest that refused to turn to violence despite brutal and deadly attacks from vigilantes and the police force. He too was killed for his stand. The list could go on. All of these examples are socially deviant Christians who challenged the norm: they stood up for justice, truth and equality against the tide of public opinion, driven by their faith.

According to the recruitment professional I met at the beginning of the chapter, all those people would fail the assessment process, simply for being too religious. They would have been sectioned or silenced in the name of the tolerant and inclusive society that Wilberforce, Bonhoeffer, King, and many others besides, fought for, and in some cases, ultimately gave their lives for.

Like so many, I became a user of Apple products not just because I believed they were better devices, but because there was an association of breaking with the norm. In fact, as I sit typing this sentence, I am wearing a black T-shirt I bought at the Apple Headquarters at 1 Infinite Loop, Cupertino, California. It has two words on the front: 'crazy one'. It's an allusion to Apple's wildly popular advertising campaign from 1997: 'Here's to the crazy ones. The misfits. The rebels. The troublemakers. The round pegs in the square holes. The ones who see things differently . . . [T]he people who are crazy enough to think they can change the world, are the ones who do.'[18] For Steve Jobs, there was something very attractive about being an outsider, a radical, an outlier. There are certainly many challenging things about being a social outsider, and yet for many it is an inspiration. Perhaps the time is right for Christianity to take on its original radical identity.

Collaboration

It has been a very long time since someone called me 'nig nog'. I have not been physically assaulted because of the colour of my skin since I left secondary school. As far as I can discern, I have not been treated differently in job interviews because I am brown. We may still have a long way to go in racial equality in the world, but I am grateful for how far we have come already. Many workplaces have equality training as part of their staff induction and ongoing staff development, and issues such as race, gender and sexuality are regularly part of those training sessions. This has changed businesses and organisations, not only in their policies and operating procedures but also in their conversations and relationships.

I have not been called a 'nig nog' recently, but I have been called a Bible-basher and a bigot. I have not been barred from meetings because of race, but I have been silenced because of my faith. I do not hear social workers naively trying to promote racially neutral or 'colour blind' environments, but I do still hear them suggesting that ideological neutrality is possible. I am often invited to speak on the radio about all sorts of contentious topics, but I am often not allowed to mention my charity work with unaccompanied refugees and children in the care system, either because it is politically sensitive or because the charity has religious connections.

It is time that our equality and diversity training included faith as well as race, gender and sexuality, in order to help expose the double standards that have emerged, and in order to promote relationships not by erasing differences, but by celebrating them. This pressing need for increased religious literacy in our multicultural society and globally connected world has not gone unnoticed by politicians.[19] For example, the All-Party Parliamentary Group for International Freedom of Religion has pointed to a lack of understanding and misconceptions of religion and belief among decision-makers working within the UK asylum system.[20] Another All-Party Group

report said: 'There is a high level of religious illiteracy which
has led to many situations where religious belief is misunder-
stood and subsequently restricted. This comes from a social
and cultural minimisation of Christianity in public life. Religious
illiteracy has led to legal restrictions on the way that faith can
be expressed. Recent changes have compelled Christians to
provide services that they had never previously offered and
which may be contrary to their beliefs.'[21, 22]

Our collaboration needs to begin by acknowledging the
growing gap in understanding between faith communities, the
Atheist community, and society as represented by public service
providers, central government, local authorities, media, schools
and businesses. Admitting that there is suspicion and exclusion
is a vital first step, providing a piece of common ground that
can pave the way for Atheists and Christians to be involved in
and served by the equality and diversity training that already
exists. Taking a closer look at some of the traditional areas of
conflict, as we will do in the rest of this book, is crucial to
see, understand and work through the very real differences
between us.

Race equality training has helped me to feel not only accepted
despite my Anglo-Indian-Sri Lankan-Malaysian heritage, but
also valued *for* that Anglo-Indian-Sri Lankan-Malaysian heritage.
Similar provision for faith literacy would enable both Christians
and Atheists – as well as those from other faith positions – to
feel accepted and valued in their diverse belief systems.

If we call this significant area of collaboration 'provision for
belief', where we recognise that our identity regarding our faith
position or core beliefs is a valuable aspect of our diverse culture
whether that is expressed as Christianity or Atheism, then we
could call a second significant area of collaboration 'suspension
of disbelief'.

When we visit our local cinema or read a novel on holiday, we have to accept that in order to enter and enjoy the imaginary worlds the author or director has made for us, there needs to be a degree of 'suspension of disbelief'. This involves a willingness to abstain from applying critique or logic for the period of engagement with the fiction in order to appreciate it for what it is. So when I watch a sci-fi film or read a fantasy novel, I don't reject it based on my understanding that I don't believe dragons exist or that it is technically impossible for spaceships to be launched with only five minutes' preparation time. Even though I fundamentally disagree with the assumptions on which the fiction is based, I can suspend my disbelief in order to appreciate other aspects of the story – the plotline, the themes or the overall message.

Now some Atheists argue that ideas such as ethics, purpose, meaning and rights are necessary fictions we have to assume in order to appreciate or manage life in our societies today. For example, the best-selling author and historian Yuval Noah Harari argues that we cooperate effectively with strangers because we believe in things like gods, nations, money and human rights. 'Yet none of these things exists outside the stories that people invent and tell one another. There are no gods in the universe, no nations, no money and no human rights . . . outside the common imagination of human beings.'[23]

Harari argues that it is fine for us to borrow ideas from one another – whether they are to do with economics, politics, compassion or human rights – because they are just temporal 'stories' with no ultimate meaning, just convenient conceits allowing there to be some level of community cohesion. This view allows Atheists to suspend disbelief about the Christian origins of values they would rather not live without. For example, someone who believes that evolutionary biology is sufficient justification for our existence might still be keen to borrow the concept of human equality. Some moral philosophers describe this as an anti-realist approach to ethics; namely, that there are no actual ethical laws or values, but we choose to accept those commonly held to make life more beautiful and fulfilling. (We will explore this further in Chapter 4.) Most Atheists would agree that a compassionate and peaceful universe is more attractive than a pitiless and indifferent one (see Chapter 8), so, according to Harari, it is acceptable to suspend disbelief in Christian faith in order to borrow that aspect of its worldview.

Atheists have often equated the Christian worldview to a fairy tale. For them, Christians seem to live in a fictional world framed by the belief in a God who does not really exist. However, and Harari admits as much, perhaps Atheists also can seem to live in a fairy-tale world when, because of intuition or socialisation, they create temporary fictions to allow them to live a meaningful life, albeit in a meaningless universe, adopting values they cannot find a reason for: right and wrong, compassion, generosity.

From this perspective it is not unreasonable to apply the same courtesy to each other that we would offer to a movie or book: the temporary suspension of disbelief, as we hear each other out.

I was invited onto BBC Radio 5 live for the morning drive-time show, to give a Christian response to Stephen Fry's outburst about God being 'mean-minded and capricious'. I had plenty to say. I wanted to sympathise with Fry's contempt for evil in the world. I wanted to question his basis for morality. I wanted to challenge his logic when it came to his view of God. I wanted to put forward a case for God being entirely the opposite of each of Fry's emotionally laden negative adjectives. But I did not have a chance to say any of those things.

The interviewer bombarded me with question after question, without giving any space for a response. Now, I can appreciate that perhaps he agreed with Fry and needed an outburst opportunity of his own. But his tactics were not going to win me or the audience over. He needed to model a willingness to suspend his own disbelief so that he could both ask the questions, and hear the answers.

Suspension of disbelief allows us the space to hear what others are saying, and gives us the opportunity to both empathise and engage with people we disagree with. By suspending disbelief, Atheists and Christians can work together. Whether faced with a personal crisis, a work project or a global or local tragedy, they will not always need first to debate the philosophical justification for compassion or diligence of action. Usually their responses will naturally cohere with the moral and ethical frameworks that we teach at school – kindness, patience, self-sacrifice, putting others first. When they do not cohere, suspension of disbelief allows them to walk in each other's shoes for a while, to see where they are coming from, and find ways to work together.

Provision for belief and the suspension of disbelief go hand in hand. We can value what the other holds to without feeling obliged to convert. We can converse over our different beliefs without resorting to cynicism and conflict. We can contend and collaborate instead of colluding and colliding. We can believe the best about one another without believing the same as one another. We can paint a picture of what each other believes without tarring everyone with the same brush. We can be provocative without being pejorative. We can be discursive without being dismissive. We can boldly hold up what we believe, while humbly allowing room for error or misjudgement.

But this is not the end of the story. The ultimate question

is not what is weird or normal; the question is whether there is a God or not. Eventually either the Atheists or the Christians will be proved right or wrong. What we believe or do not believe will one day be replaced with what is true or is not true.

If God does not exist then it probably does not matter if you live as an Atheist or a Christian, as weird or as normal. Of course, Christians may have wasted their time living for some moral ideal, and possibly had a harder life because of it.

If God does exist, then it definitely does matter if you decide to live as an Atheist or a Christian. If the Bible is true, then your choice to follow or reject God has implications for eternity.

Weighing up these two choices in this way reminds me of 'Pascal's Wager'. Born in 1623 in France, Blaise Pascal was a child prodigy and he went on to make huge contributions in mathematics, physics and philosophy. He conducted a correspondence with the mathematician Pierre de Fermat on how to solve the mathematical problems involved in gambling. One of Pascal's friends wanted to work out when was the best time to bet on a game of dice and wrote to Fermat about it. They worked on the numbers together and ended up laying the foundations of probability theory. Perhaps that is why, when considering the meaning of life and the possibility of eternal life, Pascal offered the following reason for choosing the Christian faith over Atheism: 'Let us weigh the gain and the loss in wagering that God is. Let us estimate these two chances. If you gain, you gain all; if you lose, you lose nothing.'[24]

I am careful throughout this book to indicate as clearly as I can that Christians are not intrinsically any better than Atheists. I also try my best, given my acknowledged bias, to give both Christianity and Atheism a fair and equal hearing. I attempt to give both Christians and Atheists much to think about concerning their own and the alternative worldview. In doing so I probably raise more questions than I offer answers. Although the main issue I address is how Christians and Atheists can believe the best about each other, I also have to challenge readers to consider what it means for you to believe the best for yourself. I want you to wrestle with the differences and work out which worldview best fits with your experience, with your hopes for the future, with your conscience and your common sense. Which one is best when it comes to reason and logic, and probability and potential gain? Which one is the best bet? Which one is true, and worth committing your life to?

Questions

Why have both Christianity and Atheism experienced times when they were socially deviant?

In which ways do you think that Christians and Atheists have borrowed from each other's approaches to the world?

How could the strategy of 'suspension of disbelief' help to build bridges between Christians and Atheists on contested issues?

How might Christianity benefit from embracing its socially deviant identity?

What challenges might Atheism face as it becomes the new normal?

Chapter 2

Christians are born /
Atheists are made

Collision

Over two billion people around the world profess to follow the teachings of a controversial Middle-Eastern man who lived and died over two millennia ago. He claimed not only to have personally created the entire universe, but also to hold the solution to the age-old problems of evil, suffering and death, and even to have prepared a never-ending, perfect afterlife for all who pledge allegiance to him. At the heart of these outrageous claims lies his assertion that he was not just a human man, but an all-powerful, all-present, all-knowing, all-loving eternal being, and indeed, the one and only true God. The vast majority of people who say they believe this extraordinary story are descended from other people who believe it. In other words, you could argue that most of those who call themselves Christians do so because of a prenatal lottery that has caused them to be born into a Christian family, community, country or empire.

Atheists, on the other hand, are a small, but rapidly growing, population who do not believe that there is a God at all, and definitely not one who walked on this planet as a Palestinian man two thousand years ago. This is not a decision they have come to lightly. They have looked at the cold hard accumulation of evidence, and through rigorous interrogation of data they have been able to free themselves from the confines of tradition, from emotional ties and from circumstantial evidence, and conclude objectively that God does not exist. They are thankful to have been able to break away from the indoctrination of religious beliefs pushed on them by parents, and from proselytising organisations who force-feed the myths and lies of religious dogma on impressionable children. Now they are on a quest to protect other vulnerable children from brainwashing. With no traditions, no habit-reinforcing institutions or ceremonies, Atheists, you could say, are brave, independent souls building their lives on the truth that is found in scientific and rational deduction alone.

These are the stereotypes that lead people to assume all Christians are born that way, while all Atheists have made their own way. But I know an awful lot of exceptions to the rule. Let me start with myself. I do not identify with either of these stereotypes. When my father named me Krishna, it was with the expectation that I would follow the Hindu gods he believed in. Although we lived in the UK, he took every opportunity to send me to the other side of the world to spend time with my Tamil Hindu relatives. He took me to Hindu temples to pray and to take part in traditional ceremonies. When I came of age, he offered to find me a Hindu wife. But, like many of my Atheist friends, I know what it means to break away from traditions impressed on me since birth, and to make a decision for myself based on the evidence I saw. Despite my heartache at letting my father down, I converted to what I had deduced to be the only logical path of truth: Christianity.

Professor Richard Dawkins was born into a family that called themselves Christian. He was baptised and then confirmed when he was thirteen years old, along with his peers at school. By the age of sixteen, however, he had converted to Atheism. Dawkins was for many years the University of Oxford's Professor for the Public Understanding of Science and is well known for his outspoken Atheist views and writings. In later life Dawkins has argued strongly that children should not be force-fed 'un-evidenced opinions about the nature of life or the cosmos'.[1] Perhaps this is a reflection of how he now feels about his own childhood upbringing.

At the other end of the spectrum, Professor Alister McGrath describes his earlier self as being an 'aggressive Atheist', influenced strongly by studying science at school at a time when Marxist ideals were popular and when scientists who were Christian appeared to be few and far between. But it was through an investigation of the history and philosophy of science and his studies in Chemistry at Wadham College, Oxford, that he converted to Christianity. McGrath now holds the Andreas Idreos Professorship of Science and Religion at the University of Oxford and writes prolifically on the subject of faith and science. Reflecting on his own conversion, he writes that he 'began to realize that atheism was a faith position – in other words, something you believe, not something you can prove. And I began to realize that it wasn't even a very good faith position. Christianity was much more intellectually robust.'[2]

Apart from debunking the myth proposed in our chapter heading that all Christians are born Christian, Professor McGrath's comment also raises a controversial question that it is important to consider at the beginning of this book: can Atheism be understood as a faith position? Some people would automatically categorise Atheism as a 'world religion' alongside other systems of beliefs about the existence – or non-existence – of God. However, others would contest this. For example,

Ricky Gervais argued in his interview with comedian Stephen Colbert on US television's highly popular *Late Show*: 'Atheism is only rejecting the claim that there is a God. Atheism is not a belief system. This is Atheism in a nutshell. You say, "There is a God." I say, "Can you prove it?" You say, "No." I say, "I don't believe you then."'[3]

Agreeing with Gervais, Richard Dawkins asserts generally, 'Atheists *do not* have faith.'[4] In fact, at times Dawkins and his peers seem even to take it to the next level, to say that faith is not simply something you either do or do not have; it is something you *should not* have in this enlightened day and age.

Look at how the well-known Atheist, the late Christopher Hitchens, defines faith:

> Faith is the surrender of the mind; it's the surrender of reason, it's the surrender of the only thing that makes us different from other mammals. It's our need to believe, and to surrender our scepticism and our reason, our yearning to discard that and put all our trust or faith in someone or something, that is the sinister thing to me. Of all the supposed virtues, faith must be the most overrated.[5]

Or Richard Dawkins puts it like this: 'Faith is the great cop-out, the great excuse to evade the need to think and evaluate evidence. Faith is belief in spite of, even perhaps because of, the lack of evidence.'[6]

This is the impact point of a key collision between Christians and Atheists – the question of the nature of faith. When faith is defined as a cop-out or the 'surrender of the mind' it is perhaps understandable why Atheists might have so little time for it and wish to distance themselves from any connection with the term. Faith appears to them to be unthinking dogmatism that stands in the way of progress and rational thought and common sense – or as the cynical writer H. Mencken argued in 1927, 'an illogical belief in the occurrence of the improbable'.[7]

On the other hand Christians, not to mention adherents of other faiths, can find such descriptions of faith demeaning and dismissive, as well as misrepresentative of their understanding of the world. They certainly do not tie in at all with the way that Jesus, the founder of the Christian faith, understood the nature of faith. He said: 'Believe me when I say that I am in the Father and the Father is in me; or at least believe on the evidence of the works themselves.'[8] This was Jesus' response to one of his followers who was struggling to grasp his claims – about who he was, what he was doing and where he was going. Jesus, sympathetic in his knowledge that these concepts are indeed hard for finite human minds to grasp, therefore put forward evidence. The 'works' he refers to relate to the miraculous events people had seen – resurrections of the dead, supernatural healings, and feeding crowds of thousands with scant resources. This is not the book to debate the historicity or validity of these so-called miracles. What is pertinent is the fact that even Jesus promoted rational decision-making methods when it comes to faith. He is not asking his followers to ignore or evade the evidence. He is not asking people to believe, in Dawkins' words, 'in spite of, even perhaps because of, the lack of evidence'. Quite the opposite: Jesus expects people to evaluate and weigh up the evidence and then come to personally reasoned conclusions when it comes to faith.[9]

There is sound logic at work in Jesus' expectation. If someone really did heal people spontaneously and bring them back from the dead, that would indeed be good grounds for deducing that they are more than just human. On the other hand, if those miracles were merely fables, fabrications or fakes, there would be reasonable grounds for concluding that their performer was an imposter.[10]

The first Christians understood that. One of the biographical accounts of the life of Jesus, which is included in the Bible, is John's Gospel. It was an eyewitness account written by one of Jesus' followers and includes this postscript, reiterating this logical approach and arguing that faith in Jesus was to be based on hard, reasonable, attested evidence: 'Jesus performed many other signs in the presence of his disciples, which are not recorded in this book. But these are written that you may believe that Jesus is the Messiah, the Son of God, and that by believing you may have life in his name.'[11]

This evidence-based description of faith offers a challenge to both Atheists and Christians. Some Christians feel that there is no need to search for or provide any reasons or logic for their beliefs, because they themselves understand the term 'faith' to imply the lack of evidence or rational processes to support it. Some Atheists, on the other hand, blandly assume that Christian faith is irrational and no thinking person would ever freely choose to accept its tenets, and therefore do not look closely at the evidence that does exist. As a result, both Christians and Atheists can misguidedly assume that only irrational motivations, such as family tradition, intuition or psychological manipulation, lie behind someone calling themselves a Christian, while evidence-informed belief and rational decision-making remains the sole property of Atheism.

Collusion

An unspoken agreement between many Christians and Atheists to accept that faith is based on un-evidenced opinions, a blind leap into the unknown, is a popular collusion in today's culture that may fuel the Atheist argument but unfairly misrepresents the Christian position.

I am often asked questions beginning with 'Why?' Most of the time they relate to why I became a foster parent and an adoptive dad when my wife and I had three birth children already. In comparison, relatively few people ask me why I write books, why I go running (fairly) regularly, or why I live in rural Oxfordshire. But, when it comes to opening my home to children who have had a tough start in life, my motivations and decisions quickly come under scrutiny. I explain why for me, just as for many other Christian foster carers, my desire to help provide love and security for children who have not been able to continue living with their birth families flows directly out of my experience of being loved and accepted by God. I remember giving this answer to one social worker who had been listening attentively with lots of affirming smiles and nods. She went on to respond: 'I wish I could have faith like yours, but my problem is I am too rational and logical. I can't make myself believe the things that you do.'

As someone who, through scientific training and academic research, has attempted to fine-tune my rational and logical skills, who considers myself to be sensible and educated, and who has, I believe, good reasons for faith in God, I felt her remarks were patronising and dismissive. I bit my tongue and changed the subject quickly. If only she had asked 'Why?' about my commitment to the Christian faith instead of assuming that I was a brainless idiot with a delusional belief in an unlikely supreme being! But my chewed tongue and attempt to change the subject probably only confirmed the impression that I must be a brainless idiot with no logic or reason behind my beliefs. My silence made me complicit in the myth of irrational faith. Or perhaps my choice not to respond to her comment betrayed an assumption on my part that she was the brainless one and would be incapable of thinking through the evidence and rationale that I had to offer.

The sentiments expressed by this social worker, and the silence I chose to meet it with, reflect many conversations with Atheists I have had throughout my life. Such remarks are not necessarily intended as an insult, or attack. And sometimes I am too lazy, too shy or too busy to reply by defending my beliefs. The irony is that the person saying that they are too rational to have my faith probably thinks they are being kind and tolerant, perhaps even complimentary. I, too, may think I am being tolerant and kind by not reacting to their misjudgement or patronising attitude. In actual fact, both of us are unwittingly colluding with an unhelpful understanding of faith and belief. It's a common story. The Atheist's assumption that Christians are irrational, uneducated and self-deluded goes unchallenged. And Christians return the favour. They assume that all Atheists are deliberately hostile and unashamedly insensitive to those with faith, or incapable of discussing or understanding the reasons for believing in Christianity. And so they hold back from engaging in further discussion or conversation.

But what happens if an Atheist, instead of dismissing the Christian position as irrational, does put forward a genuine question in an attempt to discover the reasons or evidence for belief in God? I have been in various debates and meetings where Atheists have done just that. In response, the Christian speakers have too often patronised the Atheists, remarking that they are too hard-hearted to understand, or, worse, that they are wilfully ignoring God. I have even heard Christians not only refuse to engage in good-natured intelligent discussion

as to the merits of and evidence for their position, but provocatively suggest they pray for the Atheist to 'see the light'.
Christians like this collude in reinforcing the stereotype that
Christianity is ultimately irrational. When a Christian is
dismissive of an Atheist, or an Atheist of a Christian, however
politely, the conversation cannot move on in a constructive
way.

Contention

In order to develop a richer and more fruitful conversation
between Christians and Atheists, we need to face up to the
problematic subject of the nature and definition of faith. While
both Atheists and Christians may agree that their views or
beliefs about God should be informed by evidence, the suggestion that Atheism is therefore a faith position can be
inflammatory. While both Atheists and Christians may agree
that each individual should be allowed to make an informed
choice about their beliefs, the suggestion that children born
to Christian parents are predisposed to choose faith because
of familial brainwashing is also inflammatory, especially when
those making the claim often seem to ignore the fact that
children born to Atheist families will of course also be exposed
to that particular view of the world. It seems this discussion
is pre-set to stir up hard feelings and conflict.

Perhaps you know the story of a speaker who had been
invited to address a conference in an African city. Trying to
build a rapport with the audience, he recounted a funny
incident that had occurred to him that day. He explained that
he had been at the check-in for his hotel and while he was
talking at the desk a tame monkey had crept up behind him
and lifted his wallet out of his pocket. Apart from the ethical

issues relating to the domestication of a monkey as a hotel pet, this was a pretty uncontroversial story. It was when the speaker made the comparison to his spendthrift wife that the reaction started. This story would have bombed in most polite company in most parts of the world, but to this audience it was particularly incendiary. People reacted by shouting or walking out. Some people picked up their chairs and started throwing them towards the front of the room. Soon the police had to be called in to quieten things down, and they tactfully explained to the visiting speaker that comparing a woman to a monkey was a terrible insult in that culture. The next day the speaker stood up to apologise for his mistake – he should never have said that his wife poached his pennies like the pickpocket pet ape. Once again the crowd were in uproar and another riot kicked off – he had made the self-same error, apparently equating his wife with a monkey. Sometimes we accidentally offend people, and sometimes even our best-intended efforts fire up controversy.[12]

This is often what happens between Christians and Atheists when it comes to speaking about faith. The term itself is so controversial that it has become a trigger word for conflict. Many Christians, hearing faith lambasted as a poor substitute for critical thinking, immediately feel aggravated. Most Atheists, hearing their lack of belief in God categorised as a faith-based position, feel similarly incensed. And the situation is only exacerbated by people like Richard Dawkins who talk about faith as a 'mental illness'.[13] This is deliberately offensive not only to Christians but also to people suffering with their mental health. Dawkins' words are as unhelpful as so-called 'faith healers' who talk about illness as a mental illusion that can be overcome by anyone who has prayer or faith. That is offensive to scientists and doctors who have spent years mastering their profession to help cure disease, and also to the sick, who are being told they just don't have enough faith to be healed.

When it comes to the Christian–Atheist conversation, collision occurs when we deliberately or inadvertently use a tone or trigger terms that escalate conflict. Contention, on the other hand, seeks to maintain a real relationship by believing the best about the other person, seeking to be sensitive in the way we use our language, and yet not backing down from trying to talk about the difficult subjects. Recognising that there are some Atheists and Christians out there who may seek to derail cooperation through inflammatory and offensive comments, most Christians and Atheists I know are prepared to have a respectful conversation even about the tricky subject of faith.

We could first of all acknowledge the two opposing *definitions* of faith that are implied by the different sides of the debate. For the Atheist, faith is synonymous with 'unwarranted belief', while, for the Christian, faith is synonymous with 'warranted belief'. Any conversation where faith is being discussed without understanding the context of the two definitions is set to be at cross-purposes. Those of us who speak English are aware of many terms that could be their own opposites, depending on context. The word 'custom', for example, can imply something that is a common practice, or an item that is specifically and uniquely made. A 'handicap' may be something that makes equality impossible, such as a disability, or something that makes equality possible – such as when playing golf. The words 'wicked' or 'sick' when I use them denote something terrible, while my children use them to denote something particularly excellent. A grasp of the different definitions, contexts and speakers enables us to understand one another as we speak about faith, albeit from opposite standpoints.

The philosopher Julia Kristeva explained: 'Whether I belong to a religion, whether I be agnostic or atheist, when I say "I believe," I mean "hold as true."'[14] I wonder if it might be less inflammatory and more helpful for both Christians and Atheists to talk about what they each 'hold to be true' instead of simply using terms such as belief or faith without clarification. Either way, it is the warrant, rationale and evidence behind what is 'held to be true' that is significant.

Second, we can acknowledge the two *challenges* of faith that are brought by the two sides of the debate. For the Christian, as Gervais said, the challenge is to prove or demonstrate the existence of the God we follow. For the Atheist, the challenge is to prove or demonstrate the non-existence of God. Neither challenge is at all straightforward.

The problem is that neither Atheists nor Christians can fully and logically, indisputably demonstrate the existence or otherwise of God. McGrath's claim that Christianity and Atheism are both ultimately faith positions derives from the fact that for both groups their belief system 'goes beyond what is logically demonstrable, yet is nevertheless capable of rational motivation and foundation'.[15] Science, sometimes portrayed as faith's great adversary, can in fact help us here.

In the field of science there is much about the universe that defies our current understanding. It is not possible to explain all the workings of our cosmos, as so much of it is unknown – indeed it often appears irrational and difficult to comprehend. Nevertheless, the operating principle that drives the scientific enterprise, or, one might even say, the often unacknowledged article of faith that is implicit in the workings of the scientific community, is that the universe can be described by a set of physical laws despite all that we don't know yet. Of course this conviction cannot be proved until the scientific enterprise has completed its task. At one level this seems to be a circular argument. The theologian and philosopher Lesslie Newbigin argued that science 'has to assume from the beginning the truth of that which it seeks to prove'.[16]

There is a naive understanding of science that assumes that scientists simply observe the universe and then generate theories that describe what they have observed. But that is rarely, if ever, what actually takes place. Scientists often develop theories and then go looking for evidence to support them. Back in 1964, a physicist wrote a paper on a mathematical question in particle physics proposing the existence of an undiscovered subatomic particle. The theory was rejected by a major physics journal, but he persisted and, indeed, a wider group of physicists made similar proposals.* Eventually the theory received enough support that funding was found to create one of the world's largest physics experiments. After billions of pounds of investment and forty-nine years of research, scientists at CERN discovered the predicted Higgs boson particle at the Large Hadron Collider. This is a truly amazing discovery and one of the most celebrated stories in modern science. It demonstrates that theory often precedes evidence. In the same way, the thinking Christian, without ultimate proof for the existence of God, nevertheless holds convictions they believe have a reasonable foundation and will one day prove true.

Science can also help in the question of faith as we weigh up the two challenges; that is, to prove the existence or non-existence of God. Even the most brilliant of scientists claim to understand but a tiny fraction of information about the

---

* Indeed it has been suggested that we should call the newly discovered particle the London-Anderson-Englert-Brout-Higgs-Guralnik-Hagen-Kibble-Weinberg mechanism.

universe. If I were to draw a circle that represents all of the information it is possible to know and ask them to shade a section to symbolise how much they have grasped, most true scientists would struggle even to justify putting a dot on the page. By most self-declarations, more than 99.99 per cent of the universe is outside of anyone's personal, or even our combined, spheres of knowledge. We can refer to this approach as the circle diagram of fractional knowledge. If we know so little about the universe, is it not logically impossible, indeed irrational, to say definitively that God does not exist? That is why most Atheists, including Richard Dawkins, ultimately admit to being agnostic. Dawkins concedes: 'I cannot know for certain but I think God is very improbable, and I live my life on the assumption that he is not there.'[17] I can mirror that sentiment with my own reverse understanding of the universe: I cannot know for certain, but I think God is very probable, and I live my life on the assumption that he is there. Scientifically speaking, it seems that our respective rationales for our convictions may not be as dissimilar as they first appear.

Third, we can acknowledge the two *implications* of faith. As a counter to the logic behind the argument proposed by those who use the circle diagram of fractional knowledge, Dawkins famously said that he is atheistic about God in the same way that he is atheistic about a Flying Spaghetti Monster: 'None of us feels an obligation to disprove any of the far-fetched things that a fertile facetious imagination might dream up. I am an atheist when considering Zeus, Apollo . . . the Golden Calf and the Flying Spaghetti Monster.'[18] Apart from the fact that likening belief in God to belief in a Spaghetti Monster is very similar to deliberately baiting an African crowd by comparing women to monkeys, implying that believing in God has the same rational value as believing in supernatural spaghetti – Dawkins himself disproves this claim by the very time and effort he has spent in fighting against faith. And more importantly, two billion people are not claiming a personal relationship with a pasta deity. Nor has Western culture been shaped by a heritage based on sentient spaghetti. For Christians there are serious and far-reaching implications for faith, and so to casually claim that belief in God has the intellectual equivalence and cultural significance of belief in a Spaghetti Monster is disingenuous. While faith for an Atheist may seem a nonsensical life choice, for a Christian, faith is a necessary life choice that affects all they think, say and do.

Just as Richard Dawkins, Ricky Gervais and Christopher Hitchens do not speak for all Atheists when they are dismissive about the claims of faith, neither do the subset of Christians who are dismissive about the claims of science speak for all Christians. There certainly are Christians who respond disparagingly about those who seek evidence for God. Indeed, some Christians go so far as to argue that there is a conspiracy within the scientific community to disprove the Bible. This needs to be called out as not just unfair to Atheists but also unfair to Christians. We must contend that, generally speaking, both Christians and Atheists are likely to be open to discussing together subjects of mutual interest – faith, belief, evidence, warrant, and the existence or otherwise of God.

Collaboration

Perhaps you remember the picture of a striped dress that became a viral hit on social media in February of 2015. It caused great debate because some people were adamant that the dress was blue and black, while others argued back that it was surely white and gold. The difference in perception had to do with the way that the brain processes colour. Some say it is related to how natural light is translated in your neural pathways, others say it is due to the variant numbers of differently shaped photo-receptors on your retina. Whatever the reason, two people could look at the same picture and see it completely differently.

In a similar way, Christians and Atheists can look at the same world, and see the same evidence and yet process it differently. This is not to say that both interpretations are correct, as they indubitably claim mutually contradictory things about the universe we live in. One day we may find out which group – which theory – was correct. But in the mean-time, just recognising that two people can see the same thing and interpret it differently, without assuming the other is stupid, ignorant or wilfully uncooperative, is a good beginning point for a conversation.

Pascal Wallisch, Clinical Assistant Professor of Psychology at New York University, describes how the controversial dress and the ensuing debate actually facilitated scientific progress, precisely because it challenged the entire understanding of the field of colour vision. Wallisch contends that up until early 2015, a close reading of the literature could suggest that the entire field had gone somewhat stale, as most scientists in the discipline seemed to assume that they knew how colour-based vision worked. But after the surge of interest, debate and speculation online over the colours of the dress, scientists began to collaborate to forge new research and theories about eyesight, perception, photography, light and neural pathways.[19] This is science at its best – conflict leading to collaboration, different findings promoting new theses, hence new discoveries and new evidence-sharing opportunities.

When scientists explore the vast, apparently chaotic, or apparently irrational, unknown universe, sometimes research and experimentation lead to theories that bring agreement across the field. However, it is not uncommon for the same experimental evidence to lead to very different, even controversial or opposing, theories.

In the world of quantum mechanics there is a very famous thought experiment involving a cat that can help us here. A cat, a flask of poison, and some radioactive material are placed in a sealed box. If a monitor inside the box detects radioactivity the flask of poison is shattered and the cat is killed. If there is no radioactivity detected, then the flask is not broken and the cat lives. As long as the box is closed, according to the prevailing interpretation of quantum physics, the cat is both dead and alive in dual superposed quantum states. When the door is opened, of course, the quantum states are made known and the cat is observed to be either alive or dead.

Now there are two important things to remember. First, this is a thought experiment, so no actual cats were hurt in the process. Second, this thought experiment was designed by Erwin Schrödinger to show the philosophical challenges of what has become known as the Copenhagen interpretation of quantum theory. Schrödinger's intentions seem to have been to encourage respected peers to collaborate when presented with opposing theories, not just ridicule and mock those they were not in agreement with. The idea that a cat could be simultaneously alive and dead seems absurd. Especially since just by opening the door it would be obvious by observation that the cat would be found in only one of those states. But then that adds the extra factor of the interaction of the observer, such that merely observing the state of the cat changes the state of the cat and so the philosophical debate continues –

alongside the scientific debates over the nature of the universe – or universes.

Those debates aside, when the scientific community is presented with opposing theories, which have far-reaching implications, but ones that are notoriously difficult to test, best practice is to find room, at least initially, for both interpretations. At their best, scientists respect and cooperate with those who hold a radically different understanding of the universe to them, and continue to search for evidence in order to further the conversation until one view or the other can be ruled out.

In a similar way, we can follow suit to acknowledge that Christians and Atheists have profoundly different approaches to the world we both inhabit. We have a different rationale for its ultimate origins, a different understanding of human purpose and meaning, and a different set of beliefs around the existence of God. Instead of trying to discredit the beliefs others hold by speaking to one another with condescension, disrespect, dismissive sarcasm – or by not speaking to one another at all – there is an alternative way forward: the possibility of striving together towards the truth.

The rest of this book is dedicated to that pursuit. In a spirit of collaboration, or, one could say, in a show of good faith, I will attempt not to assign the term 'faith' to the position of the Atheists, choosing instead to use terms such as 'core beliefs', 'worldview', 'conviction' or 'philosophy' for the things they 'hold to be true'. When I assign the term 'faith' to the position of Christians, on the other hand, I would like it to be assumed that I mean 'warranted belief', and 'evidenced conclusions' regarding the things they 'hold to be true'. Believing the best of each other in this way provides the strongest of foundations for further debate and discussion.

Let me be so bold as to offer challenges to both Christian

and Atheist readers of the book at this point. First, to
Christians, I would ask if they really understand the nature
of their faith. Do they know not just *that* they believe but
also *what* they believe, and *why* they believe? Can they articulate the basis for their faith, or have they indeed simply
inherited their faith, or 'absorbed' it, from family or friends?
The Bible demands that Christians be ready to give an answer
to everyone for the 'reason for the hope' they have.[20] In other
words, Christians need to be able to explain to enquirers and
sceptics the rational justification for their faith. At its outset
the Christian faith launched into the world what Lesslie
Newbigin termed 'public truth'.[21] From its genesis the
Christian movement, despite fierce opposition, has been confident that its message is true, that it is based on evidence, and
that it has hope and help to offer the world. The timid,
privatised view of Christianity that is so widespread in our
culture now has not just come about in reaction to the growing
Atheism; indeed, our anaemic distortion of Christianity may
actually have served to fuel the arrogance of the militant
Atheists. I would challenge Christians, in this increasingly
sceptical world: do you have a bold humility, a confident faith
that is unashamed and unafraid to present a winsome and
warranted case for believing in God?

With Atheism increasingly becoming the accepted norm in
certain sectors of our society, I would ask Atheists also to face
up to the challenge of understanding what they hold to be
true and why. I wonder how many Atheists have ever stopped
and asked themselves the reasons for their stance? If they were
asked to justify their Atheism, what evidence would they give?
To what extent is their Atheism an inherited or socially
absorbed view? I would challenge Atheists: have you gone with
the flow? Do you assume an Atheist stance because of the

newspapers you read, the family you have come from or a personal preference you settled on in childhood?[22]

Award-winning journalist Isabel Hardman put a similar challenge forward in the *Spectator* magazine:

The religious politicians are always required to explain the detail of their worldview to an extent that those who profess liberal beliefs are not . . . But I would wager that there are many more politicians who hold liberal views on conscience issues for the very simple reason that this is what everyone else believes, and potentially because expressing a different view would expose you to the fury of the mob. Surely that, too, is meekly following the views of a powerful group?[23]

It seems it is possible for both Christians and Atheists to exhibit blind, uncritical, unthinking faith which does not do justice for either cause. To prevent this we need to recognise that the Atheist or the Christian in your life presents us not with a threat, but with a fantastic opportunity. By asking one another searching questions, by not accepting simplistic answers, lazy thinking or unhelpful prejudice, but offering different perspectives and tackling new problems, we can keep each other honest. Honest to ourselves, so we do not just go with the flow, or make default choices for an easy life. Honest with each other, so we prevent the build-up of unhelpful assumptions and suspicions that encrust our relationships like limescale. When we are not afraid to talk about our beliefs, our conversations are richer as a result. When we can break out of our echo chamber, we have the opportunity to discover if what we hold to be true does in fact hold water.

It is precisely the present controversy over the nature of faith that provides the potential for collaboration. As we work together we find it is safe to test what we truly hold to be true. When we take the effort to understand and test our beliefs, ironically we are more likely to be humble about them. Instead of a vicious cycle of ridiculing and dismissing one another's views, we can revolutionise the conversation to build a virtuous cycle. Challenging one another to understand our thinking better means not only do we learn more, but we are more aware of the limits of our knowledge. In other words, the more we collaborate, the more humble we become, and that humility breeds respect, honesty and further collaboration.

Questions

How do *you* define faith?

What are the prejudices you have when it comes to Atheists and Christians?

How did you come to the beliefs you have about God – are they inherited or personally decided?

If you had to give the three main reasons why you hold to your current belief system, what would you put forward?

Chapter 3

Christians are judgemental /
Atheists are tolerant

Collision

You don't have to search very far online to hear a Christian denouncing something or someone. In fact, according to the media, Christians have a special gift for finding things to criticise. Christians appear to be anti-gay, anti-women and anti-abortion. They are even anti-cake if the cake has a pro-gay rights message on it. Christians are perceived to be opposed to basic civil liberties like choosing whom you can love and what you can do with your own reproductive organs. When they are not restricting other people's freedoms, they are often found judging those who attempt to live differently to their ancient and narrowly defined Christian rules. And when they have finished proclaiming their judgements, they stand on the moral high ground they have claimed, looking down on everyone else for the way that they live. With audacity and arrogance, these self-named 'saints' call the rest of us rule-breakers – 'sinners'. At least, that's how the stories go.

Of course, not every Christian is like this media-billed stereo-type. Some keep their opinions to themselves – or at least they try to. The problem is that even when Christians are silent, an air of judgementalism can still appear to leak out. The Christian

who won't join in risqué office banter or wild post-work cele-
brations can make everyone else feel guilty and judged without
even saying a word. And when a Christian casually asks you
what you are doing at the weekend, that innocent question from
anyone else's mouth suddenly bears down on you like a ton of
'holier-than-thou' bricks. You are not planning to go to church
and volunteer in the community like you assume they are. And
so, because of that implied, if not imposed, judgementalism,
you feel somehow embarrassed about that lie-in you were hoping
for, the party you are holding, that football game you are
attending, that shopping spree you were planning with your
daughter.

Atheists, meanwhile, are the opposite of Christians. They
are tolerant. They are open-minded people, not controlled by
the strictures of an ancient book. They have no axes to grind,
no secret agendas, no reasons to judge or look down on others.
They can affirm all people whatever their social status, physical abilities or lifestyle choices. Your Atheist colleague or friend
will accept you whatever your choice of gender, sexuality,
morals, values and priorities. Atheists will not tell you who to
marry, which candidate to vote for or when to have children.
They will not make you feel bad if you have an affair, gamble
your money away, or routinely break the speed limit. At least,
that's how the stories go.

With these kinds of stereotypes circulating, it is no wonder
that in the faith literacy sessions I facilitate, many well-educated
professionals hold the assumption that Atheists are far easier to
work with than Christians. Not only that, many of them have
bought the line that all Christians hate gay people, beat their
children, and not only have the arrogance to believe that their
religion is the only true one, but also preach that everyone else
is going to hell. This last perception is often the final straw. It

appears to be the height of judgementalism, claiming privileged access to God while pouring implicit scorn on the rest of doomed humanity. The exclusive claims of Christianity seem to give its followers a most unwelcome superiority complex.

These are some of the stereotypes and prejudices that fuel the Christian–Atheist conflict at many levels. Once these two stereotype-informed groups start to interact with one another, the fireworks go off. One reaction from Atheists to the perceived judgementalism of Christians is to berate Christians for not being loving enough. Sometimes a few Bible verses can get thrown in too. How can Christians dare to be so critical? Doesn't the Bible say, 'Judge not lest you be judged'? Didn't Jesus say, 'Love your enemies'? Surely Christians cannot oppose loving relationships, and freedom of speech and conscience? Christians should forgive their work colleagues, not judge them. Christians should turn the other cheek, not get embroiled in battles they can't win. Before long, Christians are not just being charged with unfounded judgementalism, but with outright hypocrisy.

Typically, the Christian response is to explain to Atheists that they have got it all wrong. Christians are not judgemental – no, they are very tolerant people. Churches are running the largest food distribution programmes to the needy, the largest non-state provision of children's work and youth support. Christians help those in prison and drug rehabilitation, the refugees, trafficked and homeless. Christian churches are among the most inclusive communities in our society. And anyway . . .

This is the turning point. The conversation is about to switch from defence of Christianity from the charge of judge-mentalism to an attack on Atheist claims of tolerance. And anyway . . . isn't the pot calling the kettle black?

Isn't it in fact Atheists who are taking the high ground by criticising Christians? Doesn't their tolerance display its own limits when it comes to those practising a Christian faith? If anyone is intolerant, is it not Atheists as, through the lobbying of groups like the National Secular Society, they are the ones seeking to ban Christian work in schools and prisons?[1] Is it not these judgemental Atheists who are the driving force behind movements to try and ban Bibles from being offered in hotels and schools? Wasn't it Atheists who successfully campaigned to change hundreds of years of observation of Sunday as a day of rest by allowing Sunday opening of shops – showing a fundamental lack of respect for Christians and our national Christian heritage in the process? Isn't it Atheists who seek to colonise faith festivals like Christmas and rename them Winterval or the like? If anyone is intolerant, is it not Atheists?

And so the debate goes on. Such entrenched positions are widespread, and the more they are debated, the more the stereotypes seem to hold water. On both sides of the fence, those labelled bigoted, narrow-minded and judgemental look most bigoted, narrow-minded and judgemental precisely when they are trying to argue that they are not.

On the broader stage, although Atheists have enjoyed a recent period of being perceived to be open, tolerant and accepting, the more vocal they become, the more often they too are accused of being hostile and intolerant. Journalist Stephen Glover, writing in the *Daily Mail*, wrote: 'The truth is that there is a new breed of militant atheists who are capable of being as unreasoning as the most bone-headed creationist. Their intolerance is a strange mirror reflection of the bigotry of religious extremists.'[2]

Atheists seem to be getting a reputation for intolerance because of a minority group of militant Atheists who take every opportunity to bait and belittle Christians. Perhaps that is the same way that it started for Christians. Aggressive, vocal minorities have given Christians a terrible reputation, even though they do not by any stretch of the imagination represent what most Christians believe or how most Christians behave. According to a rigorous study conducted among millennials in the USA, it was found that for sixteen- to thirty-year-olds who are not part of a church community,[3] the public reputation of the Church is summarised by three words: 'anti-homosexual, judgemental and hypocritical'.[4] These words do not describe most Christians I know – although I have to admit that I do know one or two who delight in giving this impression.

The main flashpoint of the debate over who is or is not intolerant seems to lie in differing stances on a range of ethical issues – particularly those regarding sexuality. For some Christians, it seems ironic that their long-held position, of recognising only heterosexual relationships, has suddenly gone from being universally socially acceptable to totally unacceptable. The tidal change of public opinion on these issues has been so fast and so extreme that those maintaining any semblance of what now seem politically incorrect minority opinions are vulnerable to vicious attack.

Even within the Christian community, there is a wide range of views over these issues of sexual ethics and what has now become a debate about human identity. While many Christians have broadened their views, they feel tarred with the same brush as those who vocally denounce those involved in same-sex relationships. They feel not only marginalised, but ridiculed, suppressed, censured and excluded from public discourse.

Tim Farron, as we touched on earlier, a high-profile MP with a history of fighting for LGBT rights and gay marriage and plenty of evidence to show he was a progressive and tolerant leader, was publicly humiliated because the media focused on his privately held traditional beliefs on sexuality.

What he practised and what he preached was still not enough for those on what seemed to be a witch-hunt against socially unorthodox beliefs.

Some Christians, feeling victimised by those preaching tolerance, coined the term 'totalitolerance',[5] recognising that the idea of tolerance, taken to an extreme, paradoxically promotes a new breed of intolerance. Because many Christians find themselves the wrong side of the prevailing social norms on a range of ethical and social issues, some have responded to this sense of isolation and suppression by blaming Atheists *en masse* for promoting a negative image of Christians through misguided portrayals in the media and on film and television. Some Christian groups have even instigated legal battles to force a change of perception or law following what they perceive to be overt discrimination on the grounds of their faith. For example, in 2013 the British Airways employee Nadia Eweida was told she could not wear a cross, despite BA's uniform policy which allows symbols of faith to be worn. The European Court of Human Rights ruled that her rights had been violated. Similarly, the case of Dr Drew and the Walsall NHS trust involved a medical doctor who claimed to have been dismissed because he did not keep his religious views private and refrain from referring to his faith in communication with work colleagues.[6]

Following a number of such cases, The Parliamentary Assembly of the Council of Europe at Strasbourg agreed Resolution 2036 on 'Tackling intolerance and discrimination in Europe with a special focus on Christians', based on a Report by the Assembly's Committee on Equality and Non-Discrimination. The Resolution includes the following words:

> Intolerance and discrimination on grounds of religion or belief affect minority religious groups in Europe, but also people

belonging to majority religious groups. Numerous acts of hostility, violence and vandalism have been recorded in recent years against Christians and their places of worship, but these acts are often overlooked by the national authorities. Expression of faith is sometimes unduly limited by national legislation and policies which do not allow the accommodation of religious beliefs and practices.[7]

Atheists may have often been at the forefront of the attack against Christian beliefs and practices, but they also know what it is like to be discriminated against and socially isolated for unpopular views. In the UK, a country that calls itself Christian, with over 60 per cent of people claiming some sort of Christian affiliation, Atheists have felt and still can feel that they are the ones battling the tide of public opinion. Some Atheists feel under-represented in education,[8] religious or ethical debates, or are concerned that public broadcasting is weighted against them.

Professor of Late Modern History, Callum Brown, reports that as he travels around meeting with humanist and Atheist groups, he finds many irritated and irate Atheists who feel excluded, since, for example, they have no representatives in the prized four-minute daily slot 'Thought for the Day' in Radio 4's *Today* news programme.[9] Brown also reports that in the USA, Atheists 'get hot under the collar about God on the dollar bill',[10] referring to the inscription 'In God We Trust' on US paper currency.

In its analysis of the treatment of Atheists around the world, one Atheist group described the United Kingdom as having 'systemic discrimination' towards the non-religious. They felt that there was systematic religious privilege, with evidence of discriminatory prominence given to religious bodies, traditions or leaders. They also called into question not only the fact that religious groups control some public or social services, but that government funds these either directly through salaries or indirectly through discriminatory tax exemptions.[11] The report also found that in the United States there was recurring and widespread – albeit localised or infrequent – social marginalisation or prejudice against the non-religious. Atheists reported that in America, the social and political atmosphere has meant that they have been made to feel like lesser citizens, or even non-citizens. Atheist candidates running for public office are much less likely to win elections, for example.[12] As Steven Gey summarises: 'Thus, in the United States and other countries with similar traditions of religious liberty, atheism often suffers from a quasi-legal cultural ostracism that is inconsistent with the principles that provide the justification for the formal legal protection of individual rights of conscience.'[13]

Because of the feeling experienced by both sides of being treated unjustly, and the emotionally sensitive nature of the areas of conflict, it can be difficult to have any rational, measured and fruitful conversation to forge and strengthen relationships. But unless we attempt a fresh way forward, such constant collisions as these will not help anyone. Most Atheists are not responsible for the social isolation that Christians feel, in the same way that most Christians are not responsible for the social isolation that Atheists feel.

Nevertheless, recognising that both sides have been victims as well as perpetrators of intolerance, and that tolerance is a virtue both sides claim to practise and promote, is there a way to move this conversation forward? Are there ways we can mend broken bridges, or perhaps even better, build new and useful ones?

Collusion

Before we look for positive ways the conversation can develop, we first should recognise that only a minority of Christians and Atheists end up on the collision course of public and vocal opposition. How do the rest of us, who are by nature less publicly confrontational, deal – or not deal – with the divisions caused by judgementalism and intolerance? There are two main ways we collude in trying to brush these problems under the carpet. The first has to do with absence, the second with silence.

In an attempt to avoid confrontation, conflict and collision, it may be easier for us to spend time with, live with and work with those who hold similar views to us. Sometimes people do this very obviously, by setting up deliberately isolated communities that have minimal contact with the wider world. But all of us may gravitate towards workplaces, social clubs, schools and facilities that attract people who hold to the same core beliefs as us. We choose to read books and watch television programmes that promote ideas we agree on. Some call it 'confirmation bias'.

Because of the ubiquity of the Internet and the promise of global connectivity, we may think we are more diverse and inclusive than we actually are. We overestimate the degree to which we have genuine relationships with people who are very different from us. But, ironically, even our online activity can enmesh us in its own form of isolation. Professor John Inazu of Washington University argues that 'the internet for many of us becomes a huge echo chamber in which we only hear the voices that agree with us. Everything we think, write, or say goes largely unchallenged, and our ideas become self-reinforcing.'[14]

When we surround ourselves with others who think like us,

it becomes easier to demonise people who hold views that are different to ours. We can become lazy in our thinking and just assume that people who don't share our views are intellectually backward or wilfully obtuse. It also becomes easy to exaggerate the degree to which we would be willing to hold unpopular views. During recent racist violence in the United States, one lecturer noted a paradox in the students in his class:

> Undergraduates say the darn'dest things. When discussing the history of racial injustice, I frequently ask them what their position on slavery would have been had they been white and living in the South before abolition. Guess what? They all would have been abolitionists! They all would have bravely spoken out against slavery, and worked tirelessly in the cause of freeing those enslaved. Isn't that special? Bless their hearts. Of course, it is complete nonsense. Only the tiniest fraction of them, or of any of us, would have spoken up against slavery or lifted a finger to free the slaves. Most of them – and us – would simply have gone along. Many would have supported the slave system and, if it was in their interest, participated in it as buyers and owners or sellers of slaves.[15]

Robert P. George, the McCormick Professor of Jurisprudence at Princeton University and a visiting lecturer at Harvard Law School, posted that comment on social media – alongside a challenge. Perhaps, he says to his potential readers, you would not have simply gone along in support of the slave system. Perhaps you can show evidence that you are prepared to embrace an unpopular cause right now. Perhaps this week you have stood up for the rights of victims of injustice, risking your own reputation, friendships and employment prospects in the process. Well, have you?

The likelihood is that we have not dared to go against the majority view, not braved speaking out at personal cost. By definition, most of us go with the majority. Most of us tend towards the 'average' views and beliefs of our group. We naturally narrow our field of vision to the comfortable, reduce our conversation partners to those we can speak to easily, and live life in splendid isolation from those whose views or lives are very different from ours. Whether we have done this deliberately or subconsciously, the result is that we expose ourselves to the danger of stagnation and stigmatisation. When Christians and Atheists demonise one another, the two parties may feel a level of protection in their separate groupings. But living in the isolated bubble of our own private ghettoes is not healthy for us, or for our world. Neither do we engage with the critique of our views, nor allow the richness of other people's ways of viewing the world to influence us. Not having to question, explain or defend our beliefs will make our thinking sloppy. But worse than that, it exacerbates the problem of intolerance, and runs contrary to what we actually want to stand for. As Mark Twain once wrote: 'Broad, wholesome, charitable views of men and things can not be acquired by vegetating in one little corner of the earth all one's lifetime.'[16]

The other collusive approach to avoiding collision is silence. Being silent about what we hold to be true has the benefit of our neither shunning nor seeming to want to change the people around us. Instead, though, it changes the content of the conversation. We can still live in proximity with those who hold other views to us, but we meticulously avoid any controversial topics by keeping silent about our value commitments. Sometimes this involves a personal decision not to talk about our core beliefs; at other times we do this in practice out of social expectation.

Choosing to keep quiet about what we hold to be true can

be an example of collusion with the unhealthy side of tolerance. By avoiding all mention of our values and opinions for fear of being judged or excluded, or for fear of appearing judgemental or exclusive, we deprive other people in our lives of something important. This self-editing of conversation distances us from others, and means we present less than our authentic selves to the world.

In genuine relationships we should be able to bring all that we are into every situation we find ourselves in. This does not mean that we impose our beliefs onto every situation and into every conversation. Just because I am an Asian does not mean every conversation is about that aspect of my identity. Just because I support Liverpool Football Club does not mean I can't talk about other sports and teams. Just because I love a good curry does not mean spicy food is the only thing on the menu for supper if you visit me.

But it is true that some aspects of our identity are so deeply woven into our sense of self and our approach to the world that they cannot be removed.[17] I am always a father, always shaped by my working-class origins, always influenced by my Christian convictions. There are not many topics of conversation where you will not be able to see traces of those elements in my contributions. To be silent in conversation either for fear of imposing my identity on someone else or of causing conflict is neither practical nor helpful. To deliberately withhold from each other the influence of the beliefs and values that we treasure most deeply is a form of relational withdrawal. Although it may stem from a desire to retain a healthy relationship, it can instead lead to an impoverished, neglectful, undervalued and unhealthy relationship.

As well as personal restraint when it comes to talking about our differing views, there can also be a social silencing of the expression of core beliefs. I have been in debates, training sessions and conversations where I have been told that Christian views have no place in the modern world, because we live in a tolerant and loving society. I have heard Christians being asked to keep their faith private and personal, practising it only within the confines of their own homes. And I have also seen Atheists silenced. One example of this is the 'No Platform' policy of the National Union of Students in the UK. There was an attempt to force the University of Cardiff to prohibit the veteran feminist campaigner and academic Germaine Greer from speaking because, despite her outstanding record of championing women's equality over many decades, she has stated on numerous occasions that she believes that post-operative transgender women are not women. This was deemed to be transphobic and over three thousand students signed a petition that she be disinvited to speak.[18]

This incident demonstrates a couple of things; first, that it is not only Christians who face social isolation because of their beliefs, but anyone who takes a different approach to the prevailing social orthodoxies. The second is that we need to figure out a way to disagree well, where we can be genuinely tolerant of people who hold to a different set of values to ours, and find a way to hear rather than censor different opinions. When we find ourselves in disagreement with somebody, this does not mean that all their views are written off. I respect the huge contribution Margaret Thatcher made to politics, even though I fundamentally disagree with those policies of hers that led to the mass unemployment that directly impacted on my own family. I respect Martin Luther King's stand against racism, but not his sexism. Can we afford one another the same courtesy – agreeing where possible, and disagreeing where necessary, with respect?

When there is a real danger that in the name of tolerance, we end up less accommodating, less hospitable, less able to recognise genuine difference, we need to be extra vigilant. Tolerance can be like a solvent that starts out with the good intention of dissolving prejudice, partiality, bigotry and the inhuman treatment of other people. But this solvent is so powerful that it has begun to dissolve the values that it originally sought to protect, making views that do not fit the new social orthodoxy unacceptable.

The philosopher Karl Popper put it like this:

> Unlimited tolerance must lead to the disappearance of tolerance. If we extend unlimited tolerance even to those who are intolerant, if we are not prepared to defend a tolerant society against the onslaught of the intolerant, then the tolerant will be destroyed, and tolerance with them.[19]

When it comes to faith-related topics in a multi-faith society, I have heard it expressed that any and all discussions should be discouraged for risk of offending. But when our commitment to free speech means that free speech is quashed, something is seriously wrong. When our commitment to tolerance leads to intolerance, something is seriously wrong. When our commitment to protecting relationships leads to destroying relationships, something is seriously wrong. Collusion may be better than collision when it comes to protecting relationships at a surface level, but if we are not careful this collusive approach can contribute to the further disintegration of society, the ghettoisation and marginalisation of certain groups of people and, unwittingly, to a suppression of human rights and freedom of expression.

Contention

In conversations about tolerance between Atheists and Christians, both sides have plenty of ammunition to fuel a conflict. We cannot deny examples in relatively recent history where intolerant Atheist regimes have persecuted Christians for their faith: Pol Pot's Cambodia, Josef Stalin's Soviet Union, Enver Hoxha's Albania, Kim Jung-il's Korea. Neither can we deny examples where intolerant Christians have persecuted others for their views: the Spanish Inquisition, the Salem Witch trials, or the despicable antics of Westborough Baptist Church. It is no wonder, in the light of this heritage of conflict, that temperatures and tempers quickly rise and we collide in the worst ways – ironically, often in the name of tolerance. The conflict between Christians and Atheists on this can look pretty intractable. Both sides can feel marginalised and discriminated against. Both are passionate about their right to be heard and accepted. Both sides have reason to vent anger and frustration. So how can we move forward from here?

First of all, I believe it is pertinent to reconsider our terminology. Although tolerance has been the commonly held value for both Christians and Atheists to strive towards, is it really in fact the place we want to get to?

My line of work involves a lot of travel on public transport and I am often on buses, trains and planes. As an extrovert, I feel some inbuilt sense of obligation to start conversations with my accidental and unsuspecting neighbours. Recently, on an eleven-hour flight back from Vancouver, the seat next to me was occupied by a man who, before I even had a chance to say hello, had donned an eye mask and headphones, and downed two small bottles of vodka. The message was clear. He was not in a chatting mood. He was not showing any animosity towards me. But neither was he appreciating my company. In other words, he was tolerating my proximity – no more. We spent our flight in mutual tolerance of one another; in ignorance, or even perhaps silent judgement of each other. And part of me felt dehumanised that day. I had been inches away but I had not even been acknowledged or allowed the basic courtesy of a greeting.

Tolerance is collusion. At a basic level it promotes those twin weapons of absence and silence which, as we saw, cannot lead to healthy, meaningful, impactful relationships. Genuine intimacy and honest conversation, on the other hand, even about difficult subjects where different opinions are expressed, far outweigh any benefits of mere tolerance.

Jesus did not preach tolerance. In fact, not unlike some of the Atheist critique of religion today, Jesus was aggressively intolerant of the hypocrisy of those who, in the name of religion, were so stuck on telling others what they should and shouldn't be doing that they failed to practise the most important values of grace, forgiveness and compassion. They were quick to judge and slow to help, and so Jesus damned them: 'And you experts in the law, woe to you, because you load people down with burdens they can hardly carry, and you yourselves will not lift one finger to help them.'[20]

For the Christian, there has to be a wake-up call here. The Bible calls Christians to speak out against those who take advantage of the vulnerable. The Bible teaches, not tolerance, but something higher – to 'love your neighbours' *and* to 'love your enemies'. Christians should be marked by their sacrificial welcome and service of others irrespective of economic class, ethnicity, moral history, sexuality or religion. In an increasingly fragmented world, where we have seen a spike in violence towards immigrants and minorities, it seems we need something more than tolerance to reverse the trend and build a stronger, more united society. In one of the most quoted passages of the Bible, often recited at weddings, there is a call to love. This is not supposed to be restricted to the way we treat our nearest and dearest, however, but is to define how we relate to everyone:

> Love is patient, love is kind. It does not envy, it does not boast, it is not proud. It does not dishonour others, it is not self-seeking, it is not easily angered, it keeps no record of wrongs. Love does not delight in evil but rejoices with the truth. It always protects, always trusts, always hopes, always perseveres.[21]

It is relatively easy to love people who are like us, as Jesus himself pointed out – but love is demonstrated most radically when we love people with whom we don't agree. While tolerance is a willingness to accept others at a distance, love is the hospitality that welcomes others up close and personal – even when we disagree. While tolerance is devoid of emotional transaction, love is full of emotional investment – even when we disagree.

Second, instead of simply accusing one another of being judgemental, it may be worth investing the time to unpack some of the preconceptions that we hold about each other. When I got married, I didn't realise that I had some assumptions about what would happen when I was sick. Any time I had been unwell during my childhood, my world would stop, and my entire family would revolve around me. I would take prime position in the lounge with a duvet and full authority over the TV remote control. I would order refills of ice-cream, Lucozade and sympathy at regular and frequent intervals. On the other hand, when my wife was growing up, being sick meant quarantine. She was sent to recover in the privacy of her bedroom, and all privileges and luxuries would cease. After all, if school was out of the question, then so was television, food and company. And apparently all that peace and quiet helped her to recover quickly. The problem was, I was unaware of this clash of assumptions when I got married, and so when I first got sick I got a shock. I felt deserted, unloved.

I cannot say there was no collision over this. As soon as I felt well enough for the fight, there were some insults thrown around, with one of us accused of being cold and uncaring, and the other of being lazy and attention-seeking. What could have been a marriage-breaker was saved only by some difficult but honest and deep conversations. Instead of focusing just on what we each did, and how it made us feel, we had to work through the assumptions behind our actions. We had to believe the best about each other; not only to begin to appreciate where each of us was coming from, but also to work out how we could forge a new pathway in the future.

It is this time invested in contention that is long overdue in the Christian–Atheist tolerance debate. What lies behind the anger, rejection and hurt that both sides may be feeling? How can we expose some of the root assumptions that drive our apparent and sometimes real judgementalism? Can we discuss and agree terms and goals of engagement? Can we raise the bar on tolerance to truly accept our differences? How can we move the conversation forward towards collaboration?

Collaboration

At its best a commitment to tolerance is the recognition of the value, dignity and worth of all people. Fair-minded Atheists and Christians are both committed to this. It means that opinions and views that are different to our own should be able to be expressed, heard and understood, and that those holding these views should be given the benefit of the doubt. Similarly, neither Christians nor Atheists should be willing to tolerate the abuse, denigration or exclusion of anyone else. So tolerance does not mean that 'anything goes'.

One of the areas we must work on together, of course, is identifying the correct limits to tolerance: recognising the dynamic interplay between free speech and protecting one another from hate speech or incitement to violence.

Starting on this common ground, Christians and Atheists therefore can, should and do work together to build a more inclusive and equal society. Not only can both sides affirm the Universal Declaration of Human Rights, but both Christians and Atheists make claim to the genesis of its formulation.

Article 18 of the Universal Declaration of Human Rights states:

> Everyone has the right to freedom of thought, conscience and religion; this right includes freedom to change his religion or belief, and freedom, either alone or in community with others and in public or private, to manifest his religion or belief in teaching, practice, worship and observance.[22]

For Atheists, affirming this statement might involve contending alongside Christians for the right of freedom of religious expression in both private and public. For Christians this might involve advocating for fair and equitable treatment of Atheism in religious broadcasting or political representation. Christians may need to rethink how to live out their faith in a pluralist, multicultural context, as many of the practices of the Church still assume that Christianity is the norm for the majority of the population. There are assumptions made in many of our church systems that need to adapt to the diversity of the population. For example, it is no longer widespread practice to ask someone what their Christian name is, we don't now assume that everyone can meaningfully swear on a Bible in court, and it is becoming less realistic to expect Christian worship in all school assemblies. Although these changes make sense in a pluralist society, nevertheless Christians are experiencing culture shock as the things they took for granted are no longer normal for large swathes of our population, and so we are having to work harder at finding ways to express our commitment to Christian claims in a multicultural context. Because of the large-scale shifts in our culture, Atheists, on the other hand, are finding that they are no longer a tiny ostracised minority but have instead, in some areas of life like politics, academia and the media, more social acceptability than Christians. One of their challenges in transitioning from a marginalised oppositional view to a prevalent majority is how to use newfound power and influence responsibly.

For both Christians and Atheists, collaboration with the tolerance movement at least invokes a willingness to avoid social isolation, either by absence or silence. It involves the opportunity to show genuine hospitality to each other whatever our views. It gives us the incentive to find better language to express areas of contention without unnecessary and unhelpful labelling of others' opinions, or critique of personal motivations. Instead of fighting for our own particular rights there can be a reshaping of the conversation that involves contending for the rights of all.

This struck home to me when I was on an inter-religious panel exploring the broadcasting output of a particular national television channel. The panel was made up of representatives from all of the major faith groups, as well as Atheism. As we went around the table, each group lamented their lack of representation. Each person fought for their own corner in an effort to win their slice of the broadcasting pie. By the end of the day this collision mode of interaction had achieved nothing.

Finally it was my turn to speak, and I had no solutions. I could not fix the schedule to transform religious broadcasting and keep all parties happy. There were no arguments left to back my own agenda for better Christian programming. It seemed that the loudest voice was going to win, and I did not have the loudest voice.

As I reflected on this dilemma, I realised that everyone was as frustrated as I was – each of us wanted to get what we felt was ours by rights, and each of us thought that we wouldn't get it. We were not really angry with each other – although it sounded like it. We were not really angry with the television channel – although it sounded like it. We were angry with the system. When the pie was divided up, of course we all made a bid for the biggest slice. But what if we could go back a step and work together to find a fairer system before the pie was cut? Could this kind of collaborative approach be something we all get behind?

When it comes to ethical controversies, where there seems to be an impasse between Christians and Atheists and the only recourse is to accuse one another of being intolerant and judgemental, perhaps it is time to pause and ask some questions. Are we making assumptions of each other that may actually not be true? What are the reasons behind our positions? Are we so blinded by the fight that we are losing sight of what is really important? Are we keeping quiet when we should be raising our voices? Are we raising our voices when we should be reframing the conversation? Are we prepared to invest in genuine relationships by speaking out with our views, even when they may be unorthodox? Are we prepared to respect others, by listening to, questioning and discussing unorthodox views rather than censoring them? Can we agree to be intolerant together of those who are clearly inciting

hatred and violence, while at the same time being protective
of freedom of conscience and freedom of speech? Can we
work towards a tolerance that genuinely welcomes, loves and
invests in those who are different from ourselves? Can love
win the day?

Two people who seem to demonstrate the worst of both
sides of the Christian–Atheist debate are Jerry Falwell and
Larry Flynt. Falwell seemed to delight in making shocking,
crass and provocative public statements. He blamed gay people
for the 9/11 attacks, spoke out against the *Teletubbies* children's
show because of a perception that it promoted homosexuality,
and wanted every school in America to be run by Christians.
Flynt, on the other hand, was the founder of *Hustler* magazine
and an icon of the pornography industry.[23] He seemed to stand
for everything Falwell rejected.

For years Falwell and Flynt engaged in a personal war. The
language Falwell used was every bit as bad as the language
used in Flynt's magazine. And Flynt retaliated with typical
force, not even holding back from asserting that the first time
Falwell had had sex was with his own mother, whom he labelled
a Baptist whore. He made no secret of the fact that he wanted
to destroy Falwell's character. It is hard to think of two more
diametrically opposed ways of viewing life than Flynt and
Falwell. Their mutual repulsion at one another's views was
made public in the media, in the courtroom and in the movies.
But that was not the end of the story.

Larry Flynt faced many legal battles during the 1970s, but
his fight about pornography and free speech was immortalised
in the 1996 movie *The People vs. Larry Flynt*. At some point
after this most infamous trial, Flynt and Falwell's relationship
changed. They began to seek each other out when they came
to the other's town. They would exchange greetings cards,

photographs of their grandchildren, and diet tips. They found, as they spent time together, that they had more in common than it appeared. They conversed robustly yet amicably about philosophy, politics and religion, despite the gulf of difference between them on those subjects. When Jerry Falwell died, Larry Flynt wrote a moving tribute to his adversary, concluding by saying, 'the ultimate result was one I never expected, and was just as shocking a turn to me as was winning that famous Supreme Court case: We became friends'.[24] If Flynt and Falwell can achieve something beyond tolerance, then there is hope for all of us.

Questions

In your experience are Christians judgemental and Atheists tolerant?

Are you more likely to seek to keep the peace through absence or silence?

Have you ever seen injustice performed in the name of tolerance?

What does tolerance look like in your life? Are there opportunities for you to go beyond tolerance towards love and hospitality?

Chapter 4

Christians are do-gooders / Atheists are good-for-nothings

Collision

Bill Gates, or Mother Teresa? Which one of them is the truly good person? Bill, along with his wife Melinda Gates, is fabulously wealthy and fabulously generous. He has personally given away over $28 billion to health, education and economic development. Not only that, he has started the Giving Pledge, which encourages the rest of the world's wealthiest people to support philanthropic causes. Atheist Gates is effecting change on a global scale and impacting on millions of lives. His generosity was used in a bus campaign by the Illinois Secular Student Society with the strapline: 'Bill Gates is Good without God'.[1] Mother Teresa, on the other hand, is one of the most famous Christians in the world. In 1950 she founded the 'Missionaries of Charity' in Calcutta, a home that looked after those who were dying of leprosy, tuberculosis and AIDS. She lived most of her life in voluntary poverty, personally serving 'the poorest of the poor'. She was unequivocal that it was her faith in Jesus that motivated her service: 'I see Jesus in every human being. I say to myself, this is hungry Jesus, I must feed him. This is sick Jesus. This one has leprosy or gangrene; I must wash him and tend to him. I serve because I love Jesus.'[2]

So which of these two people is really doing good: the Atheist or the Christian? Some are critical of Gates' philanthropy, arguing that he gives at a distance, donating only from his surplus wealth, while still leaving himself with more than enough to live from. Some are critical of Mother Teresa, arguing that she was motivated by a desire to convert people, and that for all her efforts, she did not lift anyone out of poverty.

One thing we can say, comparing these two examples, is that 'doing good' does not belong solely to Christianity or to Atheism. Whether rich or poor, male or female, old or young, Christian or Atheist, anybody can feel a pull to do good in society. It is also evident that anyone can get criticised for the good they try to do, and so philanthropy is not without critique and conflict. But what is it that motivates some people to promote the well-being of others around them? And conversely, why do others seem not even to notice or care about the needs of those struggling around the world? At a time when poverty and displacement, war and bullying, domestic violence and inequality are endemic and conspicuous, we need to face up to some of the challenges and opportunities of what doing good really means across the Atheist–Christian divide.

The controversy of charity is always closely accompanied by the question of morality. We don't have to look far online or wait too long in a debate for this to come up in a discussion between Christians and Atheists. When the gloves are off and the rhetoric is flowing, the controversy quickly heats up.

Although there can be no denying the charitable activity that many Christians do, the Atheist might say that there are dubious motivations behind their actions. They do it to bolster their belief that they are morally superior to the rest of humanity. Or they do it to proselytise, as a means of recruiting the most vulnerable to populate their churches. Or they do it to help them get to heaven or worm their way into God's good books. Or they simply do it because they are told to – they have abdicated their own decision-making to a religious book, which, by the way, contains all sorts of morally questionable material. And yet, if they fail to do good, they do not need to worry, because their God will forgive them anyway.

If the stereotypes facing Christians are tough, then it is not much better for Atheists. For Atheists, the Christian chips in, if there is no universal morality, just as there is no universal purpose or meaning or accountability, then everything is relative. Atheists are driven by their own personal agendas, where there is little room, rhyme or reason to care for anyone or anything but themselves and their interests unless they happen to decide they want to. As Fyodor Dostoyevsky famously had one of his characters, Mitya, say in his classic *The Brothers Karamazov*: 'If God does not exist, everything is permitted.'[3] If they can avoid interacting with the poor and needy, that's fine. Because Atheists live in a moral vacuum, they feel no obligation to participate in making the world a better place. Whatever good they do is motivated only by self-interest or self-delusion.

Suddenly it's easy to see how a conversation about doing good can quickly turn bad. And this is not just an academic issue. Whether Christians are being assessed by an Atheist social worker as a potential foster family, or an Atheist is running for election in a predominantly Christian constituency, or whether a government body is deciding between funding a faith-based or secular relief agency, or whether applicants for a counselling job are being checked out, or if a doctor begins making unscheduled house calls, it is vital to understand the fundamental motivations that can lie behind apparently altruistic activities.

But when those motivations are scrutinised and held up for questioning, the relationship can swiftly deteriorate. However much we may defend ourselves, the truth is that it is hard, perhaps impossible, to have completely benevolent intentions and morally pure incentives behind our actions. Exposing the truth of this hurts.

Collusion

Whether we recognise it or not, in our professional, personal and public lives we are constantly grappling with moral questions. How much money we spend on our house, car or laptop is a moral question. How we choose to form our families, whether we have kids, how many we have and where they come from, these are all moral decisions. Separating out our recycling, writing our will, choosing our holiday destinations – all involve complex moral challenges.

When I studied medicinal chemistry at university I was told that ethics didn't have anything to do with science and research. But I soon discovered AIDS research was receiving ten times the funding that malaria research received. Digging into why this was the case, I discovered it was because AIDS was affecting Western people more than malaria did. In 2013, Bill Gates made an even more telling comparison: the World Health Organisation reported that in 2010 worldwide spending on procedures to address the non-fatal condition of baldness was more than twice that spent on research into malaria, which kills hundreds of thousands of people a year.[4] So even within the seemingly 'ideologically neutral' world of scientific research, decisions are influenced by ethically (or perhaps unethically) assumed categories.

Moral frameworks play a huge part in every sphere of life:

in the health system, judicial system, educational system or social and political systems. Most of the time, however, these frameworks are unrecognised and unacknowledged. It is like having an accent – we only recognise that we have one ourselves when we encounter someone with a different one. And so whenever we experience a conflict of interests or when a controversy hits the headlines, the collusion begins to unravel.

Most people would agree that littering is bad and equal opportunities are good. Most people would be happy to delay their journey to allow an emergency vehicle to pass by. Most people would be outraged if graffiti suddenly appeared on their street. But when public opinion is divided – for example, on whether speed limits should be reduced, or fox-hunting should be permitted, or whether euthanasia should be legalised, or whether foreign aid spending should be increased, then it is much harder to effectively debate the issues without waking the sleeping giant of what forms the basis of our morality.

A recent case in point which illustrates this very clearly is the question of immigration controls for those caught up in the refugee crisis. Some people would argue that it is 'good' to relax our controls, because we are helping those less fortunate than ourselves; because we value diversity; because refugees often contribute skills to society; or because we should treat people the way we would want to be treated if we found ourselves suddenly in mortal danger. Other people would argue that immigration is a 'bad' thing, because we have sufficient problems in our society already without additional pressures; because a diverse society can create conflict; because refugees drain precious resources; or because of the risk of terrorists infiltrating our communities. Those on different sides of the debate argue endlessly about the pros and cons, risks and opportunities of welcoming refugees. But eventually the ethical questions have to be faced. Do we have a moral obligation to help? What is the 'right' thing to do in this scenario? And what is that sense of obligation, of good and evil, right and wrong, based on?

In the interests of not rocking the boat, discussions on ethics and morality are often avoided. This can lead to some interesting personal dichotomies, such that someone can rally round their neighbour as she desperately tries to get her 'right to remain' visa, while simultaneously sharing on social media the terrible risks that immigrants pose to our communities. We may berate those who engage in benefit fraud, while overlooking our own less-than-honest attitude to our tax return. We might 'do our bit' to support charities and community cohesion activities, criticising those who won't get involved, and yet still defend policies that widen rifts and cut services. We are far too polite to point out the hypocrisy in our friends, and far too reticent to spot it in ourselves – and so we avoid the challenge of our individually and collectively illogical moral conclusions.

Alternatively, we collude by dismissing people's viewpoints without consideration. Sometimes Christians assume that Atheists have no moral framework and are therefore only swayed by their unfounded personal opinions and are not worth engaging with. Sometimes Atheists assume that Christianity is not just morally dubious but morally dangerous, and therefore that Christians have no right to talk about morality and are not worth listening to. For example, Christopher Hitchens famously suggested in one debate that because those attempting suicide bombings or practising genital mutilation are entirely faith-based, anyone of faith claiming a moral grounding for their views can be immediately dismissed.[5]

When we are not avoiding moral debate for fear of exposing

our own hypocrisy or out of a naive dismissal of alternative points of view, we collude in allowing that moral debate to shift to a personal attack. Instead of discussing ethical principles fairly, with points put from both sides of the table, it is easier to dismiss or ridicule the proponents of the opposing view to ours. The press, media and government have often wittingly or unwittingly colluded with this approach, not only accepting the stereotypes, but turning them to their advantage to win votes, readers or kudos.

Recently, I was invited to participate in a televised BBC ethical debate programme. As the researcher checked my opinions on the pressing moral question of the day, I did my best to answer in a forthright yet gracious and nuanced way. However, by the end of the conversation, the researcher told me that, because my views were too moderate, I was no longer to appear on the show. The researcher then proceeded to seek out a more angry and angular Christian perspective on the issue, because that made for more exciting television. Commentators describe it as the 'see-saw approach' to balanced reporting, where they find vociferous extremes on two sides of the moral debate and play them off against each other. This makes for great television, apparently – the debate is energetic and heated. But the mutually dismissive, polarised argument does nothing to further true conversation and does a lot to incite division and disagreement by presenting only the ugliest version of the two views being expressed.

The see-saw approach may have a claim to be balanced, but it is nevertheless biased,[6] driven by programme makers whose criteria for success are viewing figures rather than actually finding answers – let alone encouraging community cohesion. Some may argue that our political systems are also impoverished by their intrinsic adherence to this approach, because it is easier to pit Conservatives against Labour, or Republicans against Democrats in the USA, than to fairly represent a wider range of views or parties.

This argument reveals the flaws in the 'Mother Teresa versus Bill Gates' scenario we started this chapter with. Just as these two fine examples do not (sadly) represent the approach to charity of all Christians and all Atheists, so it is not helpful to pit Christians against Atheist, as though they were on opposite sides in the debating chamber or on the outrage see-saw. We do not disagree on everything to the extreme, but nor do we have to agree with one another on everything. We can, though, agree on enough to do some good.

Contention

In order to move the conversation forward, we need to explore the differences between Christian and Atheist motivation and people's justification for doing good and knowing good. Let's begin with a look at the Christian position. Understanding the essentials of Christian ethics is relatively simple. Jesus makes it clear on a number of occasions that the two greatest principles for life are: '"Love the Lord your God with all your heart and with all your soul and with all your mind." This is the first and greatest commandment. And the second is like it: "Love your neighbour as yourself."'[7]

Love is the absolute centre and essence of a Christian understanding of life and morality. The calling of the Christian is to love God and to love their neighbour, and the Bible is clear that these two loves cannot be separated. We love those around us because we love God, and, because God loves us, we love those around us. Christianity teaches that everyone should be treated with grace and dignity irrespective of their beliefs, behaviours, abilities, sexuality, race or class. Because the pursuit of love, justice and mercy is of central significance to Christian living, there is a rich history of thousands of years of reflection and practice. Driven by the desire to love their neighbours Christians have, from the very beginning, been active in caring for the sick, vulnerable and impoverished. In the West, Christians started the first schools, hospitals and hospices. These institutions and acts of charity were never intended only to serve the needs of Christians and their families, but were to serve the needs of all, as Christians were directly inspired by Jesus' words to love their neighbour.

Ethics, compassion and doing good are therefore an intrinsically important aspect of Christian faith and worship. Here are three aspects that a Christian might cite as a rationale or motivation for doing good. The first centres on the character of God, the second focuses on the example of Jesus and the third revolves around the power of grace.

First of all, Christians believe that God's character is intrinsically and absolutely good – he is utterly fair, reliable and trustworthy, with no corruption, deference or bias in him. Because God is perfectly good, Christians believe both in an absolute moral standard as revealed by God, and also in an ultimate moral accountability.

Second, Christians believe that Jesus is God in human form and as such he provides a perfect worked example of how all of us should live. The best historical accounts of Jesus' life reveal him as having lived a life of radical sacrificial service to others. He fed the hungry, healed the sick, included the outcast, challenged the corrupt and gave hope to the hopeless. The name Christian was attached to Jesus' followers in the first century because they were attempting to emulate Jesus Christ's lifestyle, and so it has been ever since.

Third, according to the Bible every human being before or since Jesus has failed to live up to the standards set by the two commands to love both God and neighbour. It says we have not loved God with all of our being, and we have not shown the same degree of care and concern for others that we have shown to ourselves. And Christianity claims that, for this very reason, Jesus came to make us right with God through dying on our behalf so that, whatever our human shortfall when it comes to loving God or loving our neighbour, we can still be acceptable to God. If this is true, then the good things that Christians try to do in the world should not be driven by an anxious attempt to earn favour with God, but should rather stem from a response of gratitude for what God has already done for them. Christians refer to this idea as grace, and their experience of grace motivates many to pass on the kindness and compassion they have received, using Jesus as an example, and God's perfect goodness as a goal. At its best this means that Christians don't come with any kind of superiority complex or holier-than-thou attitude. They come from a place of brokenness looking simply to share the grace they have humbly received. As the Indian missionary D.T. Niles famously said: it is just 'one beggar telling another beggar where to find bread'.[8]

There are a number of areas where Atheists might dispute this kind of articulation of Christian motivation for doing good. Not least is their struggle with the fact that Christians ground their ethics in a God whom Atheists don't believe exists, following the example of a man Atheists would dispute was God in human form, and trusting his claim to have died on behalf of the world. On top of that, Atheists would question the mooted nature and character of God, questioning the evidence that points to him being morally pure.

Furthermore, some Atheists challenge God's own basis for morality. This last challenge is linked to a line of thought articulated by the ancient philosopher Plato. Through his character Euthyphro, Plato asked 'Is what is holy holy because the gods approve it, or do they approve it because it is holy?' Or to put it another way: is an action good because God commands it or is an action good in itself and God recognises it as so? If the former is true, then God could suddenly decide to decree war or child abuse as good. If the latter is true, then we don't need God to be able to determine morality.[9] Either way, it seems, Christian morality is faulty. But behind Plato's question lies an assumption. In that regard it is reminiscent of the classic example: 'Have you stopped beating your wife yet?' which has no 'good' yes-or-no-style answer. If you say yes, then you are admitting wife-beating, and if you say no then it assumes that you are continuing to perpetuate violence against women. Plato's assumption is that morality is separate from God, but Christians believe that the essential character of God is good and therefore he does not and cannot randomly decide either to make something good or bad, or to choose to approve something as good or bad. This renders Plato's question invalid. It's like asking what colour an object is in the dark. Colour only makes sense when light is involved: colour and light are inseparable. If the essential character of God is good, he will only decree what is good, and we are able to recognise it as good because God has hardwired our conscience. In other words, Christians claim it is not coincidence that what in general we find good coheres in general with what God commands. Christian morality is mostly self-evident, precisely *because* God exists.

But there are two problems here, as Atheists and Christians will agree. What happens when God appears to *command* something we know to be very bad – like genocide? And what happens when God appears to *do* something we know to be very bad – like orchestrating earthquakes and tsunamis, or as Stephen Fry accused, allowing parasitic worms to make children ill? There are many passages in the Bible and more than enough 'acts of God' and other unpleasant phenomena around the world to give us good grounds to question God's morality. In fact, it is vital that we do so. Just as a husband or wife confronts the other if they suspect they have been unfaithful, a healthy confrontation allows the truth to come out. Either the partner has been unfaithful and the consequences of that breakdown of trust must be faced, or there is an innocent explanation, which restores the marriage to a relationship of trust. If God is not morally pure, then Christians are deluded. If he is, then there must be another explanation for the evidence we see. Christians maintain that it is precisely because God is perfectly good that evil must be opposed, and that passages in the Bible that talk about God's judgement do not prove he is judgemental, but rather that he is just. However, Christians also believe that God is perfectly loving, and that he is therefore holding out on ultimate judgement, even though the consequences of human rebellion against God are having destructive knock-on effects on the planet. Of course, the arguments are much more complex, but for the sake of this discussion perhaps it is enough to show that there are reasons why Christians would defend a moral absolute based on their understanding of who God is.

Nonetheless, there are problems here too. Christians who believe that there are moral absolutes still argue and disagree. Take, for example, views on gun ownership. Many Christians in the UK oppose the personal ownership of guns in civilian homes, whereas many Christians in the USA support the ownership of guns. Christians on both sides of this debate can appeal to Scripture and basic moral principles. Does this mean the appeal to moral absolutes is flawed? Not at all. We can believe in the existence of moral absolutes without saying that any of us has an infallible grasp of what those absolutes are or how to apply them. In the same way, scientists believe that the universe is knowable and understandable and yet no one is claiming an infallible grasp of all the laws of the universe. We are all on a journey to better understanding and this means that we can have confidence in moral absolutes while also being humble about our grasp of them.

We recognise that Christians – who share a common faith and who look to the life and teaching of Jesus for wisdom and inspiration – still have a wide range of views on subjects as diverse as gun control and sexuality. Imagine how complex it is to speak of Atheist approaches to morality when there are, according to Ricky Gervais and Richard Dawkins, no unifying doctrines or beliefs apart from the rejection of the belief in God. There are no authorised spokespeople, no officially recognised canonical writings that form the basis of atheistic thought on any given issue. What follows is an attempt to map some of the most common moral frameworks that contemporary Atheists put forward.

First of all I have to acknowledge that my Atheist friends are just as passionate about social reform, justice and fairness as my Christian friends. In my experience many Atheists have a very clear and strong moral compass. They have a clear commitment to fairness and equality, to human rights and to seeking to improve society. In the work I have been involved with regarding welcoming refugees, I have found committed Atheists to be among the most passionate campaigners and activists. So how do Atheists tend to ground their moral frameworks?

Some Atheists argue that morality has no grounding, as life, the universe and everything else is ultimately meaningless.[10] In fact, if there is no such thing as morality, some would argue, then those who propose morality pose a danger, as moral virtues such as compassion and pity undermine humanity by contradicting the evolutionary principle of 'survival of the fittest'.[11] The main problem with this approach is when it shifts from descriptive to prescriptive. In other words, when we decide to give 'survival of the fittest' a helping hand – such as arguably happened under Nazi Germany, with the eugenics programmes, concentration camps and gas chambers. For this reason, there are very few Atheists in the West today who would sanction this view of morality.

Atheists like Richard Dawkins argue that while the concept of morality is indeed ultimately illusory, it can nevertheless be beneficial in an evolutionary sense. His argument is that the most effective way to ensure the survival of our genes is by being selfish,[12] but sometimes, he continues, driven by our own enlightened self-interest, we demonstrate what looks like altruistic behaviour. Sometimes our selfish genes[13] motivate us to altruism when it benefits ourselves or our kin. This derives from Dawkins' understanding of the nature and purpose of human life. In his 1991 Royal Institute Christmas lectures for children he explained:

> We are machines built by DNA whose purpose is to make more copies of the same DNA . . . That is exactly what we are for. We are machines for propagating DNA, and the propagation of DNA is a self-sustaining process. It is every living object's sole reason for living.[14]

Because gene replication is humanity's defining purpose, any form of ethical consideration must serve this greater end.

There is plenty of evidence for these two ideas in society. The first can be seen in the 'I scratch your back, you scratch mine' philosophy that might lead people to care for the elderly, fundraise for cancer research, or mow their neighbours' lawns. By doing these things for others, it is more likely that they will be done for us and our offspring in our turn. The second motivation can be seen in the drive to care for the planet or create a fairer society: we do it to optimise life quality for our children and our grandchildren. But Dawkins goes on to argue that when we are compassionate towards those who have no connection to us and offer no likely benefit to us or our offspring, this is defective morality, as we are then acting against the very purpose of our being – the replication of our DNA. He explains:

> We can no more help ourselves feeling pity when we see a weeping unfortunate (who is unrelated and unable to reciprocate) than we can help ourselves feeling lust for a member of the opposite sex (who may be infertile or otherwise unable to reproduce). Both are misfirings, Darwinian mistakes . . .[15]

Again it is hard to find many who would recognise Dawkins' Darwinian ethics as a motivatory force for social good. So we need to look further afield for a moral framework that befits the morality that drives most Atheists.

The most commonly affirmed justification for morality I have come across from Atheists that I respect is utilitarianism. This approach suggests that the ultimate point of moral reference is doing whatever seeks the greatest amount of good for the greatest number of people. You may remember the balloon debates from your school days, where a hypothetical hot-air balloon is going to crash unless one of its passengers either voluntarily jumps to their death or is thrown out. Each passenger has to justify their utility to the group and whoever is voted out is thrown overboard and allowed to die for the greater good. This lies at the heart of Sam Harris's 'scientific morality', where he argues that morality involves the 'maximization of well-being for conscious creatures'.[16]

Christians find much to critique in the nihilist-evolutionary, defective-gene and utilitarian approaches to morality.[17] Is it even possible genuinely to 'do good' for another person under any of these systems? What Dawkins calls misfirings: non-selfish, altruistic, sacrificial help to the weakest in society – are they not the very thing that enables our society to cohere and flourish and overcome tragedy? What would happen to society if we suddenly abandoned those who were weak and poor?

Jeremy Bentham, the founder of modern utilitarianism, proposed that to increase the pleasure of the majority it was necessary to round up beggars from the streets and put them into workhouses along with the 'raving lunatics, or persons of profligate conversation . . . the deaf and dumb . . . the shockingly deformed and the blind'.[18] Although Bentham's logic may seem sound, this does not cohere with the way that most Atheists choose to live.[19]

The majority of Atheists I have spoken to hold – to some degree – the idea that there is intrinsic morality. One way to explain this is to follow Sam Harris's suggestion that ethical truth, like scientific truth, has principles to be discovered, refuted or verified.[20] There are some clear advantages to this approach – it might explain why there is a general universal repulsion at murder and other violence, and a wide acceptance of charitable activity as good and beneficial. This line of thinking is particularly followed by Atheists who also identify as humanists, taking a very high view of human well-being and placing it as central to their ethical decision-making.

In fact it is echoed in the Amsterdam Declaration, which is described as the 'defining statement of world humanism'[21] and affirms the worth, dignity and autonomy of the individual and the right of every human being to the greatest possible freedom compatible with the rights of others: 'Humanists have a duty of care to all of humanity including future generations. Humanists believe that morality is an intrinsic part of human nature based on understanding and a concern for others, needing no external sanction.'[22]

However, this approach does raise its own questions. If 'ethics' are existential things waiting to be discovered, just like the laws of gravity and thermodynamics, how did they get there in the first place, and why, once discovered, are they not always self-evident? Why do some cultures propose that, for example, honour killings or female genital mutilation are morally required, while others find the same acts morally reprehensible? Why do some Atheists argue for compassionate service to fellow human beings, while others in history have opposed this on the grounds that it encourages the weak to persist instead of perish? (This latter point may be the counterpoint to the conundrum of why, if Christians believe that the Bible reveals God's laws, there is still such a diversity of moral positions held by Christians.)

We can see from this brief overview of the moral debate that this is no small subject area, and there are no easy solutions. Just as Atheists find problems in the Christian grounding of their ethics in God, so Christians find problems in atheistic attempts to ground their ethics without God. In fact, it could be said that our parallel struggle to work out our morality is the first thing that we have in common when it comes to doing good.

Collaboration

Despite the ongoing debate, and despite the fact that Christians and Atheists operate from extremely different moral frameworks, there are still many examples of common ground between them. In most everyday situations, Christians and Atheists agree on what is morally creditable and what is morally repugnant. The large overlap between the practical outworkings of these moral frameworks means that Christians and Atheists can serve together happily in our hospitals, schools, community groups and neighbourhoods. It means Christians and Atheists who are married to one another can agree when they teach their children principles of sharing, respect, generosity and forgiveness. It means that people such as Bill Gates or Mother Teresa can become aspirational role models to all of us, whether we agree with their religious stance or not.

While face-to-face philosophising about ethics can often end up being unproductive, with Atheists and Christians arguing, point-scoring and putting each other down through slurs and cheap one-liners, practical ethical conversations in a shoulder-to-shoulder context are often surprisingly productive. For example, although I was rightly challenged rigorously by social workers about my motivations for becoming a foster carer and how it related to my Christian faith, post-assessment those debates were put aside as our energies went into working together to advocate for the welfare and best outcome for the children in my care. Similarly, my work campaigning to support refugee children in the UK has opened up fruitful and respectful collaborations with Christians and Atheists alike.

We have assumed in this book that collaboration is better than conflict. If you agree with that you will probably agree that living in compassionate and considerate communities, where each looks out for the needs of the other, is better than the selfish, narcissistic, egocentric individualism of a dog-eat-dog world. Both Christians and Atheists face the daily challenge of keeping our own consciences clear, of listening to what Atheist writer Steven Pinker has referred to as the 'better angels of our nature'.[23] And for both Christians and Atheists there is a constant negative pull on us towards self-centred living. For Atheists, this might be understood as the evolutionary influence of the 'selfish gene'. Christians, on the other hand, speak of the sinful nature. It is good to be reminded of the importance of making caring for those around us a normative part of life in our society.

Without denying our differences, ignoring that ideas have consequences or seeking to close down conversation, we can recognise that Christians and Atheists share significant ethical common ground and, for the most part, a common desire to make the world a better place.[24] Even when we disagree on a particular ethical dilemma, there would still be principles over which we can find agreement. For example, while a couple composed of a Christian and an Atheist may find themselves at loggerheads over whether or not to include attending a church service as part of their Christmas Day celebration, they could find that they agree about making the day meaningful through generosity, spending family time together – including those who may feel overlooked – and much more. Or while Christian and Atheist businesspeople may disagree on whether or not to give away a proportion of their business's profits, they may well share values of integrity when it comes to investing those profits ethically.

I am not suggesting that either Christians or Atheists compromise their moral standpoints. I believe, in fact, that a moral framework worth its salt must be worth pursuing and defending, in order to prevent us from living half-hearted, 'accidental' or hypocritical lives. In this respect I have often been challenged by my thoughtful Atheist friends to re-examine some of my prejudices and assumptions. Christians sometimes like to think that virtues of hospitality, generosity, compassion belong solely to those of us who believe in God, but charitable giving and volunteering is not monopolised by those from different faith groups. In fact, many Atheists put Christians to shame with their kindness. Perhaps Atheists have unconsciously imbibed a Christian framework that recognises the drive to help those around us? Or perhaps Christians have unconsciously imbibed an Atheist 'selfish gene' framework?

In 2008 *The Times* columnist Matthew Parris, a convinced Atheist, travelled back to Malawi, the country he grew up in as a child, after forty-five years away. Parris was visiting the work of Pump Aid – a secular charity that helps rural communities install pumps which keep their village wells clean. But Parris found more than he had bargained for. As he spoke with the employees of the charity, many of whom were Christians, he noticed a discernible difference about these workers:

> It inspired me, renewing my flagging faith in development charities. But travelling in Malawi refreshed another belief, too: one I've been trying to banish all my life, but an observation I've been unable to avoid since my African childhood. It confounds my ideological beliefs, stubbornly refuses to fit my world view, and has embarrassed my growing belief that there is no God.
>
> Now a confirmed atheist, I've become convinced of the enormous contribution that Christian evangelism makes in Africa: sharply distinct from the work of secular NGOs, government projects and international aid efforts. These alone

will not do. Education and training alone will not do. In Africa
Christianity changes people's hearts. It brings a spiritual trans-
formation. The rebirth is real. The change is good.[25]

Parris humbly recognises a benefit that Christian faith brought
to a continent that he loved. A cynic might argue that Parris is
demonstrating a colonial attitude – that he thinks the Christian
faith is good for the backward people of Africa to get them
through their difficult circumstances but isn't good enough for
him and his enlightened and superior Western intellect. But
perhaps he has a point. At the very least, perhaps it is time we
started recognising the good in the worldviews and motivations
of those we disagree with and use that as a point of collaboration
for encouraging good in the world. In a world full of bad things
– tragedies, wars, famine, inequalities – one thing is certain:
whether we are Atheists or Christians, when it comes to doing
good, we could probably all be doing better.

Questions

Who is your moral hero: Mother Teresa, Bill Gates or someone
else?

What examples can you think of where the media has used the
see-saw effect? Did it demonstrate balance or polarisation?

Why do both Christians and Atheists have problems when it comes
to the justification of their ethics?

What are the principles that guide your moral decision-making?

Chapter 5

Christians are boring / Atheists are fun

Collision

Halloween is too ghoulish, Easter is too chocolatey, Christmas is too tinselly. Such sentiments generally come from the same sort of people who complain about Sunday trading, and make a fuss about the opening of new casinos, the teaching of sex education in schools, and the stocking of dinosaurs in toy shops. They are also likely to boycott popular books and films such as *Harry Potter* or *Fifty Shades*. These are the world's self-appointed fun police. Indeed, one American journalist, Henry Louis Mencken, described such Christians as living with 'the haunting fear that someone, somewhere, may be happy'.[1]

Atheists, on the other hand, live with unrestrained and uncontained hedonistic joy, driven by the supposedly epicurean axiom: 'Let us eat, drink and be merry, for tomorrow we die.' They are free to pursue their own pleasures at will, as they have no moral absolutes to limit their fun. There are no Ten Commandments for Atheists. They are the masters of their own fate and, in the words of the poem, captains of their own souls.[2] They can be counted on for enjoyable company where anything goes – at least, anything except boring, moaning Christians.

These stereotypes are pretty common, and certainly regularly drive the plotlines of movies and TV series. For example, picture a small town in America where the local high-school prom is being planned by the students – except there is a ban on dancing. Guess who has dreamt up and is enforcing this ridiculous embargo? Yes, the local church minister. But, thanks to an enlightened young Kevin Bacon, the town is liberated from its miserable conservative Christian stranglehold. The movie is *Footloose* and its central concept is a popular trope, also to be found in the children's animated film *Happy Feet* with its council of elders, in *The Shawshank Redemption* with its corrupt warden, in the judgemental and holier-than-thou Flanders family in *The Simpsons*, in the underhand ecclesiastical hierarchies of *The Da Vinci Code* or in the brutal totalitarianism found in Margaret Atwood's futuristic dystopian novel *The Handmaid's Tale*.

But most Christians resent this stereotype, and the movies that reinforce it. Their response is often to insist that they are truly joyful, and it is Atheists who are the miserable ones; they point a finger, particularly, at those angry and bitter Atheists who shout out their anti-religious rhetoric. They only have to quote Richard Dawkins' and Ricky Gervais's Twitter feeds as unequivocal evidence that Christians don't have the monopoly on being obstreperous or mean-spirited. Judging by the tone of a lot of militant Atheist spokesmen, it seems that Atheism carries with it very little joy. In fact, often it seems that the public face of Atheism looks like a lot of very rude, angry, white, old men with a chip on the shoulder and an axe to grind when it comes to faith. Ironically, some might say this is not too dissimilar to the way many people see the Church?

Some Christians argue that they are the only ones who know the real meaning of happiness. I have met many Christians who say that, after converting, everything is different – the sky is bluer, the grass is greener, happiness is . . . well, happier. Many of them claim to have discovered a previously unimaginable sense of peace, joy, contentment, satisfaction and well-being. Some of them say that they have experienced physical healing, or achieved financial prosperity like never before. Others that they have found a sense of identity, belonging, acceptance and purpose that overrides any difficulties of their personal circumstances.

Atheists can easily dismiss this sort of talk as psychosomatic – wishful thinking. What Christians have mistaken for happiness is just brainwashing into delirium. Those fake-talk-show-host smiles, overbearingly cheerful dispositions and 'Praise the Lord anyway' catchphrases are just due to Christianity being, as Karl Marx said, the 'opium of the people'.[3] Is Christianity just a legal high for the gullible or desperate? Are Atheists right to question whether Christians are really happy, or just indoctrinated and conditioned by their music or their church community? Who truly is happier: Atheists or Christians?

Collusion

You could say that arguing about who is the happier is about as productive as arguing over which ice-cream flavour is the best. However much I preach that mint choc chip is the highest pleasure possible in the realm of frozen cone-based desserts, I cannot persuade my wife to forgo the much inferior raspberry ripple she insists on. Happiness is subjective. One person's deepest joy is the awe of assaulting the north face of Everest, while for another that would be their worst nightmare. For some an adrenaline-fuelled sporting endeavour brings great pleasure, while for others it's a glass of claret and a good book every time. Just as some people enjoy the elegance of the opera, others prefer the visceral pleasure of a rock concert. Within Christianity, some love to get lost in the transcendent beauty of choral evensong at St Paul's Cathedral while others would much prefer to worship to the sounds of kerranging guitars and thumping bass. It seems to be intrinsic to happiness that everyone experiences it differently.

Nevertheless, statistics about the relative happiness of Atheists and Christians regularly make the headlines. For example, the Office for National Statistics released data in 2016 that demonstrated that religious people were significantly happier than people of no religion.[4] But soon after, secular humanist sites reported that the world's happiest countries were also the least religious.[5] Is this toing and froing just a point-scoring exercise, or is there more to it? Social scientists sometimes use happiness indicators such as personal satisfaction, smiling, low levels of cortisol and the like to try to measure happiness. But there is much debate as to the accuracy and relevance of the statistics. The annual World Happiness Report[6] analyses average scores on the following indicators: income, life expectancy, social support, generosity, freedom and trust. The list regularly sees rich Western countries top the list for happiness and poor African nations come at the bottom. However, there is anecdotal evidence that suggests the opposite might be true – that people from financially impoverished nations exhibit a happiness, contentment and generosity despite adversity that can far outweigh their rich counterparts in the West despite their relative prosperity. Happiness inhibitors such as mental health problems, obesity, job dissatisfaction, peer pressure, propensity to lodge complaints and lawsuits, divorce and family breakdown are much more rife in richer, so-called 'happier' countries, but these are rarely taken into consideration in the analysis.

Perhaps the report reflects more about what the compilers of the list value than the existential experience of happiness from actual people. Or perhaps their indicators are designed to reflect their stated motivation to drive political change and aid investment.[7] Nigerian political commentator Dr Jideofor Adibe argues:

> The World Happiness Report may unwittingly be reinforcing an essentialist construction of Africa and the narratives and innuendos that go with it. Since its chosen variables can only measure well-being, wealth and democracy (freedom), which are areas that actually define Africa's condition of underdevelopment, it becomes axiomatic that African countries will not do well in such rankings.[8]

While we may never agree on whether religion or lack of it, or wealth or lack of it, makes us happier or not, what is commonly accepted is the right to pursue happiness. In fact it is acknowledged as a basic human right in the Declaration of Independence of the United States of America, which frames happiness in the following way: 'We hold these truths to be sacred and undeniable; that all men are created equal and independent, that from that equal creation they derive rights inherent and inalienable, among which are the preservation of life, and liberty, and the pursuit of happiness.'[9]

There is no shortage of ways for human beings to pursue happiness. Each of us seeks our own personal happiness, whether it be through sport, art, food, diet programmes, relationships, sex, cosmetic surgery, academic study, family-building, spas, holidays, drugs or other mood enhancers – the list is long. The pursuit of pleasure is an all-consuming passion for many of us who live in the Western world. This applies equally to Christians and Atheists. Side-by-side comparison of a Christian's social media feed with an Atheist's might show more similarities than you would imagine. So many of us, whatever beliefs we hold, share a common image of what the good life we are seeking to achieve really is, and much of it is simply a composite image created out of all the marketing materials we are exposed to. We receive the same gifts on our birthdays, we drive the same cars, wear the same clothes, eat the same meals, post the same pictures from our travels on our social media feeds, and celebrate the same achievements of our children and grandchildren. In fact, on any given day of the week (perhaps excluding Sundays), if you were to track the lives of most Christians and Atheists they might look almost identical. Christians and Atheists respond with similar passion and compassion to the same global disasters, attend the same parties, jump onto the same bandwagons, and jump off the same sinking ships.

So we certainly seem to have lots in common when it comes to our pursuit of happiness. Is this a form of collusion from the Christian side? The prevailing culture we live in, with its individualistic consumerism, often shapes the lives of Christians more than the tenets of the Christian faith. This is a major challenge to Christians who claim to follow Jesus, who, after all, calls his followers to a radically counter-cultural way of living. Just as Jesus challenged the social norms of his day – calling for and showing kindness towards foreigners, dignity towards women, value towards children and compassion towards the needy, so if Christians are to follow in his footsteps, we cannot just go along with the values and expectations of our culture.

I feel the finger pointing at my own life here. I sometimes catch myself taking more pleasure from the purchase of a new tech gadget than I do in serving the needs of others. The advertising bombardment that says I should ditch my trusty phone for a new model, or exchange my second-hand car for a new upgrade, colonises my imagination and I find myself spending far more time thinking about how I can increase my own personal pleasure than I do thinking about those around me. I am ashamed to say that I am often more inclined to be keeping up with the Joneses, than keeping up with Jesus. 'What would the Joneses do?' is often higher on my happiness agenda than 'What would Jesus do?'

Sometimes, though, there may be an implicit collusion from the Atheist side, with the Christian moral and cultural heritage of the Western world shaping their lives more than the logical expression of their Atheism. The end result is that some Atheists live more 'christianly' than some Christians, while some Christians seem to live more 'atheistically' than Atheists.

One benefit of this implicit collusion means that it is easier for us all to get along. If we both splash out on the same luxury items then there is no guilt when we both drive our new cars into work. If we both join in a charity fun run raising money for the same cause, there is the added benefit of the feel-good factor that comes from doing not only the right thing, but the in-thing. If there is a particular drinking or social-climbing culture at work, or an expectation of financial extravagance within the family, then it is often easier to go with the flow than to stand apart because of our convictions. Nobody wants to be the social outcast, after all. Sometimes Christians compromise their standards and values because they don't understand them well enough, or because they don't value them strongly enough. In the same way, perhaps Atheists compromise the outworking of their worldview to conform intentionally or unintentionally to the wider culture.

Contention

So, how can we graciously untangle the potential prejudice and misunderstanding that exists, not just about the moral frameworks that Christians and Atheists hold to, but about the real-world lifestyle choices that Christians and Atheists make in their pursuit of happiness?

Let's imagine a social worker looking to place a child for adoption. Two families seem equally suitable – one is Christian, the other is Atheist. They both have passed their assessments with flying colours and both have a good support network. They are both financially secure. They are both well regarded in their communities. Now the social worker has to make a choice about where this child will be happiest and best able to thrive. When all other factors are equal, imagine this social worker decides that the Atheist family is a better match for the child because they do not have a 'restrictive religious background' that he feels may stop the child from experiencing fullness of life.

Now, at one level, this may seem fair enough to a social worker who has the child's best interests at heart. Atheism is widely perceived to be open-minded and non-judgemental, and therefore seems more supportive of the child's future flourishing, whatever choices they may make. But from a Christian perspective, this is discriminatory. The rejected family claim their faith is liberating, not restricting. In fact, for them, it is precisely their faith that makes them other-centred, happy and compassionate, intent on practising and promoting unconditional love, making them at least equally supportive when it comes to including a child in their family and able to make the child happy and secure. And what if the child in question has a faith of their own, or may at some point in their life develop a curiosity about faith? Perhaps a Christian family would be better placed to meet that need.[10]

Let's imagine for a moment that the differentiating factor between the two families was not faith, but race. Imagine the social worker placed an adoptive child with a white family based on the view that white families are happier because they have more progressive views than black families. This (hopefully) would be instantly identified as racial discrimination. We cannot attribute a negative characteristic to a whole segment of society because of race alone; such is the essence of racism. In the same way, to assume Christians will be boring and restrictive is a prejudicial position to take, because it is to assign a negative characteristic to a whole segment of society. In the UK there is legislation to protect people from this kind of discrimination. Being rejected as a potential adoptive match for a child solely on the basis of religious convictions contravenes equalities legislation, which says that faith is a protected category and cannot be the basis of discrimination. Equally, if the social worker was a Christian and chose the Christian couple over the Atheist couple because he assumed the latter held atheistic views that were fundamentally selfish and uncompassionate, this would be just as wrong, prejudicial and illegal.

Nevertheless, from the way Christians are regularly treated in the public arena and the media, it seems to be socially acceptable to stereotype Christians as culturally conservative and restrictive. Faith is regularly showcased as having a negative influence on the world. This is not just a critique of those who use faith to excuse violence, but is applied to all who adhere to a faith. Sam Harris said 'the greatest problem confronting civilization is not merely religious extremism: rather, it is the larger set of cultural and intellectual accommodations we have made to faith itself'. Or even more forthrightly, Richard Dawkins in an interview with the BBC, when asked if religion was a force for good or evil in the world, replied, 'for evil, on balance'.[11]

Again, we can see how prejudicial this is if we apply such language to issues of gender or race. Imagine an educated person claiming that men are, on balance, a force for evil. Or imagine an interviewee claiming on the BBC that black people are, on balance, a force for evil in the world. They could even cite evidence that in the USA men make up 93 per cent of prison inmates, but only make up 50 per cent of the population. Or that African Americans account for 35 per cent of prison inmates compared to only 12 per cent of the general population. It would be seen as outrageous. Most reasonable people would recognise the fatally flawed logic. There are many contributing factors to the mass incarceration of black men in the USA. To move from anecdote or unfiltered statistics to make generalised discriminatory assumptions about a whole group of people is not what a tolerant progressive society does. Yet, somehow, it is currently deemed acceptable for sweeping statements about the negative impact of religion on the world to be made in our mainstream media. We will spend time looking directly at the problem of religious-based violence in a chapter of its own, but at this juncture it is worth exposing the illogic of linking all those who have faith with the minority of those who perform evil in the name of religion, or with the stereotypes that often get recycled by lazy journalists or film directors.

Just as there have been breakthroughs in recent decades in

combating prejudice when it comes to gender and race, so now it is time to forge a breakthrough in combating prejudice when it comes to faith. It is wrong on many levels to claim that Christianity is a force for evil. It is wrong to claim that Christians make intrinsically worse (or indeed better) parents than Atheists or provide an unhappier (or happier) home. It is time to expose some of the prejudices that are often fuelled by the media, and take a closer look at what lies behind the claims Christians and Atheists make.

Is the widespread perception that Christianity is rather boring and restrictive a true reflection of the essence of the Christian faith? Is it indeed repressive and opposed to people's happiness? Or, is it a crutch, encouraging people to feign happiness in the same way that a bar of chocolate or glass of wine or a 5K run might buoy someone up? After all, it is not hard to find examples of either one of those glass-half-empty, killjoy Christians, or of those glass-half-full, fake-smile Christians.

The stereotypes do not portray Christianity either as it was meant to be, or how most Christians understand it. So what is the connection between faith and happiness, according to the core teaching of Christianity itself? The best way to determine the essence of the Christian faith must be to explore the life and teaching of its founder. Here are three central themes of Jesus' life and teaching that help us to triangulate where the Christian faith should lie when it comes to the portrayal of happiness. The three themes are celebration, sacrifice and liberation.

First of all, Jesus brought celebration. One of the main criticisms levelled against Jesus was not for being an ascetic but for liking his food and drink a bit too much. He was chastised for attending not too few parties, but too many.

Indeed, Jesus likened the coming kingdom of God to a party on numerous occasions. Jesus' first public miracle was providing liquid refreshment for a party when they ran out of alcohol, by turning ordinary water into the finest of wines. The strange thing about the parties Jesus went to was the guest list. Jesus made sure that the forgotten, the marginalised, the outcast and the disreputable were welcomed. Jesus' words and actions tapped into an ancient Jewish expectation that when the promised Messiah came there would be feasting and celebration. He indicated this not just by the miraculous provision of food and drink, but by the magnanimous provision for everyone, especially those who had felt excluded by race, class, gender, disability and faith. This was supposed to be a revolution bringing the most happiness to the least happy people in society.

Second, Jesus was not afraid to teach about sacrifice and hardship. For many people Christianity is seen as restrictive because of 'all the things you have to give up'. Even though we have seen that, on the surface at least, Christians and Atheists seem to live very similar lives, the decision to become a Christian is perceived to imply losing a great deal. At one level this is true. Jesus taught that being a Christian could cost effort or well-being or possessions or family, or one's very life. It could mean laying aside personal ambitions and desires. It could mean working against unhealthy habits or selfish acts or ungracious attitudes. It certainly is not just a bolt-on extra to add to life – a get-out-of-hell-free card, a crutch when you need one, or an insurance plan against bankruptcy or sickness. Faith is supposed to percolate through the whole of life, affecting everything – motivations and morals, views and values. The great cost of becoming a Christian might seem to be at odds with the party theme. But great sacrifice does not negate great joy, as Jesus indicates in these two illustrations:

> The kingdom of heaven is like treasure hidden in a field. When a man found it, he hid it again, and then in his joy went and sold all he had and bought that field. Again, the kingdom of heaven is like a merchant looking for fine pearls. When he found one of great value, he went away and sold everything he had and bought it.[12]

The first illustration is of an honourable man who gladly empties his bank account to gain legitimate ownership rights over the treasure he had located. The second man also willingly sells everything he owns to acquire a valuable gemstone. Both images clearly indicate the great personal cost involved. But there is also a glad, unrestrained and joyful exchange of everything they had to get what they longed for most.

Many people would see marriage in a similar way, where the partners willingly promise all their worldly goods and exclusive faithfulness to another person. Perhaps you have met the cynic sitting at the back of the wedding – muttering what a terrible institution it is that restricts people's freedom, reducing men's chances of proliferating their genes through multiple sexual partners, and repressing women economically and socially. But that is not how the couple getting married see it. Giving up everything for the sake of the other is not a burdensome sacrifice but such a joyful commitment that they invite all their friends and family to celebrate it. The happiness of a life together, companionship, family and security are all seen as a treasure worth giving up the freedoms of singleness to attain. In the same way, the joys the Christian faith promises – intimacy with God, being welcomed into a community of love, forgiveness from wrongs committed, a purpose in life that is bigger than self-fulfilment, and the hope of eternal life – are all shown to far outweigh the sacrifices the Christian faith requires. If God exists, and there is a better way to live both now and after death, then what is too precious to us to exchange for it?

Third, Jesus knew that there was corruption in the system and condemned the restrictive practices of the holier-than-thou religious elites. He acknowledged that in the name of religion, some so-called believers were piling on the guilt, adding rules and other religious expectations, and stealing the joy and freedom that was always supposed to come with a relationship with God. He made it very clear that the hypocrisy of the self-serving religious types was not true faith. He taught liberation not only from the power of evil and death, but also from the shackles of legalistic religion. Because Jesus spoke out very critically of the narrow-minded approach to faith, he was in constant battle with the Pharisees and religious leaders of his day, who seemed to know little of joy but lots about laws, rules and judgementalism. If Christians were as quick to quash restrictive and rule-bound forms of our faith today, then we might have quite a different reputation.

These three principles – of religious liberation, willing sacrifice and inclusive celebration – point to a faith that is far from boring and restrictive. This does not mean that Christians have only one emotional state, of ceaseless and unbounded happiness. But it does mean that joy and gratitude is such an essential part of Christian living that it should be hard to miss.

Sadly, there are far too many churches where these principles have been forgotten or neglected, despite them lying at the very core of the Christian faith. There are too many Christians who have neglected Jesus' example and teaching and who inadvertently misrepresent the Christian faith. It may be time for the Christian community to consider a major facelift in order to put right the wrong perception we have given of our faith.

If Christianity is not as dull and miserable as it sometimes appears, then maybe the public perception of Atheism's unrestrained hedonism is also misaligned. As we have already seen in the previous chapter, the vast majority of Atheists live within a moral framework. And so (to return to our case study), a child placed for an adoption in an Atheist family, like any other, will experience times of boredom and restriction. Whether it's mealtime etiquette that needs to be learned, or screen time that gets curbed, or chores to be completed, or curfews that are agreed, each family will have their own boundaries and prohibitions, when it comes to ensuring a child's safety and well-being, that the child itself may not be too happy about.

Hedonism may also have been widely misrepresented. In the Western world, at least, the unrestricted pursuit of pleasure is seen as synonymous with the freedom of individual consumerism. The emphasis on the personal amassing of wealth and material possessions, leading to an ever-increasing gap between rich and poor, does not guarantee happiness, however. Some people call this the pleasure paradox. Victor Frankl argues:

> Don't aim at success—the more you aim at it and make it a target, the more you are going to miss it. For success, like happiness, cannot be pursued; it must ensue, and it only does so as the unintended side-effect of one's dedication to a cause greater than oneself or as the by-product of one's surrender to a person other than oneself.[13]

Wimbledon Champion Boris Becker discovered the elusive nature of pursuing happiness at a great cost. After achieving all the goals he had set himself at such a young age, he found himself close to suicide. He had won Wimbledon twice over, once as the youngest player. He was rich and he had all the material possessions he needed. But he had no 'inner peace'.[14] This is not an unusual sentiment for the rich and famous – Whitney Houston, Michael Jackson, Prince, Kurt Cobain, Heath Ledger, are just a few of those with glittering careers who ended their lives either deliberately or accidentally as a result of addictions to mind-altering drugs. All of them had hugely successful lives by the standards of Western consumer society, yet despite their extravagant lifestyles, their commercial or critical success, they did not find the happiness they sought. So many celebrity lives (and deaths) provide evidence that pursuing happiness rarely leads to its discovery.

If Becker and Frankl are correct, then true happiness comes not from the pursuit of pleasure at all. Rather it comes almost incidentally when we pursue something altogether different. The British economist Richard Layard, who has devoted much of his life to the study of happiness, observed, while writing a critique of Jeremy Bentham's utilitarianism, that 'the pursuit of happiness is self-defeating: the only way to become happy is do something else – happiness is a by-product'.[15]

This begs the question, then: what is happiness a by-product of? We find a clue by looking back at the American Declaration of Independence. Protecting the pursuit of happiness as outlined in that document was not originally intended to mandate individuals to do whatever they pleased. Rather, framed within the assertion that all people are created equal, it was always supposed to be a mandate for everyone to work together to create a society where each other could be happy and enjoy freedom, independence and equality.[16] In other words, it suggests that it is when we seek the common good, or the happiness of others, that we perhaps can chance upon happiness ourselves.

Jesus wrote a similar manifesto linking happiness to social inclusion, and finding happiness where it is least expected.

Happy are the oppressed, because to them belongs the kingdom of heaven.

Happy are they who grieve, for they shall be comforted.

Happy are those who have been humbled, for they will inherit the earth.

Happy are those who hunger and thirst after justice, for they shall be satisfied.

Happy are those who show mercy, for they shall be shown mercy.

Happy are the pure in heart, for they will see God.

Happy are those who are peacemakers, for they shall be called children of God.

Happy are those who are persecuted for righteousness' sake, for theirs is the kingdom of heaven.

Happy are you whenever they reproach you and persecute you and speak all kinds of evil concerning you for my sake.[17]

This series of apparently paradoxical statements shows that Jesus' promise of happiness has two dimensions: hope and help. It suggests that happiness can be a by-product of hope when our current circumstances, however bad, are seen as temporary.[18] Second, it suggests that happiness can be a by-product of helping others. There is a significant amount of anecdotal evidence to support the theory that those who show mercy, seek justice and make peace not only offer the possibility of greater happiness to others – but also find a greater degree of happiness themselves.

Collaboration

Caring for an elderly relative, being generous towards those who are in need, comforting a grieving friend, standing up for those suffering injustice – these are not always easy things to do. They can be costly in terms of time, emotional and physical energy and finances. However, by making a difference to other people's lives, people of all faiths and none have discovered that we bring as much pleasure to ourselves as to the other person.

I remember once returning home from a particularly dispiriting day in the office, having attempted – and failed – to facilitate a joint project between various charities. Arriving at the front door rather dejected, my young foster child launched himself enthusiastically at me with a hug, begging me to take him to the local playground. Tired from the day's disappointment, it was with a reluctant spirit that I dutifully took him out – I would have much preferred to slouch down on the sofa miserably for the rest of the evening. Yet that was the day my foster son mastered cycling for the first time. Years later I don't remember much about the meeting that went so wrong, but etched on my mind is the indelible image of my boy zooming across our local park at full speed, punching the air and shouting 'Awesome!' loudly and repeatedly for all to hear. It could well have been the best hour of his life. It is certainly one of mine. I was not looking for happiness that day but I found it accidentally, in sacrificing my self-pity in favour of helping a young boy learn to ride a bike. The memory of that occasion still brings a smile to my face.

There's a Chinese proverb that states: 'If you want happiness for an hour, take a nap. If you want happiness for a day, go fishing. If you want happiness for a year, inherit a fortune. If you want happiness for a lifetime, help somebody.'[19]

Winston Churchill put it this way: 'We make a living by what we get; we make a life by what we give.'[20]

Christians need to rediscover the challenge of Jesus' words in his manifesto and take seriously his promise that genuine happiness is to be found in serving others. Too often we get side-tracked by our culture's messaging that happiness is to be found in the accumulation of stuff, or the upward mobility of a career, or the adrenaline-fuelled collection of experiences. Jesus was unequivocal that genuine worship of God must involve meeting the needs of others, and states that the way we treat those who find themselves without food, or clothes, or freedom, or care is a measure of the reality of our love for God. By investing in others in this way Jesus offers an invitation almost too good to refuse: to 'share in your Master's happiness'.[21]

But this form of pursuing happiness through service is not the sole province of Christians. I know many Atheists who willingly give up their time after work to run charity fund-raising events, help their neighbours or run community activities. I have good Atheist friends who regularly attend my church because they find pleasure and satisfaction in supporting the youth work, offering their professional expertise to those in need, raising money for local causes, or enriching a sense of community.

Whatever our motivation for pursuing happiness for others – whether it be the manifesto and example of Jesus, an accidental misfiring of our selfish gene, or the ultimate expression of a selfish gene – because it does make us happy in the giving, it is something that Christians and Atheists can do together. Pursuing happiness for others is good socially, it is good personally and it helps to develop stronger relationships across the Atheist–Christian divide.

My experience and my faith tell me that our country will be happier not when taxes are lowered, living standards are raised, unemployment figures are reduced or borders are closed, but when looking out for those around us who are in need becomes normal. This is why I am passionate about ensuring that every child who needs one gets a home, and about welcoming child refugees and providing them with a safe place to belong. This is why I will speak up for people with dementia and their carers, or for children with autism, Down's syndrome or learning difficulties. And in order to help those at risk of being marginalised, I will gladly work together with those who hold to different beliefs, whether Atheists, Muslims or Hindus.

As the conversation around happiness increases in breadth and influence[22] there are exciting possibilities available to Christians and Atheists globally as well as locally. There is already a movement to encourage nations to stop measuring the health of their populations in economic terms such as Gross National Product, national income or unemployment. Economist Richard Layard[23] argues strongly that economic growth, though important, is far too limited a political goal, and would like to see national happiness measured and analysed to the same degree. There are dangers here, of course: taken to the extreme, it might be argued that the happiness of the majority justifies the oppression of the minority. However, a happiness index, or well-being scale, offers a complementary perspective on the state of our nations that could be hugely beneficial. Christians and Atheists, with their differing perspectives, could add much to the development of this exciting new trend. As we see the possibility for the world to shift in its understanding of happiness, success and wealth, this could have massive knock-on effects in all sorts of areas, including the environment, peace-building, mental health, parenting and education.

Questions

What makes you happy?

In your experience is there any evidence for the stereotypes: 'Atheists are Fun: Christians are Boring'?

How do you think Christian and Atheist approaches to the world influence one another?

When do harmless religious stereotypes cross the line to become illegal discrimination?

How does Jesus' model of happiness through sacrificial service challenge you?

What do you think will make our country a happier place?

Chapter 6

Christians are Bible-bashers / Atheists are bus-bashers

Collision

Walk through any city on a busy day, and someone, somewhere will be trying to convert you. Some have megaphones, some might have sandwich boards. Some have tracts. Some have clipboards. Some are standing alone. Some are in pairs. Some have enlisted a crowd. Some have free coffee. Some have free samples. Some have free childcare. Some have choirs, jugglers or fire-breathers. All of them harangue unsuspecting passers-by in a bid to divert their attention briefly from their daily activity in order, ultimately, to get them 'saved'.

Most people in this day and age are quite adept at avoiding salespersons of all varieties, and religious evangelists are usually duly dodged, along with those selling conservatories, insurance and roadside assistance. But a few years ago Atheists decided to take a more evangelistic approach themselves. An anti-religion advertising campaign launched by *Guardian* newspaper journalist Ariane Sherine bought space on the sides of buses to proclaim a message of their own. The slogan that they chose was: 'There's probably no God. Now stop worrying and enjoy your life.' The campaign was duplicated around the world in a number of countries where there is a high number of

Christians – in Brazil, the USA, Canada, Switzerland and Australia.

It was a bold tactic, but one that may have backfired somewhat. First, thanks to this committed group of Atheists, it seems more discussions about the existence of God were provoked than by any campaign spearheaded by Christians in recent years. Second, it appears that Atheists themselves became the very street evangelists they so despise, pushing their opinions and beliefs on others – 'There's probably no God' – and telling people how to live their lives: 'Now stop worrying and enjoy your life.' Third, the campaign only ramped up the conflict, fuelling the fire instead of dousing it. Some Christian groups bought their own bus adverts to present their response. Others – Christians and Atheists alike – have used social media to further the debate.

For example, comedian Ricky Gervais tweeted provocatively to his 12 million followers: 'Imagine if you carried on believing in Santa and the tooth fairy into adulthood. And even killed and started wars over it. Ha ha. Imagine that.' Richard Dawkins sent this tweet: 'Many people are stupid anyway, and many religious people are not stupid. But religion is an organised licence to be acceptably stupid.' Clearly, offensive tweets like these are designed to attract plenty of equally offensive retorts, and so the battle lines are drawn.

Collusion

Most of us – Christians and Atheists – feel very uncomfortable about this ideological warfare, which seems to show a starting position of arrogance on both fronts. Rather than get caught in the vicious philosophical and theological crossfire that goes on between the vocally aggressive strands of our communities, we usually choose one of two very different collusive approaches. The first is a presumptuous pluralism; the other is a naive secularism.

The first collusive strategy is *religious pluralism*, which cloaks itself in a position of quiet compromise. We agree to disagree by saying something along the lines of 'It doesn't matter what you believe as long as you are sincere.' Or, 'I choose what is right for me – you choose what is right for you.' Or, 'All religions are basically the same at heart.' This position may appear the epitome of humility, but certain forms of it are actually the quintessence of arrogance.

The thinker Lesslie Newbigin describes religious pluralism as

> The belief that the differences between the religions are not a matter of truth and falsehood, but of different perceptions of the one truth; that to speak of religious beliefs as true or false is inadmissible. Religious belief is a private matter. Each of us is entitled to have . . . a faith of our own. This is religious pluralism, and it is a widely held opinion in contemporary British society.[1]

A classic example of this kind of thinking is illustrated by the well-known poem about four blind men and an elephant. Each stanza of the poem shows how, using only their sense of touch to encounter the beast, each man draws their very different conclusions about what it could be like. One man feeling the elephant's side describes it as similar to a wall. A second man happens on a tusk, which reminds him of a spear. The third man feels the trunk and declares the elephant to be like a snake. The fourth man grabs the elephant's leg, and so likens it to a tree. So far – so good. The problem comes when they

compare notes, and inevitably an argument ensues. The poem
concludes:

> And so these men of Indostan
> Disputed loud and long
> Each in his own opinion
> Exceeding stiff and strong
> Though each was partly in the right
> And all were in the wrong.[2]

This poem seems to be an ideal parable for living humbly in
our pluralistic, multicultural and multi-faith society. If God
is like an elephant and the blind men represent those of
different faiths, then we can see that each religion may hold
some element of truth, but in isolation each one only grasps
a partial picture. Any debates and arguments as to what God
is really like are laughably pointless. If we can just admit that
we are 'partly right', then this should allow us all to live in
harmony and mutual respect for one another – it is a clarion
call for humility, community and pluralism.

But there is a paradox here. The poem only works because
the author and the audience see the whole of the elephant. We
are in on the secret. We have special knowledge that the poor
blind men in the poem do not have. We know in full what they
are only grasping at. If we apply this to the field of religion,
then the only people who truly see and understand what God
really is are those who claim that all religions are basically the
same. This approach seems both humble and inclusive, but is
actually the opposite. It claims that religious people are intellectually disabled and lack the necessary vision or insight – while
pluralists are intellectually clear-sighted and enlightened. So
it begs the question: how do they know? Where has *their* special

knowledge come from? What is it that gives them a better understanding of God than all of the individual adherents and believers of the world's religions?

Do they realise that instead of their ostensible respect for Christians and Muslims and Buddhists alike, they are in fact implying that all of them are blind, or blinkered or ill-informed? What sounds like a politically correct, tolerant approach, actually conceals a patronising and arrogant dark side. It claims an intellectual superiority over practising Christians and those of other faiths, all without any evidence or justification. There is an irony here: in a bid to avoid arrogant statements about which position is or is not true, the course of least resistance is to take up a position that is arguably even more arrogant.

Imagine a hypothetical Brit taking a holiday in a hypothetical Far Eastern country. Visiting a local (similarly hypothetical) restaurant, the tourist peruses the menu and then calls the waiter over with that portentous phrase: 'With all due respect, sir . . .' He continues: 'All this huge variety of food, with their nice-sounding names, and helpful pictures, and translation into English. Well,' (cue another fateful phrase) 'that's all very well, but . . . do you possibly have egg and chips? You really should have egg and chips, you know; it is not hard to have egg and chips; everyone loves it; you just can't beat it; and since it is the best food on the planet, as you really ought to know, then I assume you can bring me egg and chips. And I think you'll thank me – because everyone will want egg and chips instead of all this spiced stuff that nobody likes. It will be the making of your business. Thank you so much.' However polite and friendly the diner appears on the surface, the language only cloaks the arrogance and prejudice and ignorance of his position.

The other collusive strategy we use in an attempt to avoid potential conflict in religious dialogue is *naive secularism*. At its best, secularism is supposed to prohibit religion from exerting unhelpful controlling influence over political power. For example, one Atheist philosopher writes: 'The overwhelming majority of atheists do not want to see an atheist state but a secular one, in which matters of religion and belief are not regulated by government but left to individual conscience, in line with the broadly liberal tradition of individual liberty.'[3] Secularists are not seeking to ban religion, rather to create a neutral space in public life so that no single religion dominates. There is a helpful aspect to this approach, of course. The imposition of extreme religious laws and values on a diverse population is not helpful. For example, Sharia law as imposed by the Taliban in Afghanistan or ISIS in parts of Syria left no room for dissent or diversity. Similarly, you could point to the intolerance demonstrated by Christians in the Salem witch trials in 1692, when women were summarily executed because of alleged witchcraft. So secularism offers the possibility of a safe space for public life where a non-religiously partisan set of laws can operate for the common good.

However, some have gone on to interpret secularism as the suppression of the expression of religion in public. Take, for example, a recent occurrence at Balliol, one of the colleges of Oxford University. The Christian Union, a student-led society, was banned from the Freshers' Fair by other students who wanted it to be a 'secular space'.[4] Although they recognised the advantages of having a Christian Union at the university, they nonetheless felt that it presented a 'potential for harm to freshers' because 'Christianity's influence on many marginalised communities has been damaging in its methods of conversion and rules of practice, and is still used in many places as an excuse for homophobia and certain forms of neo-colonialism.' However, the governing body of the college saw this as discrimination, a violation of free speech and religious freedom, and duly prohibited the barring of official religious societies from future Freshers' Fairs.[5]

It is true that differing religious views can cause violence and offence – as can differing political views, or even allegiances to different football teams. But creating a safe space cannot involve silencing the expression of different views.[6] The naivety shown in the Balliol College students' attempt to ban Christians demonstrated that secularism can be a guise by which religion and free speech are suppressed.

However, it is not only Atheists who may be guilty of over-enforcing this secularist line. Many Christians have colluded with secularist tendencies. Some Christians have tacitly accepted the notion that faith has no place in public life, and should be restricted to personal beliefs and practice. Like a black person trying to change the colour of their skin so that they fit into a white workplace, however, privatising faith is a denial of the dignity of their identity. It is an attempt at integration by obliteration. It exposes the naive assumption that society is better off if difference is wiped out and diversity is banned.

I once lived in a country where this stance was formally adopted by a totalitarian regime. In Albania, between 1967 and 1990, all religion and forms of religious expression were made illegal. It had started many years earlier with low levels of coercion, intimidation and violence against those who practised Islam, Orthodox Christianity and Roman Catholicism. Religious education was banned in schools and replaced with anti-religious education. In 1967 Albania became the 'first atheist state in the world', and religion was officially relegated to being a private matter, although in fact there were severe punishments and violent consequences if anything remotely religious was found, even secreted away in personal homes. Bibles, beards, icons, crucifixes, carvings on tombstones, and 'offensive' names were all outlawed. Churches, mosques and monasteries were repurposed. Former clergy and those related to them were isolated.[7]

Despite this anti-religious onslaught over a couple of decades, evidence came to light that the campaign was in fact counter-productive. According to one study, more young people were choosing spouses of the same religious background in the 1980s than they were prior to the legislation. During traditional periods of fasting such as Ramadan or Lent, there was a notice-able drop in demand for produce, while there was an increase around Christmas and Easter. And when religious bans were eventually lifted, numerous artefacts were suddenly miracu-lously 'discovered', and people flocked to places of worship, as though starving the people of religion had in fact increased their appetite for religion.[8]

Despite the collusion that seems to suggest that both Christians and Atheists are leaning towards a privatisation of religion in the UK, when it comes to legislation there is much that has been learned from the Albanian experience. Both Christians and Atheists[9] are likely to affirm that freedom of conscience and conviction remain a vital part of a democratic and progressive culture.

If the collusive approach is unhelpful, we need to seek another way forward that avoids the pitfall of ideological warfare – whether on the sides of buses, or in social media feeds – and also does not take us down a road towards totali-tarian ideological suppression. How can Christians affirm their identity and be open about their beliefs, without being accused of Bible-bashing? How can Atheists affirm their identity without unwontedly provoking the Christian community?

Contention

I do understand why people don't like religious groups and their attempts to convert unsuspecting passers-by. I, too, do not like being shouted at by a man with a megaphone on Oxford Street telling me I am going to hell. I resent answering the door to Jehovah's Witnesses, who do not really want to talk about the health implications of eating meat, but are intent on persuading me to join the waiting list of the 144,000 Jehovah's Witnesses they believe are going to heaven. I also resent being deliberately misquoted in a student newspaper by Atheists who wanted to ridicule Christian belief in order to attract extra members to their own group. Too often, passionate people forget that the ends do not justify the means.

Sadly, there are believers (and non-believers) of all varieties who are dismissive of other people's views, antagonistic in conversation, mean-spirited, judgemental and aggressive. The same is true in the political sphere. I have come across politicians from all sorts of different persuasions who are judgemental, spiteful, dismissive, antagonistic and angry. There are plenty of examples of politicians using hate tactics, insulting and belittling their opponents. Those aside, most politicians are capable of informed, insightful, robust, gracious debate. The abuse of political debate does not mean political debate has no place. It would be ridiculous to ban all public political disagreement, or hustings events, or televised policy debates live from the House of Commons. It would be wrong to prevent politicians from participating in public life, or asking people to restrict their political conversations to the privacy of their homes or within the walls of the party head-quarters. Just because there is sharp disagreement that sometimes crosses the line and becomes offensive does not mean those disagreements should not be aired at all. In fact, it is not only an expectation but a foundation of our political system that opposing views are raised and debated. It provides accountability, balance and representation.

Why should this not be equally true of opposing religious views? This airing of differences that is deemed more than welcome in the political sphere, in the scientific community and in the media world is currently made to seem unwelcome when it comes to religious diversity in public life. And if even the presentation of alternative religious opinions in public debate is contested, how much more controversial is the attempt to persuade others to consider the Christian faith for themselves.

Christians are indeed on a mission. Jesus mandated his followers to go and tell the world through word and deed about who he was and what he had done. The small band of Jewish disciples took Jesus' mission seriously and today there are 2 billion people, from every country of the world, confessing Jesus to be the defining person in their lives. The Bible recognises that those Christians will be living in pluralist contexts, where there will be relationships between Christians and those who do not share their core beliefs. It does not demand that Christians seize power or force their religion on others, but teaches they should play their role as good, peace-loving citizens, without denying their Christian identity.[10] The mission remains to tell others about the good news of Jesus, and to demonstrate the validity of his message by living in radically counter-cultural ways.

Some Atheists are also clearly on a mission. Just look at the titles of the best-selling Atheist books:

The God Delusion by Richard Dawkins
God is Not Great by Christopher Hitchens

The End of Religion by Sam Harris
Breaking the Spell by Daniel Dennett

All of these titles make obvious the persuasive purpose of the books in question. They are unashamedly inflammatory and defamatory. They seek to end, break, deny or refute belief in God. They claim that religion is dangerous, the root cause of suicide bombers, terrorist attacks, crusades, witch hunts, massacres and wars.[11] The authors are on a mission to persuade the world that Atheism is good and religion is bad. They are writing to persuade, to change people's minds, to proselytise, to evangelise and ultimately to convert. Perhaps, if they truly think that religion is the cause of all evil in the world, then I have some respect for their motives – they believe they are making the world a better place by eradicating religion and promoting Atheism. However, I still do not respect the rhetoric. Imagine if it was applied to other categories protected by equalities and human rights law. Imagine a book titled *The Gay Delusion* or *Black is not Beauty* or *The End of Transgender* or *Breaking the Feminine*. We would be rightly concerned about our culture if these titles were on the bestseller lists.

When it comes to Atheists and Christians on a mission, there are some serious dichotomies in play. It seems to be perfectly acceptable for an Atheist to vigorously persuade someone to abandon their faith, but it is socially unacceptable for a Christian to put forward persuasive arguments for belief. Promoting an Atheist philosophy is positively presented as informed debate or education. Promoting Christian belief is pejoratively presented as proselytism, indoctrination, brain-washing or plain Bible-bashing.

Why is there such a backlash against Christians presenting their faith to others? It must first be noted that there are some legitimate concerns about the way that some, I would argue the minority, of Christians go about their mission. The high-pressure 'hard sales' or cold-calling techniques employed on vulnerable people have been learned from unscrupulous business practice, not from the practice of the earliest Christians. Similarly, the manipulative forms of sharing faith that require conversion as the condition for receiving practical help and assistance are not found in the teaching of the Bible. Both of these practices should attract widespread condemnation from both inside and outside of the Church. Sadly, we must also face up to historic abuses by the Church in this kind of way. The history of the Church has some dark examples of forced conversions, as when, in the eighth century, Charlemagne used force to coerce the conversion of the Saxons, or when Spain and Portugal led the colonisation of South America in the fifteenth century.

But even after we have challenged the unscrupulous practices of minorities and acknowledged the historical examples of inappropriate methods of promoting the Christian faith, we are still confronted by those who would critique any attempt by Christians, no matter how gracious, winsome or humble, to persuade someone to change their views about faith. There seem to me to be three reasons for this type of reaction. The first is the problem of imposition: it is considered intolerant or even immoral to tell others what to believe. Second comes the problem of indoctrination: it is deemed wrong and offensive to pass on Christian beliefs to children. And third is the problem of imperialism: it is arrogant to claim that your beliefs are superior in some way to someone else's. Let's take a closer look at these three objections.

The first objection is based on a paradox. The problem with the statement 'No one should tell anyone else what to believe' is that it in itself tells me what to believe. In that regard it is a self-refuting statement. But it is also a self-deluded statement. All human communication, by its very nature, involves a degree of persuasion. When we wave at someone we seek to persuade them that their attention is worth giving to us. When we make someone laugh we are persuading them to change their feelings. When we say to our children, 'Dinner is ready!' we are persuading them both of the veracity of the statement and also of the urgency of action that is needed to leave what they are doing and eat with us. Whether we are discussing our own personal experiences or global politics, our questions, reactions and opinions all involve some form of explicit or implicit persuasion.

Persuasive, responsive communication is not a bad thing. Not only is all communication inherently persuasive – whether for good or ill, all communication brings out a response in us, whether resistant or open. One of the highest values of democratic free market economies is freedom of speech. What society needs in order to flourish is not the eradication of persuasive communication but effective, ethical conversation and debate engaged in by open-minded and discerning participants. It is not immoral or intolerant to try to persuade people what to believe. It is only immoral or intolerant when there is undue pressure involved. As we said in the introduction 'There may be persuasion, but never pressure. There may be mission, but never manipulation. There may be conversation, but never compulsion. There may be disagreement, but never disrespect.'

The second common objection to Christians sharing their faith is that it is wrong and offensive to pass on beliefs to children. This is an overspill of the previous objection, recognising that children are less able to respond to persuasive communication with discernment. On one hand, we do want to protect children from those who could easily manipulate them. That is why we teach them to question whether the stranger on their group chat is indeed a thirteen-year-old Justin Bieber lookalike or actually an impersonator with evil intent. Children are more susceptible to illegitimate advances by a kind-looking man with a handful of sweets. On the other hand, we send children to school, where they are faced with plenty of persuasive communication – despite their lack of discernment. They are taught to obey rules, and not answer back to those in authority. They are taught theories of history and science and geography and maths despite the controversies that may be attached to each one.

Schools and parents expect children to accept the curriculum. But imagine a relentlessly inquisitive child who breaks the rules, interrupts their teacher, and questions all assumptions:

Teacher: Today we are going to learn about a newly discovered subatomic particle – the Higgs Boson.
Child: Can I see it?
Teacher: No.
Child: Has anyone ever seen one?
Teacher: No. It is too small to observe with the eye.
Child: So how do you know it's there?
Teacher: Because scientists have collided protons together at the CERN facility in Switzerland – and they interpreted the complex data from the ATLAS calorimeter and deduced that it must exist.
Child: I don't understand the maths to be able to interpret the data, so I have to rely on the expertise of the scientists?
Teacher: Yes.
Child: So I should believe in the Higgs Boson particle because I have confidence in the trustworthiness of the scientists?
Teacher: Yes
Child: Do scientists ever lie?

Teacher: Err . . . Yes, to be fair scientists have sometimes faked their results or claimed credit for things they haven't done, or cheated on their taxes, or misinterpreted data.
Child: So why should I trust them?
Teacher: Because not all scientists are liars.
Child: Are you telling me to have faith in scientists, to trust the scientific method, despite not having first-hand access to the data, and despite the fact that some scientists lie and cheat?
Teacher: Yes, I guess I am.

I am not suggesting at all that the Higgs Boson is superstitious nonsense or that scientific discoveries are to be dismissed. The point of the exchange is to demonstrate how teaching children and discussing faith are not as different as we assume. Education often involves trusting sources and suspending disbelief. Our willingness to believe in many scientific theories despite being unable to do the experiments ourselves involves taking on trust a tradition of thought from people we respect.

We could take a geography lesson as another example. Most of us come to believe that Ouagadougou is the capital of Burkina Faso not through personal experience, or even speaking with eyewitnesses, but by trusting the reliability of a textbook – the writer of which has probably never been there either. School and family are unlikely to encourage a child to question this teaching, so this too could be seen as forcing a belief. But I am yet to meet a parent, Christian or otherwise, who would challenge schools about their dogmatic approach to geography. It is implicitly understood that education of any kind involves persuasion and relies on the ability to bend the free will of the child to not question which parts of the curriculum they are going to accept and engage with.

These two examples can help us understand how many

Christians actually come to faith. Yes, someone did suggest that I read the Bible. And yes, I was persuaded by what I read that Christianity was true. On the other hand, I had many questions, and I had to do my own research about the historicity and accuracy of the Gospels. But eventually the description of who Jesus was, and what he said about me, God and the world we live in finally convinced me to make what I considered to be a discerning, independent choice to become a Christian.

So how do we help our children? We want to be responsible parents and protect them from exposure to harmful or hateful material. We want to protect them from being radicalised by fundamentalists or anarchists. We worry about their security and take some protective measures, but we also don't want to censor their exposure to the good things of our world. We want to help our children to be both discerning and open-minded. An emphasis on discernment on its own can become judgemental and narrow-minded. Open-mindedness alone can become gullibility and open up the danger of being manipulated. We want our children to balance the two, to be open to people from different cultures, to be hospitable, generous and kind to everyone no matter what they look like or where they are from, and yet to be cautious, protected from paedophiles and fundamentalists and those who could take advantage of them.

Parenting is both a great privilege and a huge responsibility. It is inevitable, whether we are Atheists or Christians, that we will to some extent pass on our defining beliefs to our children through our words, as well as through our actions, that often speak louder than words. If we have children, then we have a responsibility to help them develop a healthy sense of both humility and discernment, learning to be open to different viewpoints, ideas and theories, and to ask critical questions. As a child gets older, they will develop the skills of independent thinking that should allow them to make their own decision about what they believe about God. Some born in Christian families will choose to become Atheists. Some born in Atheist families will choose to become Christians.

Third, what about the objection of arrogance or superiority? Is it true that those who try to persuade someone to believe in the Christian faith are claiming some kind of moral, intellectual or spiritual superiority to others? Again, by applying this same logic with other forms of persuasive communication it may be easier to discern our prejudice – our prejudging of the situation. Would we accuse the following people of parading a sense of superiority?

> You really should sign up with my dentist – the staff are really understanding with their nervous patients.

> Hey, have you seen the latest Christopher Nolan film – I saw it last night and it was fantastic. I'm going again on Sunday – you must come with me!

> You are really in the dark ages with your Blackberry smartphone. I've got the latest Samsung and it is so much easier to use – do you want to take a look?

Inviting someone to church, to engage with the Bible or to take a look at the claims of Christianity cannot in and of itself be equated with a claim to spiritual superiority or imply arrogance on the part of the Christian. So why is this criticism so pervasive?

The accusation of arrogance or cultural superiority is often connected with the practice of Western colonialism that has stained history. At the height of imperialism colonists deliberately and routinely imposed Western culture and values in the places they conquered. Colonialists did many terrible things in their snatch-and-grab takeovers of other people's lands, and the Christian Church has been rightly criticised for its involvement in this process. But other institutions were also involved. Educationalists were involved, for example, using draconian and manipulative methods and propaganda.

My mother, who was born and grew up in India, often told me cruel stories of her life in a brutal boarding school on the border with Tibet. Her white Western teachers used to hit her if she didn't sleep in the right position at night. She was forced to play outdoors in the cold Himalayan mountains without shoes or socks. Despite these clear violations of power, however, my mother grew up to make decisions for herself. She chose not to reject the foundations of the science she was taught and went on to use it in her career as a nurse caring for the elderly. She chose to reject the violent and bullying forms of parenting she experienced, and became a mother who was particularly patient and loving. She chose to reject the power structures of the Catholic Church, but did not reject the fundamental values of the Christian faith.

Philosophers call it the 'genetic fallacy' when the veracity of a belief is rejected based on where it came from rather than on its merits. The Church, the state and every other major Western institution were implicated in colonialism, and there must rightly be acknowledgement of the mistakes made. Ideas of cultural superiority, racist and degrading attitudes and practice should be rejected. However, these crimes do not warrant a wholesale rejection of travel or international politics or charity or education or faith, just as no one thinks that the recent disclosures of sexual abuse of young boys by football coaches should warrant a total embargo on football as a sport.

Interestingly, many Atheists have more recently distanced themselves from Richard Dawkins because his own posture is frighteningly reminiscent of colonial superiority. His critique of religion as backward, superstitious and culturally outdated, compared to progressive, enlightened Atheism is distasteful to many Atheists as much as Christians. This is especially condescending when it is applied to third-world countries where religious practice is predominant, or when it is applied to individual people who are scorned for their ignorance or foolishness.

The contention against proselytism and mission and arrogance that has for so long been levelled by Atheists against Christians may therefore now be coming back to haunt Atheists. As we saw earlier when reviewing the titles of some Atheist books, there is a clear agenda for proselytisation. In my children's secondary school, Atheists have been invited to give lectures about the benefits of Atheism, while Christian speakers have not been given the same platform. In the realm of medicine, doctors are allowed to prescribe therapies of meditation and mindfulness, a secularised version of Buddhist techniques,[12] to their patients to help them relieve stress, but if a nurse offers to pray for a patient or a teacher with a pupil, it may now be a sackable offence.[13] So atheistic practice and persuasion is currently socially acceptable, while Christian persuasion and practice has become socially suspect or deviant; although perhaps the tide will turn when more people realise that evangelistic Atheism is little different from the evangelistic Christianity they have so long disparaged. Whichever direction it comes from, imposition, indoctrination and imperialist attitudes are not acceptable.

Collaboration

Christians and Atheists are both on a mission, but silencing one party – or both – is not a helpful answer. Voltaire once reportedly said, 'I disapprove of what you say, but I will defend to the death your right to say it.'[14] Freedom of speech is critical, and talking about the things that matter most to us is a good thing. The core beliefs that drive us in life may not be the things we want to ram down people's throats or stick on the sides of buses – but neither are they things to be ashamed of or to hide away. Instead, they are significant aspects of our identity that we should feel free to bring into the relationships and contexts in which we live.

This is the revolution that has taken place in our Western culture when it comes to human sexuality, race and gender identity. In many parts of public life, whether in politics, media or the academy, it is no longer acceptable to discriminate against someone because of aspects of their human identity that were once deemed shameful or unacceptable. We don't want gay people to go back into the closet. We no longer think women should just stay at home. Why on earth would we want to go back to the dark ages when black people could not share public transport or public conveniences with white people? Or when B&Bs in the UK used to put signs up in their windows 'No Blacks or Jews'. Similarly, however, why should we expect people to be silent about what they believe? This, too, is a denial of someone's identity, a form of neglect, control or discrimination. When we promote freedom of speech and freedom of religion, that comes with the expectation that relationships and conversations and interactions will include speaking out about our faith or our core convictions, ideally with grace, humility and sensitivity.

I think some of our public Atheist spokespersons could benefit from employing a little more grace, humility and sensitivity. When the mere title of a book raises the hackles of those with faith, it will certainly do little to win people over. Yet the questions that lie behind the rhetoric and propaganda do include some important ones. Is religion just a social club for the lonely? Where is the evidence for God? How should we be helping our children be open and discerning, not just blindly accepting, when it comes to faith?

Mind you, Christians could benefit from employing a little more grace, humility and sensitivity too. Street evangelists who collar unsuspecting shoppers in our cities and seem to be expecting instant conversion have not endeared the Christian community to the general public. And yet Christians, too, raise important questions. What if there is a God? Who wouldn't want to be given a clear conscience and the hope of life beyond the grave? What have you got to lose by checking out the validity of the Christian message?

The prospect of recovering and exploring true freedom of speech and persuasion is an exciting point of collaboration for Christians and Atheists when it comes to their mutual drive to persuade others to see the truth they have discovered. It does not matter that our views differ. In fact, the very difference of opinions both demonstrates and validates the reality of the right to freedom of expression.

Andrew Rosenthal, former *New York Times* editor, argues, 'The right of free speech cannot be parcelled out based on whether we want to hear what the speaker has to say or whether we agree with those views. It means, quite often, tolerating the expression of views that we find distasteful, perhaps even repugnant.'[15] George Orwell similarly states, 'If liberty means anything at all, it means the right to tell people what they do not want to hear.'[16]

In order to know that we live in a country where freedom of speech is upheld, there must be evidence of freedom of conscience, belief and religion. The evidence of this freedom is that people can and do debate and change their religion or belief, both in community and alone, both in public and private, as stated by the Universal Declaration of Human Rights:

> Everyone has the right to freedom of opinion and expression; this right includes freedom to hold opinions without interference and to seek, receive and impart information and ideas through any media and regardless of frontiers.
>
> Everyone has the right to freedom of thought, conscience and religion; this right includes freedom to change his religion or belief, and freedom, either alone or in community with others and in public or private to manifest his religion or belief in teaching, practice, worship and observance.[17]

Let us give two Atheists the final words in this chapter, both of them publicly acknowledge the rightful place of freedom of expression when it comes to religious diversity. The first is the magician and stand-up comedian Penn Jillette, who was once given a Bible by an appreciative audience member at the end of one of his shows. In a live-streamed video, Penn appeared very touched by this act. Reflecting later, he said:

> I don't respect people who don't proselytise. If you believe that there is a heaven and hell and people could be going to hell or not getting eternal life or whatever, and you think that it is not really worth telling them this because it will make it socially awkward – how much do you have to hate someone to not proselytise? How much do you have to hate someone to believe eternal life was possible and not tell them that? If I believed that a truck

was coming at you and you didn't believe it there's a certain point where I tackle you. This is more important than that.[18]

The second voice is from a parent whose twelve-year-old daughter Una wanted to become a Christian. What should an Atheist mother do in this case? She writes:

> We all approach it with common sense and Una's best interests at heart. It seemed obvious that my role was to support her journey to discover herself and I didn't consider it until a Muslim friend said she thought it was admirable. 'If a child wanted to explore a religion other than their own I don't know too many families who would support that,' she said. Since childhood indoctrination is one of the things I like least about religion, I'm proud of Una for challenging my own atheist indoctrination of her.[19]

Questions

What has been your experience of someone trying to persuade you to change your core beliefs?

How can pluralism become arrogant and secularism be naive?

What would you say to someone who said, 'It doesn't matter what you believe: all religions are basically the same'?

What is the difference between proselytism and persuasion?

How can we make a society that neither banishes religion nor gives priority or preference to one belief system?

What advice would you give to parents seeking to raise children who are inquisitive and open-minded?

Chapter 7

The Bible is inspired / The Bible has expired

Collision

As I emerged from the Land of Nod this morning and glanced at the unopened Bible on my cabinet, I realised another lifelong habit had bitten the dust. A sign of the times, perhaps. Having children leaves me at my wits' end most of the time. These days there is indeed no rest for the wicked. By the skin of my teeth I managed to get myself dressed just before the apple of my eye came storming in to my room demanding breakfast. The root of the matter is that modern parenting often feels like the blind leading the blind. But today I was determined to go the extra mile and put my house in order . . .

If the above feels slightly forced it's because I have squeezed in at least ten idioms which, like so many others in our everyday language, are taken directly from the 1611 King James Version of the Bible. The publication of this royally 'Authorised Version' of the Bible proved a massive turning point in British literary history. It is not only the best-selling book of all time, but it set a standard for linguistic excellence that has permeated down through the centuries, shaping much of our language and culture today.

The King James Version of the Bible directly impacted on

the formation of the highly influential scientific academy known as the Royal Society, the language and values of Shakespeare, the canon of Western literature, and the social reforms of Wilberforce and Shaftesbury.[1] In December 2011, then Prime Minister David Cameron said that he believed the King James Version of the Bible was one of this country's greatest achievements:

> The Bible is a book that has not just shaped our country, but shaped the world . . . a book that is not just important in understanding our past, but which will continue to have a profound impact in shaping our collective future.

He went on to say:

> In making this speech I claim no religious authority whatsoever. I am a committed – but I have to say vaguely practising – Church of England Christian, who will stand up for the values and principles of my faith but who is full of doubts and, like many, constantly grappling with the difficult questions when it comes to some of the big theological issues. But what I do believe is this. The King James Bible is as relevant today as at any point in its 400-year history.[2]

Even Professor Richard Dawkins has on several occasions challenged people to read the Bible, saying: 'surely ignorance of the Bible is bound to impoverish one's appreciation of English literature'.[3] Understandably he gets frustrated debating the Bible with Christians who are less familiar with this important book than he is himself. I share Dawkins' frustration – sadly many Christians do have a limited grasp of the Bible and frequently misquote or misrepresent it. Similarly, though, many Atheist

critics of the Bible seem to have read very little of it for themselves and bring out only the same old tired partial quotes, or
anachronistic criticisms. Professor Terry Eagleton, arguably
Britain's leading Marxist critic, laments that much of the Atheist
critique of Christianity lacks the necessary engagement with
what Christians actually believe. Most critics, he writes:

> buy their rejection of Christianity on the cheap. When it comes
> to the New Testament, at least, what they usually write off is
> a worthless caricature of the real thing, rooted in a degree of
> ignorance and prejudice to match religion's own. It is as though
> one were to dismiss feminism on the basis of Clint Eastwood's
> opinions of it.[4]

There are many Atheists and Christians who have never studied
the Bible as a piece of literature, let alone as a source that is
unavoidably foundational to their viewpoint on the world. Most
of the time people talk about the Bible in a relatively uninformed
way, borrowing arguments that they have absorbed from others.
For example, many Christians say that they believe the whole
Bible is from God, yet have barely read, let alone studied, much
of the Old Testament. I hear many Christians say they take the
Bible literally, yet then fail to engage with the different literary
genres that the Bible is written in, stating as historical fact
things that are written in poetic form, for example. I hear many
Atheists claim that the Bible contradicts itself, but then struggle
to point to any clear examples. I hear many Atheists claim the
Bible is irrelevant, yet not only fail to put forward evidence of
their own as to why this should be the case, but prove unwilling
to consider evidence to the contrary.

Fair enough. Reading the Bible is difficult. It is long, its
content apparently collected piecemeal, and it is diverse in

its styles, even when read in an accessible translation. And then, despite the seminal role the Bible has played not just in the English language but in Western culture, politics and society, it does find itself at the axis of some huge controversies. Is the Bible to blame for the maltreatment of women through the centuries? Isn't it naive to think that such an ancient text could provide help for modern living? Does the Bible in fact contradict itself? Is the Bible historically accurate? Doesn't it promote sexism and arrogance? Does it endorse slavery and homophobia? And what about the God it presents at times – how are we supposed to understand this person? Perhaps it is no wonder that pretty much everyone struggles to engage with the difficulties that reading the Bible raises.

Christians nevertheless claim the Bible is inspired by God. They defend the Bible, not only as a sacred text, but as a guide for living, a source of comfort and a gift from God himself. On the other hand, many Atheists think it is well past its expiry date, not fit for purpose, perhaps even toxic. They dismiss it as being ancient, outdated and offensive, the source of blame for the ills of society. A notorious quotation from Richard Dawkins epitomises the views of some Atheists towards the Christian scriptures:

> The God of the Old Testament is arguably the most unpleasant character in all fiction: jealous and proud of it; a petty, unjust, unforgiving control-freak; a vindictive, bloodthirsty ethnic cleanser; a misogynistic, homophobic, racist, infanticidal, genocidal, filicidal, pestilential, megalomaniacal, sadomasochistic, capriciously malevolent bully.[5]

It is no wonder that Atheists and Christians often collide over the Bible. There are what we might call theoretical problems over whether or not the text is moral and sacred and believable, but then there are practical considerations over the role of the Bible in guiding our life decisions. Imagine an Atheist–Christian couple considering marriage. The Christian wishes to wait until after the wedding ceremony to consummate the relationship. The Atheist wishes to check that they are sexually compatible before entering a lifelong commitment. The Christian claims their opinion is based on their understanding of the Bible's teaching on God's design for sexual intimacy to be protected within a marriage relationship. But the Atheist does not know if the Bible teaches this or not, and more significantly the Atheist does not believe that the Bible contains God's instructions for life. What is written in an ancient book certainly makes no difference to the Atheist. There is no alternative textbook for the Atheist to quote from, so they have no source from which to claim authority – but they don't care. There is a debate over the validity of the Bible, and there remains an impasse over its role.

Collusion

The irony is that although Christians and Atheists have different starting points when it comes to discussing the Bible, the truth is that both Christians and Atheists struggle with the Bible's content and controversies. The same questions that bother the Atheists bother Christians too. Is it relevant? Is it true? Is it reliable? The adjectives that Dawkins uses to question God's character are the same ones that Christians have to face as they read the Bible. Is God in fact misogynist, violent, homophobic?

Because we all face the same problems, we end up colluding in two equal and opposite ways.

The first way we collude is by cherry-picking things that we can agree on, although we may not give the Bible too much credit for these. For example, we elevate certain biblical principles such as forgiveness, humility, sacrifice, compassion and integrity. These values may not sit well within a purely materialist or atheistic view of the world, as they have no firm philosophical or ethical basis without their spiritual origin, but they are comfortably borrowed from the moral framework of the Bible even in secular dialogue, and many Atheists demonstrate these qualities in an exemplary way. We also cherry-pick certain Bible quotes that we like and read them out at weddings, post them on social media or recycle them in popular books and films. For example, a moving scene in the original movie *Jungle Book* famously quotes Jesus: 'Greater love has no one than this – that he lay down his life for his friends.'

This approach to reading the Bible, a little as though it were a browsable book of quotations designed for after-dinner speeches, is a bit like producing a résumé, where only the positive elements of the person's job history need be highlighted. It is not untrue, but it is not a fair representation, as anything awkward and ambiguous is omitted. In this way we gloss over the difficulties presented by the Bible by agreeing to agree on what we can agree on. It is a very comfortable form of collusion.

The second way we collude also involves cherry-picking. This time we cherry-pick opposing views. While a Christian may choose only to focus on the uplifting, readily comprehensible texts, an Atheist may choose only to focus on the problematic, controversial texts. We see this in the way militant Atheists quote the Bible – using texts that involve genocide, or the stoning of adulterous women or unruly children. Again, this is an unfair representation, with neither side really getting to grips with the Bible in its entirety. When we use the Bible in this way, it inevitably leads to confusion and distortion. For example, the Christian quotes: 'For God so loved the world that he gave his only Son, so that whoever believes in him should not die but have eternal life.'[6] The Atheist has picked up a verse about not dying too: 'Anyone who beats their male or female slave with a rod must be punished if the slave dies as a direct result, but they are not to be punished if the slave recovers after a day or two, since the slave is their property.'[7] While the Christian claims the Bible is teaching love, sacrifice and forgiveness, the Atheist claims the Bible is teaching slavery, corporal punishment and how to get away with manslaughter.

Like the blind 'men of Indostan' we considered in the last chapter, the identification of separate distinct parts of an elephant will not help you appreciate the elephant as a whole. It leads only to confusion or distortion. With limited biblical literacy on both sides, as well as prejudice and preference, it is no wonder that debates concerning the veracity, validity and value of the Bible seem to go nowhere.

The Bible could be likened to the small print of a software licence: Christians are the sort of people who scroll through as quickly as possible before hitting the button 'I Agree'. On the other hand, Atheists scroll through, notice a few question-able clauses, and quickly hit 'Cancel'.

When neither side reads the Bible thoroughly, carefully or thoughtfully, there is little room for discussion. Each side takes a position and sticks to it, thereby avoiding the need for deeper thinking or true discussion. If the first form of collusion is agreeing to agree on what can be agreed on, this second form of collusion is agreeing to disagree. Neither approach tackles the elephant in the room.

Contention

A teacher introduces a new book to her A-Level students. One pupil vociferously objects to reading it. The author promotes patricide, teenage suicide, witchcraft, sexism, marital infidelity, murder, religious and race-based violence and discrimination. She claims that she is not alone in calling for this author to be removed from the core curriculum, especially as the work is difficult to understand, the themes are complex and the language is outdated. But another pupil comes up with a strong counter-argument. This author is one of Britain's greatest ever. His work has shaped our culture and language. The themes he deals with not only provide insight into the historical problems of his day and age, but actually still exist today. The author is not endorsing the evils he describes; he invariably works the plot to show the devastating consequences of immoral actions. Yes, there are complexities of themes and language, but these only make it more rewarding to study and discover the meaning behind them.

This is not a debate about the Bible, but about *Romeo and Juliet*. Who wins this argument? The fact that Shakespeare's plays are still studied at schools across the country is testament to the fact that preconceived ideas, prejudice and preference should not deter us from promoting literacy about the texts that have informed who we are today.

But perhaps there are some works of literature that are worth avoiding. I have not read *Fifty Shades of Grey* because I believe it promotes sexual violence against women, and I avoid reading Enid Blyton books to my children because of her supposed racist and snobbish views. Of course, by not reading these books I cannot be sure that my preconceptions are valid. But if I do read them, I or my family may be exposed to something

I believe is toxic. And so some Atheists object on similar grounds to reading the Bible.

In her beautiful and powerful 2015 novel *Station Eleven*, Emily St John Mandel imagines a dystopian future where a virulent flu strain wipes out 99 per cent of Earth's population. A young man finds a Bible and manages to build a brutal death cult around himself. The resistance movement to this death cult is focused on a small travelling Shakespearean company who are performing *King Lear* wherever they go. St John Mandel's insinuation is clear – some texts are good for the flourishing of society and others will inevitably bring only more pain and suffering. For her, Shakespeare and Scripture are at opposite ends of the spectrum.

On the other hand, Christians claim that despite the brutality of many parts of the Bible, and the fact that it has been used as a justification for all sorts of wrong attitudes, from apartheid to rampant consumerism, it does in fact offer a realistic view of human society and offer wisdom for a better life, a moral framework for human flourishing, not to mention a way to get to know the creator of the universe at an intimate relational level.

Moreover, it has also been the reason behind all sorts of good in human history – from the abolition of slavery, to welfare provision, to Martin Luther King's 'I have a dream' speech, to the most beloved of Renaissance art and music and architecture. Christians believe that the Bible is more than just words on the page. They believe it is dually authored – both divinely inspired, and human-penned – by shepherds and sages, prophets and poets, kings and slaves. They believe it provides a guide to this life and the next, contains the solution to all the evil and violence and death in the world, and presents a radical and counter-cultural way of living.

Christians and Atheists definitely believe different things
about the Bible. If there is no God then of course the Bible is
not inspired by God. But authorship aside, there can still be
room for an intelligent engagement that brings together what
Christians claim about the Bible and the Atheist critique of it.

First of all, both Christians and Atheists can agree that it
is wrong when the Bible, or indeed any text, is used as a
justification for evil action. The racist bigotry of the Ku Klux
Klan is wrong. Apartheid in South Africa and the conquis-
tadors' atrocities in South America were wrong. These cited
the Bible in defence of their actions. But it is not only the
Bible that has inspired wicked things. Noted Atheist Daniel
Dennett describes another book that has been the inspiration
behind other atrocities, including the Eugenics movement
that saw millions of Jews exterminated under the Nazi regime:

> From the moment of the publication of *Origin of Species* in
> 1859, Charles Darwin's fundamental idea has inspired intense
> reactions ranging from ferocious condemnation to ecstatic
> allegiance, sometimes tantamount to religious zeal. Darwin's
> theory has been abused and misrepresented by friend and foe
> alike. It has been misappropriated to lend scientific respecta-
> bility to appalling political and social doctrines.[8]

Dennett argues that the atrocities inspired by *Origin of Species*
are owing to the text being abused and misrepresented. Darwin
is not responsible for the atrocities that were committed in his
name and with the justification of his theories. Millions died
over the misappropriation of his work. Similarly, Christians
may argue that the crimes against humanity committed in the
name of the Bible have been due to the text being misread in
a similar way.

If you have ever been misquoted in an interview, or been struck by the 'fake news' claims of some political parties, you will know that it is relatively easy to misconstrue or to deliberately misrepresent someone else's words. The best way to avoid this is by making sure we understand three important concepts: context, style and intention. These 'fair reading' strategies of the discipline of hermeneutics ('the science of interpretation') can help us discover best-practice interpretive skills that allow for a fair reading of any text.

Recognising *context* means we make the effort to try and understand the way any statement, quotation or other piece of 'data' fits into the larger whole. We should be wary of isolated proof texting, or of snatching a sentence from a larger argument and repurposing it as ammunition in a different argument. Recognising *style* means that we consider the type of literature being examined and allow that to influence how we read it. No one looks for poetry in a shopping list, or dials phone numbers quoted in a novel. Because the Bible utilises many literary styles, including historical reporting, ancient legal codes, formal letters and erotic poetry, the meaning of the text is not always obvious. Recognising *authorial intent* is also important. Imagine you were to visit my neighbour and discover some rather violent material that she has been writing. Before you dismiss her as certifiable, perhaps criminal, a closer look would reveal that the material is not there for pleasure but as part of her work as a forensic scientist. This changes the way you would look at the text – what she has written is not an expression of her life-choices or her desires, but rather a recording of something that has taken place – a report of something real that she has to engage with. It changes the way you would react to this neighbour – not in shock or suspicion, but with respect for a job few of us could stomach. Recognising style, context and intention helps us to understand how to approach a text and not to misrepresent or misappropriate it, but it also helps build bridges in relationships.

Let us take a classic example used by Atheists to criticise the Bible, in order to try out these principles. We may not agree on the claims or conclusions reached on each side of the debate, but we owe it to one other to at least attempt to try and hear each other properly. Sam Harris suggests that slavery is condoned by the Bible, and that this is evidence of the Bible being a bad moral guide.

> In assessing the moral wisdom of the Bible, it is useful to consider moral questions that have been solved to everyone's satisfaction. Consider the question of slavery. The entire civilized world now agrees that slavery is an abomination. What moral instruction do we get from the God of Abraham on this subject? Consult the Bible, and you will discover that the creator of the universe clearly expects us to keep slaves.[9]

So let's take up Harris's challenge to consult the Bible and let's engage our three considerations of context, style and intention. First, it is possible to find Old Testament laws that govern slave ownership: for example in Leviticus 25:44–46.

> Your male and female slaves are to come from the nations around you; from them you may buy slaves. You may also buy some of the temporary residents living among you and members of their clans born in your country, and they will become your property. You can bequeath them to your children as inherited property and can make them slaves for life, but you must not rule over your fellow Israelites ruthlessly.

This passage seems to unequivocally confirm Harris's point. So if God allows his people to own slaves, is it because he condones treating people as property? The wider context of the Bible would claim not. The Bible starts out in Genesis by portraying life as God intended it. God created all human beings equal. Women and men are given a unique status of being made in the image of God, which confers on all human life intrinsic worth, dignity and value. But between Genesis 1 and Leviticus 25 there's a major plot development in the Bible, which is known as the fall of humanity. Sin, injustice and evil have tainted God's perfect world, and so God makes laws for his people to help them live in this temporarily skewed situation. That's why a God who abhors war, marital infidelity, murder and all other dehumanising practices including slavery makes provision for how to deal with these social evils.

Now this all might sound rather convenient. How do we know that slavery is not something that God intends? After the laws in Leviticus we have hundreds of years of history and then there is another major plot development – the coming of Jesus into the world marking a new phase in God's dealing with humanity. In the New Testament we are given a trans-formational view of slavery. In the letter to Philemon, for example, the Apostle Paul tells a slave owner not to punish his runaway slave, but to receive him back as a brother.[10] Again, in a different letter, Paul explains that in God's new kingdom there is neither Jew nor Gentile, slave nor free, male nor female, because we are all equal.[11]

These were socially radical views in the first century and they provided the basis for a new diverse and inclusive community that found its unity not in a shared status, demographic or economic position, but in the love its members had for God and for one another.

Accusing the Bible of endorsing slavery is like arguing that Greenpeace endorses polluting the environment because it describes the amount of plastic that has entered our oceans. The grand trajectory in the Bible precludes cruel and restrictive practices against fellow human beings and promotes the intended freedom of all. And it was this that provided the motivation for abolitionists such as William Wilberforce to fight against the transatlantic slave trade.

While Atheists may see the Bible as containing an immoral endorsement of slavery, Christians who dig deeper and uncover the Bible's radical approach to slavery will see something completely different. The Bible does not provide an injunction to traffic and exploit and abuse the vulnerable, but rather a mandate to protect the vulnerable, to care for victims of family breakdown or those unable to work and provide for their basic needs, and to give them the dignity of somewhere to work and somewhere to belong, a place of equality within a family or community.[12]

This quick case study on slavery shows that although it is likely that Christians and Atheists will disagree when it comes to the Bible, there are some positive outcomes. First of all, the differing views regarding the Bible's engagement with slavery can be invoked using evidence and logic that do not just sweep the problem under the carpet, pretending that slavery then and now is not a problem. Second, both views conclude that slavery is, as Harris says, an abomination, and therefore we are all motivated to help the 27 million people estimated to be in slavery today.[13] Third, both views are built on the basis of taking a closer look at the Bible.

Sometimes Christians think that if Atheists just read through the Bible carefully, they would see that it is a true account and become Christians. Equally, some Atheists claim that if

Christians were to read their Bibles more carefully, they would have to acknowledge the problems, and become Atheists.[14] We may come at it from different directions, but if both sides are in agreement that reading the Bible is going to be helpful, then there is nothing to lose.

Collaboration

I believe it is possible to live in a way that treats the words of others and the texts that they value with respect, recognising and honouring the humanity of those we disagree with. I remember one occasion when we got a call at midnight. My wife answered the phone, and two hours later a police van was pulling up outside our house. Two female police officers got out and escorted four frightened children into our house – three boys and a girl. This was an emergency foster placement; the children were from a Muslim family. Most of them had never been in the home of a non-Muslim before, and they were certainly not used to speaking English in a home environment. The first night they were so scared that all three boys huddled in the same bed and hardly slept. The youngest refused to speak at all for the first twenty-four hours. Part of our job as foster carers is to look after all of a child's needs while they are in our care: physical, social, practical, cultural and spiritual. The morning after they arrived, we asked, through our social workers, how the family would like us to honour the children's religious heritage. For the next few weeks we cooked with halal meat and gave the children space to pray and access the Qur'an. We dusted off a copy of the Qur'an we happened to have in our house and left it available for the children to read. Despite being in disagreement about the claims of their religious text, we nevertheless made every effort to respect those who followed its teaching. While those children were in our home during a particularly traumatic few weeks of their lives, what was valuable to them had to be valuable to us.

Last year I spent a whole day hunting in the grounds of a school for a ring that my friend had lost. It had no value to me whatsoever. In fact it had no monetary value either – it was a cheap ring that might have been picked up at a flea market somewhere on the other side of the world. But to my friend, it was priceless. It had been given to her by her late grandmother and it was the last tangible thing that connected them. She had worn it for years in memory of that relationship. I am sure you can think of similar occasions when you have sacrificed time and energy for something you had no connection to. Finding that lost soft toy that a child can't sleep without. Smiling through that tasteless, bland meal someone had made especially for you. Oohing and aahing over photographs you did not take. When we can show that we value what others value, it can bring so much to a relationship.

Showing respect for the Bible as valued property for others, if not for yourself, is a good start. At a basic level, this could mean refraining from making unfounded negative judgements about it. However, there is a more exciting point of collaboration. I have often read the Bible with Atheists. I find it very enlightening – they ask questions I would never have considered. They don't just accept easy answers. For example, it was through studying the Bible with an Atheist friend at university that I was challenged to pursue a more socially engaged outworking of my Christian life. My friend was the leader of the local green action group and as we studied the

Gospels together he asked helpful questions that challenged my reductionist understanding of Jesus' life and teaching.

Literary scholars call the practice of reading with people who are ideologically or sociologically different from you 'increasing your hermeneutical circle'. This allows other people to help us to see fresh angles and perhaps new meaning in the texts that are important to us.[15] It benefits the Christian hugely because it acts as a 'is that really true?' filter, and prevents us becoming blinded by wishful thinking. It also benefits the Atheist. It acts as a 'what if this were true?' filter. Neither of us would wish to discover too late that we were wrong all along – it is worth asking the most difficult, most challenging questions now.

It is recorded that the Scottish philosopher and sceptic, David Hume, who wrote scathingly about the Christian claim that miracles actually took place in the Bible, was once recognised in a crowd of listeners to the preaching of the famed British evangelist George Whitefield. Someone asked Hume: 'I thought you didn't believe in the gospel?' 'I do not,' Hume replied. Then, with a nod towards Whitefield, he added, '*But he does.*'

Hume had enough respect for Whitefield – as a man or as a preacher – to listen to what he had to say. If we can learn to listen to one another, to hear the passion and commitment, to value what others value even when we do not agree or share their convictions, to check that what we believe is really true, then there is a way forward for us. Yes, the Bible has been the cause of much division throughout history. And yes, people will still be divided on where it has come from and what it means for us today. But those divisions do not have to be the end of the story.

Questions

Which of the Bible phrases did you recognise in the opening para-
graph?

How much of the Bible have you read?

How can we avoid the cherry-picking approach to reading the Bible
either to promote reading the Bible or to criticise it?

What would you say to someone who said: 'The Bible supports the
practice of slavery and therefore it is a tool of oppression?'

How could reading the Bible with people who are different to you
help you?

Chapter 8

Christians are warmongers /
Atheists are peacemakers

Collision

At twenty to ten on a Friday evening, while a rock concert was in full swing, a car pulled up and three men wearing dark clothes entered the venue wielding assault rifles. The men went up to the mezzanine level and opened fire down onto the crowd. Over the next twenty minutes the attackers reloaded their weapons three to four times as they calmly and systematically attempted to kill as many people as possible. In all, eighty-nine people were killed in the horrific Bataclan theatre massacre in Paris in November 2015. Two of the attackers exploded suicide vests and the third died when his vest exploded after being hit by police gunfire. The next day the Islamist terror organisation ISIS claimed responsibility for the attack.

Twenty-one months earlier some men pretending to be guards broke into a government girls' school late at night. They rounded up hundreds of the girls and loaded them into trucks. That same night many houses in the village were torched. Two hundred and seventy-six girls aged between sixteen and eighteen were kidnapped and the majority of them were still missing two years on. Eyewitness reports from girls who managed to escape told how they were taken to military camps and were subjected to physical abuse, forced to take part in military operations or into early marriage, many sexually abused. The girls had been at school in the town of Chibok in Northern Nigeria. The leader of Boko Haram, Abubakar Shekau, confirmed that his men had carried out this attack and that the girls had been forced to convert to Islam.

These are by no means isolated incidents. There is clear documented evidence that thousands of men, women and children have been executed by Islamic State in the Syrian conflict and by Boko Haram in Africa. Mass beheadings have not only been carried out, but recorded and broadcast through social media channels in celebratory videos. Elsewhere around the world, tanks have been used to run down victims, homosexual young men have been thrown to their deaths from tall buildings, and a captured Jordanian pilot was doused in petrol, put in a cage and burned to death. All of these horrifying atrocities have been done in the name of God.[1]

There is overwhelming, undeniable and uncontested evidence that these particular events were religiously motivated – the perpetrators recorded and broadcast their cruelty, clearly articulating that this was done to honour God. Although most of the religious violence reported in Western media has involved those claiming Islam as their inspiration, Islam is not the only religion facing the challenge of religiously motivated violence. In India the war in Kashmir, which has seen around 50,000 casualties over the years, pits the Hindu majority in India against the Muslim majority in Kashmir. The atrocities of the Balkan conflict included unspeakable massacres of Muslim Kosovars by Orthodox Christian Serbs. And sadly, the current prevalence of religious violence is only part of a long history. The Crusades that took place in Europe between 1096 and 1487 or the pogroms in the nineteenth and twentieth century in Russia, where Orthodox Russians helped massacre thousands of Jews, are ample evidence that Christianity has plenty of its own skeletons, not in the closet but strewn across the battlefields of the world throughout history.

These shameful events serve to strengthen the case of those who oppose religion. Atheists have long been arguing that religion is not a benign influence on the world but an intrinsically evil one, and these sentiments have become particularly acute in the wake of Islamist extremism. So, for example, Richard Dawkins explained: 'Many of us saw religion as harmless nonsense. Beliefs might lack all supporting evidence but, we thought, if people needed a crutch for consolation, where's the harm? September 11th changed all that.'[2] Mind you, five years before 11 September 2001, Dawkins had clearly stated his views on the harmfulness of religion in a statement to the American Humanist Association: 'It is fashionable to wax apocalyptic about the threat to humanity posed by the AIDS virus . . . but I think a case can be made that faith is one of the world's greatest evils, comparable to the smallpox virus but harder to eliminate.'[3]

What can Christians say when faced with this damning indictment of faith and the evidence that we are confronted with all too regularly, not only in the pages of our history books but also on the nightly news? I know of many Christians who have thrown in the towel at this point. They concede the battle and wave a white flag of surrender, giving in to the Atheists' argument. They simply cannot keep defending God when the evidence of God-inspired evil seems to be all around them. They are ashamed of their faith, as though they feel a degree of guilt by association. They certainly do not want to be implicated in the root of violence that seems to be inherent in religion.

I can understand why faith seems difficult to hold on to

when faced on the one hand with the conflicts in the world around us undertaken in the name of faith, and on the other by the conflict with Atheists, who attack Christians at arguably their point of greatest vulnerability. When we believe there is an overarching battle of good versus evil taking place in the world, and have chosen to stand for the side we believe is good, our whole foundation is rocked by the accusation that we may actually be on the side of evil. By choosing Christianity, we want to stand for compassion and sacrifice and mercy and love and peace and joy. We do not want to be associated with violence, war, hate crimes and brutality. And we certainly do not want to do go into verbal conflict against Atheism, when it is blatantly clear that combat in the name of faith has had such horrendous consequences.

Collusion

Every Christmastime we are reminded that Jesus was born to be the 'Prince of Peace'[4] and that the angels announced 'Glory to God in the highest heaven, and on earth peace'.[5] Jesus commanded his followers to be peacemakers.[6] Thus, according to the Bible, Christianity is supposed to be a religion of peace. But with all the conflicts around the world in the name of God, that positive association definitely feels like it is shifting to equate all religious people with warmongers. Atheists are just as keen to see themselves as peacemakers, despite their own tough histories and atrocities committed by past atheistic regimes.

Blame-throwing, the use of dehumanising language, and prejudicial assumptions when it comes to Christians and Atheists, only serve to scale up the conflict rather than help to build bridges. When religion is blamed for all violence, when faith is labelled as effectively the root of all evil, when every act of violence is seen as a point-scoring opportunity, it seems as though neither Atheists nor Christians can claim to shine as peacemakers.

Even when trying to avoid confrontation, party lines can still be painfully obvious. One form of collusion is competitive peace-making strategies. I have seen this on a local scale. For example, a local church puts on a Bollywood event or creates a pop-up restaurant or holds a service or prayer walk for those involved in a recent tragedy. Some months later secular groups cooperate to organise a street party, a peace walk, a candlelit vigil, a Bollywood event, or a pop-up restaurant. Although on one hand the duplication of initiatives may be frustrating because it reveals deliberate non-cooperation, on the other hand, there is a positive outcome: a multiplication of opportunities to promote peace. And with each group trying to outshine the other, there is an increased profile of the message of peace and community cohesion – even if this is, ironically, based on fundamental division between the sacred and secular groups in question.

Contention

Temporarily setting aside all differences in a crisis is vital, but in the longer term it is also important to sit down and set out our differences in conversation, in order to prevent further crises down the line. When the crisis is over, it is right that questions are asked. Was the ISIS bomber in Manchester, acting in the name of faith, proof that religion is ultimately the cause of evil? Could the twenty-two deaths have been averted if the country was more secular?

Terrible things have been done, are being done and, sadly,

will be done in the name of God. Around the world there are ongoing conflicts between religious groupings. But it is not only religion that causes wars and violent conflicts. In his polemical book *Death by Government*,[7] Rudoph Rummel provides a harrowing 'butcher's bill' of the death toll attributable to atheistic regimes:

Regime	Number of victims
Josef Stalin, USSR	42,672,000
Mao Zedong, China	37,828,000
Adolf Hitler, Nazi Germany	20,946,000
Chiang Kai-shek, China	10,214,000
Vladimir Lenin, Soviet Russia	4,017,000
Hideki Tojo, Imperial Japan	3,990,000
Pol Pot, Cambodia	2,397,000

Rummel, who wrote his book to highlight the non-violent nature of democracy, in contrast to dictatorships, uncovered a litany of what he calls democide, death by government. He concludes that in the twentieth century alone:

Almost 170 million men, women and children have been shot, beaten, tortured, knifed, burned, starved, frozen, crushed or worked to death; buried alive, drowned, hung, bombed or killed in any other of the myriad ways governments have inflicted death on unarmed, helpless citizens and foreigners. The dead could conceivably be nearly 360 million people. It is as though our species has been devastated by a modern Black Plague. And indeed it has, but a plague of Power, not germs.

Another point some Christians have made is that the four bloodiest conflicts in history took place during the period we might most easily label 'secular modernity' and none of them had a clear religious motivation. The Second World War claimed around 60 million victims; the T'ai-Ping Rebellion in China around 20 million; the First World War around 15 million; and the Russian Civil War around 9 million.[8]

But a straight-out numerical battle is not sufficient to consider this argument properly. Modernity has mechanised the process of war such that it has become a ruthlessly efficient process capable of killing larger numbers of people than ever before. Mike Pearse writes: 'The wars of secular modernity . . . were more catastrophic not because they were secular but because they were modern.'

This point is even more pertinent than in its straightforward sense. Defining the conflicts listed as having either religious or secular motivations is in fact far more complicated than it appears, and they cannot be labelled based on simplistic assumptions. By looking more closely at the relationship between religion, ideology, and war and terror we could contend – whichever side of the argument we are coming from – that a statistical correlation may not demonstrate causation; second, the confession of a belief may not equate to genuine belief; and, finally, conscription of a religious or ideological cause to support violence may not entail the agreement of that view with said violence.

First of all, we should consider correlation and causation. Militant Atheists like Harris and Dawkins claim that because wars involve religious people, it must be religion that causes war. This demonstrates an attempt to convert a statistical correlation into a ground of causation. But that is fallacious logic. Just because a statistical connection is made between two variables does not mean that one causes the other. A classic example of this involves windmills:

> When windmill sails are observed to rotate faster, a faster wind-speed is recorded.
>
> Therefore wind-speed is increased by the rotation of windmill sails.
>
> In other words: windmills generate wind.

Obviously, this is not the case; just as the increased number of candles on my cake has not caused me to get older, or the increasing numbers on my bathroom scales caused me to become heavier. We must be very careful as we move from finding a statistical correlation to attributing causation.

When it comes to explaining violence in the world, a number of other correlations might be observed. For example, imagine someone claimed that 'People of colour are statistically more likely to be involved in war and violence – they are to blame, and we should try and ban people of colour from taking part in the political and public life of a nation.' Or, 'Men are much more likely to lead countries into war than women, and more likely to become radicalised than women, so for that reason men are to blame for war, and masculinity is inherently evil.' The immediate response would be that both of these categorisations are not only simplistic but also offensive. It would be right to challenge, in these instances, whether correlation does anything to explain causation. Yes, most conflicts have involved men as instigators, the vast majority of atrocities have been carried out by men and most wars have been fought predominantly if not solely by men. But there are complex social and historical factors that have led to the dominance of men in global politics and thus give men more opportunity and influence to carry out violence. Similarly, there are parts of the world where conflicts primarily involve people of colour, but this needs to be understood in the light of global demographics, as well as the historic role that Western colonialism has often played in triggering conflicts in the first place.

What does this consideration of demographics bring to the 'religious wars' argument? Since there has never been a time in history when wars have not been taking place somewhere – and the vast majority of the people on the planet profess some kind of religious affiliation – statistically speaking, wars are most likely to involve religious people. We cannot therefore jump to the conclusion that religion has caused all war, just as we should not link the increase in global conflict with the dramatic rise in Atheism. Both arguments wrongly attribute causation to correlation. Nonetheless, we cannot rule out religion as a cause of war because, as the next two points demonstrate, religious ideology and rhetoric is often used during wars.

The second point is that confession may not mean conversion. I once asked a Marxist why they still believed that Marx offered a workable system for governance in our world when so many Marxist-inspired governments led to dictatorships that committed horrendous crimes against their populations. For example, I could mention the communist leader Pol Pot, whose policies saw millions of Cambodians die from execution, starvation, disease or hard labour, or the Communism of the Soviet Union where millions of peasants lost their lives primarily from state-directed famines, in some cases arguably deliberately inflicted for purposes of ethnic cleansing as 'terror-famines'.[9] My Marxist friend explained to me that the problem was not the ideology of Marxism, but faulty practical expressions of Marxism.

The logic behind his defence was that confession does not equate to conversion. Just because someone claims to be a Marxist or to follow Marxist ideas, this does not mean they are really pure practising Marxists. This same line of argument is used by both Atheists and Theists. The Spanish Inquisitors were not really Christians. Stalin was not really an Atheist. Pol Pot was not really a Marxist. Many people would argue that Islamic State are not true Muslims. The problem is not the belief system – whether Islam, Christianity or Atheism: the problem is that their adherents are not living out the ideals and implications of these systems of thought.

There is some merit in this division between declared belief and true belief, confession and conversion. Jesus was very clear that not everyone who called themselves his followers really were his followers. 'Why do you call me "Lord, Lord" and do not do what I say?'[10] he asked on one occasion. In Jesus' famous Parable of the Sheep and the Goats, the distinguishing factor between true believers and fake ones is not their doctrinal affirmations but the degree of compassion and mercy they show to people in need.[11] In other words, Jesus clearly taught that the test of the authenticity of a confession lies not in the declared sincerity of one's beliefs or how loudly they are confessed, but rather in behaviour and whether it is in line with the core teaching of the beliefs. The proof of the pudding is in the eating, we might say, or as Jesus put it: 'By their fruit you will know them.'[12]

There is a general recognition that there must be a distinction between nominal believers – those who hold to a set of beliefs in name only and do not attempt to live consistently with those beliefs – and what we might call committed believers, who genuinely try to prioritise putting their faith into practice. Similarly a distinction can be made between committed believers and extremist believers, those who have radicalised their belief system to the point of psychopathy. And of course, this same generosity should be afforded not just to Christians but to those of other faiths and those who claim no faith at all. We must be careful not to compare the most consistent practitioners of our beliefs against the most inconsistent expressions of another set of beliefs. For example, if we set up Mother Teresa as the normative Christian, and Heinrich Himmler as the representative secularist, we have unfairly loaded the dice, just as badly as if we compare the generosity of Atheist Bill Gates against the mean-spirited Westborough Baptist Church.

Just because someone claims to be acting on their beliefs, or to be representing their belief system, does not mean that they actually are. So when it is asserted that religion causes war and violence, we must bear in mind the possibility that the religion claimed could be merely a confession in word alone, or a personal interpretation of a faith, and not a genuine conversion to the belief system under debate. Sometimes religion is a front, excuse, label or masquerade for a more sinister underlying ideology, whether consciously or unconsciously held to.

This brings us on to our third point: that when it comes to religious violence, conscription may not mean consent. Like a car on a speeding highway commandeered by an FBI agent to pursue an escaped assailant, so religion has often been conscripted for personal and political ends. For example, in 1991 Saddam Hussein, then Iraq's president, called on Muslims to respond to the conflict in Kuwait: 'We tell all the Arabs, all the believing strugglers . . . wherever they are to rise to *jihad* (holy war) and struggle by targeting the forces of evil, treachery and corruption everywhere and targeting their interests wherever they are. This is your duty.'[13]

This statement was seen by the Arab states as a cynical ploy to drag Iraq's neighbours into a conflict that Hussein had initiated not for religious ends, but rather to acquire the oilfields of Kuwait. Hussein's regime was, in general, widely acknowledged as one of the most secular in the region. Religion was being commandeered to disguise selfish, political motives. The decision-making at the heart of that conflict was not in any way motivated by faith commitments at the heart of Islam or, in truth, against any other faith.

Similarly, the conflict in Northern Ireland between Catholics and Protestants had little to do with a clear understanding of differing views on church governance, or the theological differences about salvation or the perpetual virginity of Mary. The conflict owed far more to political and genealogical divisions. When asserting that religion causes war and violence, we need to discern when religion is merely being conscripted as a disguise for more sinister motives, or as an additional incentive in drawing a wider group of people into a conflict. Richard Dawkins concedes this point in his book *The Devil's Chaplain*, where he presents a more nuanced view of religious violence and advocates a position that has a lot of merit. Dawkins proposes something that is ironically very similar to that put forward by the UK's previous Chief Rabbi, Jonathan Sacks, as outlined in his book *Not in God's Name*: 'My point is not that religion itself is the motivation for wars, murders and terrorist attacks, but that religion is the principal label, and the most dangerous one, by which a "they" as opposed to a "we" can be identified at all.'[14]

Religion has often been conscripted to serve the purpose of dehumanising another group of people, in order to reinforce a 'them and us' mentality. But this conscription does not necessarily come with the consent of or any correspondence with the religion or ideology in question. We would need to explore the core elements of a religion before we could decide if the conscription was consistent and consensual, or contradictory and conflicting. And this is often tricky, as we cannot assume, either, that all devotees and adherents to a religion interpret their faith in the same way. The differences between Catholic and Protestant Christians or Sunni and Shia Muslims are cases in point.

Atheists and Christians can both agree that terrible things have been done in the name of Atheism as well as in the name of Christianity. We can also agree that the cause of violence may well not be the presenting religious or atheistic affiliation, that sometimes religion or ideology is conscripted to serve other agendas, and that such agendas do not always reflect the true nature of the religion or ideology.

But if faith and Atheism are not the cause of war, then what is? Christians would point to human nature and their belief that all of us are in a constant battle between doing what we know to be right and our selfish, self-serving desires. The Russian dissident Aleksandr Solzhenitsyn put it like this:

> Gradually it was disclosed to me that the line separating good and evil passes not through states, nor between classes, nor between political parties either – but right through every human heart – and through all human hearts. This line shifts. Inside us, it oscillates with the years. And even within hearts overwhelmed by evil, one small bridgehead of good is retained. And even in the best of all hearts, there remains . . . an uprooted small corner of evil.[15]

Some Atheists might logically attribute war to the principle of natural selection, where the strong naturally survive and the weak naturally perish. John Keegan, the military historian, argues that the Greek and Roman view of war was that it was an integral and necessary part of human existence. Keegan argues that eventually Christianity challenged the morality of war, and it became more widely seen as an unwanted evil. Despite some significant blips, this view was a strong undercurrent through Western history. Arguably, the influence of Charles Darwin played its part in dismantling this orientation towards peace, with his conception of life as a process of permanent struggle, a competition for survival.[16] Mike Pearse argues:

> The Darwinian direction of thought, in which history is impersonal, people are mere products of nature, conflict is the engine of the universe and the keys to understanding its complexity . . . had 'its direst outcomes' in the totalitarian creeds of the twentieth century, particularly the Bolshevism of Lenin and the National Socialism of Adolf Hitler.[17]

Some dispute the link between Darwin and social Darwinism. Some might argue that it is a distortion of Darwin's own thinking for quite different ideological ends. I recently came across this quotation that challenged my own understanding. In *The Descent of Man*, Charles Darwin stated: 'At some future period, not very distant as measured by centuries, the civilised races of man will almost certainly exterminate and replace throughout the world the savage races.'[18]

While we may be familiar with Hitler's denunciation of the Jews as *Untermenschen* or 'subhumans', Lenin also dehumanised his opponents to justify the killing of vast numbers of civilians, describing them as vermin, scoundrel fleas, and the bedbug rich.[19] The same approach was taken by Chairman Mao in China's Cultural Revolution, when he essentially suggested that those who opposed the revolutionaries did not count as people.[20]

As part of our contention over this issue of violence, Christians should acknowledge that on many occasions our faith has not been the peace-making religion it should have been. Violence and atrocities have been committed in the name of God, and this goes against everything that following Jesus should mean. Atheism, too, though, should be prepared to hold up its hands to the violence that has arisen due to its promulgation of ideas that lead to the dehumanisation of our fellow human beings under unfettered materialist and evolutionary teaching. The scientific pursuit which Atheists often seek to defend and celebrate has not only saved lives through vaccination programmes and medical research, but has also caused countless deaths, whether it is the Nazis' despicable scientific experimentation with Jews or the unnecessary bombing of Nagasaki with an atomic weapon that killed tens of thousands.

I believe we need to refrain from finger pointing when both faith and Atheism have been commandeered to promote war, when both Christians and Atheists have committed heinous acts of terror and violence, when both science and God could be blamed as the root cause of tragedy. And perhaps we need to be more willing to defend the truth of our faith, and its true ideals, against those from within our ranks who misrepresent it so horrifically.

Collaboration

It is possible for Christians and Atheists to put aside differences for the cause of peace. When the two groups come together to preach peace in their communities, a powerful message is communicated. One recent example of this was the charity concert in Manchester on a warm Sunday evening in June 2017 following a terrorist attack in the city. A suicide bomber who attributed the inspiration for his atrocity to ISIS blew himself up at an Ariana Grande concert, which had primarily attracted an audience of young teenage girls. Among the 50,000 attendees at the charity concert were survivors and their families. I was one of the 10 million worldwide viewers to watch the concert live as it was broadcast on the television network. One by one the singers performed their acts and spoke their message of peace from the stage. Some borrowed Christian language and values, others broadcast their personal Christian beliefs without shame. Marcus Mumford, lead singer from the band Mumford and Sons, performed a song called 'Timshel'. The title comes from a Hebrew word found in the early part of the Bible. He ended his performance with a quote from the end of the Bible: 'Love casts out fear!'[21]

Bono, Robbie Williams and The Black Eyed Peas all talked about love, prayer and angels. And former child pop sensation Justin Bieber gave the clearest articulation of the Christian message at the event. He said, to general agreement and rapturous applause: 'I'm not going to let go of hope. I'm not going to let go of love. I'm not going to let go of God. Put your hand up if you're not going to let go. God is good in the midst of the darkness. God is good in the midst of the evil. God is in the midst, no matter what's happening in the world; God is in the midst and he loves you and he's here for you.'

These clear expressions of Christian faith in the middle of a tragedy provided a common language of solidarity and comfort to those of all religions and none. It did not matter whether the people at that concert had attended church that Sunday morning or not. Differences were put aside and overtly religious views were welcomed for the expressions of hope and faith that they were, without criticism or complaint. I found this particularly interesting in light of the fact that the attack was clearly carried out by someone who thought they were serving their religion. This could have been the perfect opportunity for anti-religious rhetoric, yet the performers and the general public did not assume that all faith was to be written off in the wake of this religiously motivated attack. Christian voices joined with Muslim voices both to express outrage at the attack and to bring compassion and comfort. Stories emerged of Muslim taxi drivers helping concert-goers caught in the pandemonium to get home safely for free, of rough-sleeping men offering first aid and other practical kindnesses, of churches collecting the tributes and opening their doors to those who were distressed. The combination of the putting aside of differences to help in a crisis with the refusal to tar all people of faith with the same brush sent out a powerful message against religious violence and for religious cooperation.

I've always been moved by accounts of the horrors of the First World War, by the terrible loss of life as enemy forces lined up in trenches metres from one other separated by the barbed-wire-laced no man's land and unleashed a seemingly unending barrage of machine-gun fire and mortar attacks. The numbers that died in the conflict are beyond imagination. In my own family we remember a kind and gentle great-grandfather who fought in the first and second battles of Ypres, and at Passchendaele. Three times he was wounded and three times he was sent back to the front. He saw his own brother die in the trenches, and was plagued by nightmares about them for the rest of his life, although he never spoke about it.

Fighting in the First World War was unimaginably horrific for all of the 65 million men mobilised to fight.

One day the two implacable enemies momentarily stopped fighting. Some candles were spotted on top of the German trenches, followed by the sound of men singing carols. It was 25 December 1914. Stories are told of an unofficial truce that day, with soldiers crossing no man's land to shake hands with those from the other trenches, some swapping buttons from their coats; apparently one English soldier gave a German soldier a haircut with some automatic clippers. There is even a report of a football match between the two sides. Somehow, on this holy day, common ground was found between mortal enemies. Somehow the most dangerous place, where no man was supposed to stand, became a place where men could embrace and see each other not as combatants and enemies but as fellow human beings. It probably felt very strange after the months of conflict. But equally strange is that the next day they were back to trying to kill each other again. They had no choice – they were under orders, and would have been shot for desertion had they refused – but perhaps it was harder for them to pull the trigger that Boxing Day, knowing what the other looked like, sounded like, felt like.

Unlike soldiers conscripted into service to fight for a cause in war, Atheists and Christians have a choice when it comes to the verbal warfare we engage in. There is no order to say that we have to speak in the lowest terms of one another. There is no rule stating that we need to patronise, berate or belittle each other. Our interaction should not be the stuff of nightmares, watching as the casualties stack up around us. Although there are real and important differences between Christians and Atheists, there is a place where we can meet. If we can leave our trenches and make our way up to no man's land, we will find that we do not have to give up our identity, but we may find our humanity.

I have been in a book group with a mix of Christian and Atheist men for the last ten years. We have met faithfully every six weeks to discuss the non-fiction books we have been reading together. We have studied politics, philosophy, history, art, economics, travel, mathematics, science, technology, aid and development, the refugee crisis, artificial intelligence and a whole host of other topics. Despite coming from opposite sides of the 'faith divide', we have found common ground together. And that common ground has not been restricted to talking about books. In ten years we have shared many life events – personal illness, bereavement, unemployment, our children leaving home, marriages, significant birthdays – and we have found a common humanity in one another. There has been a sense of generosity among us that sometimes outstrips the generosity I have seen in the Church. We share political views, a keen sense of justice, a similar life stage, a concern for the well-being of our children, as well as the occasional meal and bottle of wine. The conversation is robust and our respective beliefs are neither suppressed nor shot down. We may not share a common understanding of the universe, but we could certainly solve the problems of the world in that group – if only we had the power to make it happen.

Looking around the world right now, there are more ongoing conflicts than ever before. In 2016 it was calculated that there were twenty-eight armed conflicts taking place in twenty-six countries around the world, which involved a combined population of nearly 2 billion people.[22] It is esti-mated that global military spending in 2016 was some 1,504 billion dollars.[23] Despite increased human development, massive scientific progress and ongoing UN peace missions,

warfare is a perennial human problem and it doesn't seem to
be going away any time soon. The ongoing existence of conflict
is a challenge to all of us, both Christians and Atheists. For
Christians, Jesus is very clear in his teaching: 'Blessed are the
peacemakers for they will be called the children of God.'[24]
Making peace for the world cannot be achieved by us sitting
in a peaceful corner somewhere on our own. It is not enough
to hide in church and pray about peace. Christians are called
to an active involvement in resolving conflict. This is the family
business. We need to be there, in the most dangerous places
in the world, making a stand for humanity. For Atheists, the
challenge is to live up to their belief in our common humanity
to help create a safe world where we can thrive. Whether this
means resolving conflict in our homes, communities, towns or
nations, it is worth bringing both parties together again.

The Atheist *Washington Post* columnist Alana Massey puts
it well, in her challenge to Christians and Atheists alike:

Believing Christians need not water down the fact that God
is at the root of their commitments and traditions to accom-
modate nonbelievers. And nonbelievers need not make a point
of telling their believing brethren that general goodwill or
humanism is a better motivation for good works. As Maguire
points out, the biblical metaphor for society is a household,
not an institution but a dwelling place for a family. Though
families will quarrel over what they don't have in common,
they are meant to come together for what they do: an ancient
story of a new family formed in a place most of us will never
go and a call to peace in the world that none of us can ever
entirely live up to. And that is worth keeping alive for its
radical, enduring and miraculous love.[25]

Ninety-nine Christmases after the football match in no man's land, Pope Francis issued a call to action to both Christians and Atheists alike: 'Peace is a daily commitment. It is a home-made peace ... I invite even non-believers to desire peace. (Join us) with your desire, a desire that widens the heart. Let us all unite, either with prayer or with desire, but everyone, for peace.'[26]

Massey and Pope Francis do well to remind us of home and family. Peace is not about grand gestures or great pronouncements or deep thoughts or lively debates. Peace begins on our doorstep or around our kitchen table. Peace develops through a game of football, or a haircut. Peace is, as Ronald Reagan famously said, 'not the absence of conflict, but the ability to cope with conflict by peaceful means'.[27] Instead of fighting against one another, perhaps Atheists and Christians can fight for this cause together.

Questions

Do you think religion causes war? Why?/Why not?

What is the danger of assuming that because over the centuries many wars have been fought by religious people they must have been caused by religion?

What does it mean that both faith and Atheism have been commandeered by other agendas in order to carry out violence?

How might Christians and Atheists genuinely work together to promote peace?

Do you think peace is possible? What gives you most hope for peace in our world today?

Chapter 9

Christians are immortal /
Atheists are mortal

Collision

The world was watching when terror hit Mumbai in November 2008. A small group of criminals from the Lashkar-e-Taiba, an Islamic terrorist organisation based in Pakistan, carried out twelve attacks in a four-day period. It was horrific. I thought about my mum, who had been born in that country, but in the Assam region, far away from Mumbai. Perhaps I would call her later. Then I thought about my children. I was in charge for the weekend, as my wife was away. I had to make breakfast. I had to clear up. I had to get everyone to church. I turned off the news and pushed the awful scenes to the back of my mind.

That afternoon, my mum phoned me. One of my aunties had been in Mumbai on business, staying in the Taj Mahal Palace Hotel. Nobody had heard from her, and everybody feared the worse. I turned the news back on again, and listened with an even heavier heart. Gunmen had entered the hotel grounds, opened fire on guests swimming in the pool, and then gone inside to maim and murder. They had set fire to large parts of the hotel, set off explosive devices, and were holding all the survivors under siege. As the world media covered the event, my uncle was interviewed on the BBC and

CNN as he anxiously waited to hear news of his wife. When the terrorists were finally overcome after a sixty-hour siege, rescuers went from room to room, searching for survivors. That's when they found my aunty. She was in her room, stretched out on the sofa in a state of rest, with a towel on her chest. She had been overcome by smoke. She was one of the 164 people killed in that attack.

All the lives mattered, all the deaths were tragedies, of course, but hers was the story that most affected me. My aunty had a wicked sense of humour and could fill a room with laughter. Although she had visited me only a year or two earlier, my most lasting memory of her is from back when I was a teenager. She had come to the UK to pick out some clothes for her upcoming wedding, and she wanted our opinion on everything. My aunty was so full of energy and excitement it was infectious and this marked her life. Her murder robbed her two teenage children of a mother and took a lovely person from the world. While I grieved her sudden death, the world moved on. I was not only angry at the cruel and pointless loss, I was angry at people who walked around my neighbourhood laughing and joking as if life was normal. I was angry at Christians singing their happy songs in church. I was angry with Atheists saying there was no God to hold the terrorists accountable. I was angry with God for letting this happen. And I was angry at myself – shouldn't I have talked more with her about my personal hope for life after death?

Death is certainly an emotional subject – both for Christians and Atheists. Instead of offering one another comfort when faced with mortality and sudden bereavement, Christians and Atheists can often offend each other, either intentionally or accidentally.

The worst excesses I have seen from those claiming to be

Christians is from Westborough Baptist Church. This is a tiny family cult in the USA that has developed savvy media skills when it comes to faith conflict. Despite having fewer than fifty members and no connection with any other Baptist or Christian denominational group, this cult has made headlines around the world for its callous and cruel publicity-seeking stunts, burning Qur'ans or waving anti-Semitic slogans. For example, the very next day after Adam Lanza killed twenty young children in the Sandy Hook elementary school shooting in Newtown, Connecticut, the group threatened to picket the vigil for the funeral. But gross insensitivity is not monopolised by people who claim faith in God. One of the worst examples of tactlessness and callousness I have seen from an Atheist, on the other hand, was Christopher Hitchens' reaction to the deaths of Mother Teresa and Princess Diana, which both happened in the same week in 1997. Hitchens called Mother Teresa 'Hell's Angel', and ridiculed Princess Diana's mourners in Kensington Gardens, telling them to 'get a life'. He also wrote the following critical statement in a diary column in *Vanity Fair* magazine:

> Words to avoid this week, or perhaps any week from now on: 'idol' and 'icon'. These once meant only the show-biz versions of graven-image worship, or the cult of mortal beings. Now they mean the real thing. And spiritual and secular leaderships compete to prostrate themselves. By the way, what have we 'chosen' for our idols and icons? A simpering Bambi narcissist and a thieving, fanatical Albanian dwarf. Nice going.[1]

The overwhelming majority of Christians and Atheists do not respond to the grief of others with such callousness and lack of sympathy. Most of us take a more sympathetic approach, although it may still be collusive, gliding over difficulties rather than facing them.

Collusion

Showing true sympathy is much harder than it seems, as those of us who have been bereaved will recognise. Even well-intentioned words can smart, as people around tell us they 'know how we feel', or 'time will heal', or perhaps, 'at least she didn't feel any pain' or 'she is in a better place'. And platitudes of cultural conformity such as 'I'm sorry for your loss' or 'deepest condolences' or 'rest in peace', which seem to come from every corner, make not the slightest difference to our grief. It is no wonder that death is a taboo subject in polite conversation. Mortality as a subject is too painful for words, for most of us.

One American psychological study, aiming to uncover the reasons for anti-Atheist prejudice, found that for many people even the concept of Atheism unavoidably raised the uncomfortable issue of mortality.[2] It is an interesting thesis. Does the mere existence of Atheists make people nervous about their eternal destiny? Isn't that what Christians are often accused of doing? Is it only in the United States, where there is a greater sense of the social acceptability of faith, that Atheists are treated with greater negative prejudice because they subconsciously arouse a fear of death with no hope of an afterlife?[3] What about elsewhere in the world – is it Christians or Atheists who raise the thorny subject of death most often?

Ask anyone what is going to happen to them when they die, and most people will say they do not know, or shrug their shoulders – then most likely walk away, laugh off the question or change the subject quickly. However, it seems to me that this claim of ignorance is disingenuous. The vast majority of us must hold some sort of view, however unjustified, un-evidenced or unarticulated. The non-committal reaction reminds me of waiting on the evening train for it to depart from Marylebone Station. Inevitably, just before the train is due to pull away, someone leaps onto the carriage and breathlessly asks: 'Do you know where this train is heading?' Every time this happens, the questioner is met by silent shrugs, rolling of the eyes, sometimes even a straight 'No'. Why would these intelligent, business-suited professionals be sitting on this train if they had no idea where it was headed for? Why would they run the risk of being taken to the wrong place? They must know very well where the train is going. Or at least, they hope they know. Or perhaps they thought they knew, before the element of doubt was raised. Either way, when the moment comes, very few people have sufficient confidence to reply, and even fewer get off the train to check.

It seems to me that this silent uncertainty is felt in the same way every day when people make decisions about their lives and their futures. We must have some sense of our mortality when we decide to take out health or life insurance, when we celebrate yet another birthday, make memories, save up for our retirement or blow our savings on the here and now. Because our experience of time as human beings is linear, we cannot avoid knowing we are moving forward in an unstoppable and irreversible manner, propelled into our futures on a one-way journey to our own death. But we don't like to think about it. Most of us probably have some idea, hunch, impression or hope of what happens next – whether that be heaven or hell (however we think of those disputed concepts) – or total unconsciousness. Nevertheless, very few of us are willing to admit or debate these things. It is easier not to talk about our mortality at all, thereby reducing the risk of offending our sensibilities, or those of our friends and neighbours. We thereby collude by making it a quasi-taboo subject, one to be easily shrugged off.

Contention

Because all of us have lost loved ones, talking about death and mortality can be a profoundly uncomfortable and emotionally turbulent thing to do. Because we all have beliefs, suspicions and aspirations regarding life beyond death, challenging someone's cherished hopes for themselves or their family members is a very sensitive thing to attempt. But, just as with so many of the topics we have explored so far in this book, the fact that this subject is important to us, and has emotional resonance or consequences for us, in fact gives us all the more reason to find ways to talk about it.

Even Richard Dawkins shows an appreciation of this, in his reaction to a very bizarre practice he came across when he once visited a church in the Bible Belt of America. It involved its leader, Pastor Roberts, exposing young people to a 'Hell House' that had been designed to portray graphic depictions of eternal torture. It included sulphurous smells evoking burning brimstone and the sounds of agonised screams of 'the forever damned'.[4] I have been a Christian for over thirty years and have visited hundreds of churches around the world, and have never once come across anything like this bizarre and manipulative practice. Although I could never advocate such an approach to forcing people to face up to their mortality, Dawkins does recognise that there may be some degree of integrity in this macabre practice: 'I suppose that, if you really and truly believed what Pastor Roberts says he believes, you would feel it right to intimidate children too.'[5]

At one level our society is becoming more permissive when it comes to exposing younger children to frightening and upsetting images. I have seen many a parent take toddlers on the ghost train at the fairground, or encourage the smallest children to dress up in morbid costumes for Halloween. And I am convinced that the certification boards that govern the ratings that films receive for cinematic or online release have relaxed their thresholds since I was a child.[6] At their schools, my children are regularly exposed to stark photographs and videos of the terrible things that will happen to them if they do not brush their teeth, if they do not wear a cycling helmet, or if people use their mobile phones while driving. These horrific, emotionally jarring images are designed to etch themselves into their memories – to scare children, or intimidate them even – into keeping safe. Although, arguably, eternal safety is even more critical, in the same period the idea of hell has ironically become a toxic subject, one that mustn't be talked about in any serious way. Christians themselves these days would be far more likely to want to present the benefits of faith than scare people into belief. I would not endorse scare tactics when it comes to talking about death and mortality; however, I do believe that our beliefs about these things are important to talk about, and to talk about well.

But many, even most, Christians, do not talk about the afterlife at all. This may be part of the collusion we looked at in the previous section – a reflection of our cultural taboos. Or it may be out of fear of being tarred with the same brush as Pastor Roberts – using immoral scare tactics to intimidate people into converting. Many Christians would agree with Dawkins that such scare tactics, particularly used on children, are an abuse of power. However, Dawkins takes it much further when he writes: 'I am persuaded that the phrase "child abuse" is no exaggeration when used to describe what teachers and priests are doing to children whom they encourage to believe in something like the punishment of unshriven mortal sins in an eternal hell.'[7]

Mind you, Dawkins is not afraid to employ some scare tactics of his own. As the speaker for the Royal Institution's Christmas Lectures for Children in 1991, he warned the young audience of a 'mind virus' called Islam, likening it to Nazism and exhorting them to grow out of parochial, supernatural and superstitious ideas – by which he meant religion of any kind.[8] In the accompanying study guide for the Christmas lectures he wrote that children have no purpose in life and should aspire to have no purpose in life other than to replicate the species – in other words, to have sex and have children.

But this kind of narrowed vision is exactly the kind of thing one could imagine informing a paedophile's self-justification. Using Dawkins' own words, some might argue that the phrase 'child abuse' is no exaggeration when used to describe what our science gurus are doing to children when they encourage them to believe that sex is the only reason to exist and there is nothing beyond this life.

Most Atheists, it should be said, do not agree with Dawkins' moral reductionism here, and when it comes to human existence and mortality they are both more sensitive and more honest, admitting that they don't have definitive answers. Some do concede that there may well be further existence in some form after this life. After all, millions of years of evolution during which things that haven't been useful to our survival should have been bred out of existence has not dampened what Julian Baggini calls 'the natural tendency to be bewitched by wonder and mystery, which gives us a strong desire to believe tales of the extraordinary'.[9] This persistent belief is what

Richard Dawkins calls 'the God gene'. So, ironically, Dawkins himself has to acknowledge that religion is strangely resilient. Indeed, according to the Atheist philosopher John Gray, Dawkins' 'God gene' theory suggests that even though religion is an illusion, there must be some evolutionary value in believing in God that is conducive to our survival.[10] On the other hand, Christians like C.S. Lewis counter this line of thought with a simple explanation that the persistence of religion is a demonstration of the innately human desire to satisfy a thirst for the divine:

> Creatures are not born with desires unless satisfaction for those desires exists. A baby feels hunger: well, there is such a thing as food. A duckling wants to swim: well, there is such a thing as water. Men feel sexual desire: well, there is such a thing as sex. If I find in myself a desire which no experience in this world can satisfy, the most probable explanation is that I was made for another world.[11]

The explanation for the persistence of religious belief in the modern world will no doubt be a constant debate, but interestingly both Dawkins and Baggini agree that it would not be hard to believe in life after death if there was even the slightest bit of evidence. Baggini writes: 'a single survival of death alone would be enough to make the atheist reconsider their belief in human mortality'.[12] And Dawkins writes: 'God's existence or non-existence is a scientific fact about the universe, discoverable in principle if not in practice. If he existed and chose to reveal it, God himself could clinch the argument, noisily and unequivocally, in his favour.'[13] On this Christians and Atheists agree. For Christians, the existence of God and the possibility of life beyond death can both be demonstrated through a single historical event, satisfying both Dawkins' and Baggini's stated criteria. That event was the resurrection of Jesus from the dead – which brings us on to the Christian contention for immortality.

Christians believe the resurrection of Jesus three days after his recorded death to be the paradigm-shifting historical event through which God announces loud and clear to the world that he is here, that he is all-powerful and that he is good. The fact that it is otherwise virtually unheard of for anyone to rise from the dead does not weaken the case, but strengthens it. If it is true, then Jesus has done something revolutionary, must be unique and can be trusted in his claim to be God. It is on this single event that the claims of the Christian faith are either refuted or verified. This is acknowledged in the Bible itself, as explained by the Apostle Paul:

> For what I received I passed on to you as of first importance: that Christ died for our sins according to the Scriptures, that he was buried, that he was raised on the third day according to the Scriptures, and that he appeared to Cephas, and then to the Twelve. After that, he appeared to more than five hundred of the brothers and sisters at the same time, most of whom are still living, though some have fallen asleep. Then he appeared to James, then to all the apostles, and last of all he appeared to me also . . .
>
> If there is no resurrection of the dead, then not even Christ has been raised. And if Christ has not been raised, our preaching is useless and so is your faith. More than that, we are then found to be false witnesses about God . . . And if Christ has not been raised, your faith is futile; you are still in your sins. Then those also who have fallen asleep in Christ are lost. If only for this life we have hope in Christ, we are of all people most to be pitied.[14]

There are a number of quite astonishing claims here that would have run counter to what the people of the time – both Jews and Romans – might have expected. First of all, the claim that Jesus died 'for our sins' is large in scale, but simple in practice. On one hand it asserts that his death has changed the way God sees humanity, but it is an 'invisible' claim – there is no way to test it. I could say I was the king of an invisible land in another dimension, but what is easy to claim is harder to validate. So Paul follows up this outlandish claim with a second one, which comes with testable evidence. When Paul claims that Jesus rose from the dead, he doesn't assert that Jesus was seen by a few of his followers, in private, in a dimly lit room. He writes that over five hundred people saw him on numerous occasions and in many locations, often in broad daylight, over a forty-day period – thereby providing a visible, fully falsifiable claim. And he freely admits that if tested and found false, then all the teachings of Christianity are empty and hollow.

Paul seems to anticipate critics, such as some of today's Atheists, who say they pity Christians for basing their lives on wishful thinking. He does not dismiss their views, instead agreeing that they make a fair point. This does not sound like the ranting of a lunatic, or someone asking people to believe and hope for the best. Put yourself in these early Christians' shoes: if you were living in the ancient world and became convinced that you had seen someone who was dead not just resuscitated but actually resurrected, how might you go about convincing people? I am not sure you would do much different to what the Church actually did.

Paul invites his audience to put Christianity to the test. If tested and proved false, then he will gladly admit his mistake. If tested and found true, however, then, as he demonstrates, the hope of life beyond death is not an irrational leap into the dark. If Jesus' resurrection really took place then this provides exactly the evidence that Dawkins and Baggini require – a single, clear, historical event of someone who not only survives death, but defeats it.

There are a number of prominent Christians whose spiritual journeys began with a thorough-going scepticism towards faith but who, through investigation of the evidence, changed their minds. For example, Lee Strobel, after completing a Master of Studies in Law from Yale Law School, worked as a journalist for the *Chicago Tribune* and other newspapers for fourteen years and was presented with an award for his public service in that regard. Strobel was a convinced Atheist but after his wife converted to Christianity he started to research the evidence. In his best-selling book *The Case for Christ*, he traces his journey to becoming a Christian.[15] Strobel explores the reliability of the eyewitness evidence of the biographical accounts given in the Gospels. He examines the documentary evidence to assess the reliability of the Bible in general, and investigates the historical and archaeological evidence to assess its support for the existence of Jesus outside of the Bible itself. He then goes on to explore the Gospel accounts, with particular reference to the evidence for the resurrection. Strobel's conclusion surprised him: the evidence pointed to the reality of the existence of God, the resurrection of Jesus and the genuine hope of life after death.

Professor Alister McGrath of Oxford University explains that he grew up as an Atheist, and yet it was through his exploration of science and philosophy that he came to ask questions such as: 'What if this world is only part of the story? What if there is something more wonderful beyond it?' He became interested in the resurrection of Jesus and wrote:

If the resurrection didn't happen, then the New Testament could not be trusted. If it did, the New Testament was to be trusted . . . I could not help feeling there was rather more to the resurrection of Christ than the validation of the authority of Scripture . . . After several years of wrestling with these issues, I came down firmly on the side of Christian orthodoxy. I became, and remain, a dedicated and convinced defender of traditional Christian theology.[16]

If the Bible is clear about the basis of the Christian hope of life beyond death, it also has some pretty clear things to say about what it may look like. Jesus was not afraid to speak about the realities of heaven and hell, and yet he didn't do it in a manipulative or abusive way. Jesus' teaching about hell seems to be restricted to those conversations with the self-righteous and judgemental religious debaters who felt not only that they had a right to go to heaven, but also that they would be the ones who got to exclude others they did not like. With children, and all those who deemed themselves unworthy or unlovable, Jesus speaks at great length about the compassion of God and how they will be welcomed into God's kingdom.

We have spent a long time looking at the Christian claims and evidence for an afterlife. A sceptic might class this as wishful thinking. The idea that our eternal destiny could be in the balance may be criticised as uncomfortable reading. But the Atheist view could also face similar critiques. Isn't it just another sort of wishful thinking to suggest that there is no ultimate moral accountability for what is done in this life? Isn't it an uncomfortable thought to think that there is nothing beyond the grave and no chance to see our loved ones again?

Some automatically tend to think that because a belief has an outcome we might prefer, it must therefore be true. Others think that because a belief has an outcome we might prefer, it must therefore be untrue. There is faulty logic on both sides here. Just because a belief has a questionable originating motive,[17] or seems too good to be true, or fits with our preconceived ideas, does not in any way guide us as to its truth or falsehood. True truth must be a mind-independent reality, not dependent on preference. Therefore we cannot automatically dismiss the claims of Christians who may want to believe in the afterlife, or the claims of Atheists who may not want to believe in an afterlife.

Steve Jobs, the late visionary and Chief Executive of Apple, the company he helped found, openly admitted to his struggles with the idea of an afterlife. Like many Atheists, he did not believe in the soul, and spent most of his life thinking that life ends when brain activity ends. He said, 'You're born alone, you're going to die alone. And does anything else really matter? . . . What is it exactly that you have to lose? . . . There's nothing.'[18] However, he also found this view profoundly uncomfortable. So much so that, for a while, he refused to give many of his Apple products an on/off switch because a one-click shut-down function seemed to him to be a stark reminder of the suddenness and finality of death. When Jobs was diagnosed with pancreatic cancer, he found himself 'believing a bit more' in life after death. His biographer quoted him as saying: 'I want to believe in an afterlife . . . That when you die, it doesn't just all disappear. The wisdom you've accumulated. Somehow it lives on.'[19]

Collaboration

Looking closely at what Atheists and Christians believe about life after death reveals that we have two significant points of convergence.

First of all, death puts things into perspective. When another aunt of mine was diagnosed with cancer and was given just three weeks to live, death suddenly became the topic of every conversation we had. Sometimes it was emotional – how much we would miss one another, the milestones of her grandchildren that she would not live to see. Sometimes it was spiritual – she spoke of her firm belief that she was going to heaven, and who she was looking forward to seeing there. Sometimes it was practical – she worried about who would take care of the cat, inherit the money and pick the raspberries she had been cultivating. Sometimes we laughed – at the futility of the bathtub in the basement that would now never be plumbed in, or at the curious expression of the baby playing obliviously with her medical aids. Sometimes we cried – as she thanked us for coming, as though our visit had been a perfectly ordinary one, or as we broke the news of her worsening condition to her elderly father. Such intense conversation about life-and-death matters put things into perspective. Cross words and differences of opinion that had been exchanged in the past were forgotten. The house improvements she'd been planning became trivial, what and when we were going to eat was unimportant, whether or not we personally preferred cremation to burial or a poem to a prayer – these things were irrelevant. As we gathered to say our goodbyes, both before and after her death, the only thing that mattered was that we were together. And in those moments, relationships and conversations felt genuine as never before. They say death is a great leveller, and facing up to our own mortality means that the conversation between Christians and Atheists takes place in the light of these bigger questions. All of us are dying, whether quickly or slowly. Each morning all of us are a step closer to the end of our days. This means we need to value the time we have with one another, believe the best, and find honest and respectful ways to talk about the things that really matter. If we can talk about death, then we can talk about anything. If we can be there for one another in the face of death, then we can be there for one another whatever happens.

Second, there is nothing to fear in death. A recent study conducted by researchers at Oxford University found that both those who practised religion and those who declared themselves as committed Atheists shared the common trait of not fearing death as much as people who declared no strong commitments to faith or Atheism.[20] For the Christian, Jesus' death on our behalf and his resurrection that conquered death itself are grounds to trust his promise of eternal life for all who trust in him. As one well-known psalm in the Bible puts it: 'Even though I walk through the valley of the shadow of death, I will fear no evil.'[21] Atheists may argue that there is no need to be afraid because there is nothing beyond this life to be afraid of. If we are unafraid about death, then of course we should be unafraid about discussing death and issues around our mortality.

If Jesus did not really, historically and physically defeat death, then Christianity is fake news, its followers are wasting their time and all ideas about heaven can be discarded. But if Jesus did really, historically and physically survive death, then Christianity is good news, and its followers are absolutely right to believe everything Jesus said about God and the afterlife. Even though Atheists and Christians may disagree on the conclusion, at least they can agree on the terms and logic of the argument. Christianity makes a truth claim about the identity of Jesus based on the historicity of the resurrection of Jesus. That is not illogical or anti-intellectual. Whether you believe it or not, it is at least understandable.

When we have shared respect for the logic, at least, we have grounds for conversation and relationship that can genuinely help in the face of tragedy, death and mortality. Christians can attend an Atheist funeral, respecting the choice of the family. Atheists can find comfort at a Christian funeral, as they understand the reasons behind the convictions held by the deceased.

Christians are often not very good at emulating Jesus when it comes to grief and death. Jesus openly shed tears at a funeral, mourning the loss of a friend and lamenting the tragic state of the world. But Jesus also talked about life beyond death as a positive thing. He described death as a homecoming where those who have faith in him are welcomed into God's family home to be with him forever. Jesus talked about life beyond death as a reunion with lost loved ones. He talked about bodies that would be fixed and a home that nothing could destroy – not fire, nor cancer, nor terrorists. The rest of the Bible describes life beyond death as a welcome into a community, a renewed place where there will be no more pain or tears, where wrongs will be righted, and everything is renewed and restored. For the sceptic could this be more than pie in the sky when we die? For the suffering, could this be the good news worth waiting for?

After the horrors of the 2008 Mumbai terror attacks, news began to spread about the amazing bravery of the staff team at the Taj Hotel. Stories circulated of employees who formed human barricades to protect the guests, staff who came from other locations to the Taj to assist guests with water and food, telephone operators who returned to the Taj to help instruct people in what to do in the emergency. A *Harvard Business Review* case study showed that employees went above and beyond any training they had received or the expectations put on them by their superiors. In fact, many managers found the bravery of their employees beyond comprehension. The *HBR* investigation attributed some of the behaviours exhibited to the hotel's unusual hiring practices. The Taj is listed as one of the top twenty international hotels, yet they recruit not from the larger cities but instead go to small towns and semi-urban regions. They do not recruit those with the best grades or even the best spoken English, but look for candidates of good character, and, specifically, those who demonstrate respect and empathy.[22] The management of the hotel found that these traditional values, along with honesty, discipline and humility, held sway more in the hinterlands of India than in the cities, where young people learned to cut corners, driven more by money than by loyalty or empathy with their customers.[23] This policy paid dividends when the crisis came. Staff were willing to put their own lives at risk even for the sake of their guests, wealthy people from different countries and cultures, with opposing values and beliefs.

I have seen something of this unifying compassion in the face of tragedy in my own town. When there have been children in our local schools who died through sickness, accident or suicide, suddenly and pointlessly, I have seen Atheists and Christians work together to rally around the families, and those grieving in the community. I have seen churches offer a place of genuine refuge and reflection open to everyone, regardless of whether or not they have faith. I have seen community spaces offering a place for people to gather, to leave flowers or a note in a memorial book or a message of sympathy, and to talk.

Struggling to talk about death seems to me better than struggling in silence over the subject. We all know something of bereavement and we will all die. We will all grieve and be grieved. We all need answers to ultimate questions. What unites us far outweighs what divides us.

President John F. Kennedy, who was open in office about his own Catholic heritage, said this:

So, let us not be blind to our differences – but let us also direct our attention to our common interests and to means by which those differences can be resolved. And if we cannot end now our differences, at least we can help make the world safe for diversity. For, in the final analysis, our most basic common link is that we all inhabit this planet. We all breathe the same air. We all cherish our children's future. And we are all mortal.[24]

Kennedy's sudden death shocked the world. In that light his words seem to carry more weight, and an important challenge when it comes to collaboration. Even if we don't share beliefs about life after death, we all believe in life before death, and it is in everyone's interest to build a world that is 'safe for diversity'.

Questions

What experiences have most challenged your own views about life and death?

Do you find it easy to talk about death? Why do you think this is?

How would you summarise the Christian and Atheist views about death?

Why is the historicity of the resurrection so important to Christianity?

How can empathy be transformational for Christians and Atheists as they serve people who are grieving?

Chapter 10

Suffering necessitates God / Suffering negates God

Collision

When James[1] was diagnosed with bone cancer at the age of twelve, it was a terrible blow not only to him, but to his family, his church and the wider community. The following four years were hard to go through as the tests, the treatments, the operations, the progress and then regression and the sickness took their toll. The one thing the family held on to during those difficult months was their faith. They read the Bible together, which gave them strength and determination to carry on, as well as easing the waiting and the pain. They hoped and prayed for miraculous or medical healing, and they trusted that even if that didn't happen, then ultimately James would end up in a better place. When praying was difficult, they asked others to pray for them. They talked frankly about dying and funerals and heaven, and when James died he did so without fear. James's family continue to talk about how their faith helped them – helps them – cope with their pain and loss.

Around the time that James seemed to be dealing with the greatest pain and uncertainty, the actor, comedian, presenter and all-round British national treasure Stephen Fry spoke about bone cancer. He was being interviewed live on Irish national television and when asked what he would say to God if he met him, replied:

> I will say bone cancer in children, what's that about? How dare you, how dare you create a world that has such misery that is not our fault? It is not right. It is utterly, utterly evil. Why should I respect a capricious, mean-minded, stupid God who creates a world that is full of injustice and pain?[2]

Fry's outburst went viral very quickly. His pain and anger seemed to touch a nerve with many. Over 7 million people watched it on YouTube, with many more hearing it or reading it in the national press. He went on to give a particular example of suffering that he found particularly repugnant – child blindness caused by insects burrowing into their eyes. 'Why did you do that to us?' Fry asked poignantly as he forcefully articulated the age-old problem of suffering.

One viewer was outraged by the outburst and complained under Ireland's 2009 blasphemy laws,[3] which prompted an investigation of Fry by the authorities that was later dropped. Knowing what James and his family were facing at the time, I felt something of the insensitivity of having beliefs ridiculed on live television by a well-respected public figure, when faith was the only thing keeping that family going. On the other hand, I also found some resonance in Fry's anger. The Bible records people expressing similar sentiments to God: 'Why did you do that to us?'[4]

If Stephen Fry gives one public, angry and insensitive response to the problem of suffering from an Atheist perspective, then at the other end of the spectrum there have been some unhelpful public pronouncements from people claiming Christian faith. For example, American pastor and media mogul

Pat Robertson announced to the world, a few days after 1,836 people had died, that he believed that Hurricane Katrina's decimation of New Orleans was God's punishment on America because of its abortion policy. He did not explain why he thought God predominantly targeted impoverished African Americans. Similarly, days after an earthquake in Haiti killed more than a hundred thousand people, Robertson blamed the suffering on Haiti's 'pact with the devil', which the country had apparently made in the eighteenth century. Many people, including both Christians and Atheists, were outraged by Robertson's comments, calling them insensitive and inaccurate.

Fry and Robertson present a clear-cut example of the collision between Atheist and Christian over the problem of suffering. But you don't have to be live on national television to get mixed up in this conflict.

For many Christians and Atheists, the issue of undeserved suffering, so closely related to that of death, is *the* big question that clinches the choice one way or the other in determining their ultimate beliefs about God, life, purpose and faith. This cry, 'But why?' is the question that we all confront in the middle of disaster and tragedy. This is the question we ask after receiving bad news at a medical consultation or at the graveside of a loved one. Christians struggle with this question as much as Atheists. The question cuts to the very heart of what they say they believe. Sometimes when Christians cry out 'But why?' they feel guilty – shouldn't they just trust in the God they claim is working everything out for good? Sometimes when Atheists cry out 'But why?' they too feel guilty – shouldn't they be ready to accept these random twists and turns of fate without question?

Sometimes this question changes people. One of my friends has vowed never to give God the time of day again, for taking away the life of his brother, killed in a motorcycle accident. Meanwhile another friend, struggling to find meaning in the tragic loss of her son in a car accident, began to attend church and now calls herself a Christian. Many people in my church have suffered tragedies and have found their faith strengthened. Yet other people, who used to attend my church, now cannot face it, because they cannot square faith with their terrible personal circumstances. One friend started coming to church after praying that God would make a way for her to adopt her foster son. But when her brother-in-law died suddenly, she stopped believing in God. Some years later, faced with a false criminal allegation, she found herself in the court toilets begging God to see past her criticisms of him and to help her prove her innocence. She might come back to church. But what happens if he lets her down again?

We see, in these different responses, collisions between competing ways of facing up to the reality of suffering. This is an important question for us to grapple with because in our work, social and family life we will all come across people who are suffering, and understanding how to relate to people who deal with tragedy differently to us can help us avoid adding miscommunication, insensitivity or ridicule to their pain. It is also a vital question to face because, sadly, all of us will face tragedy of some sort in our lives, and thinking these things through in advance can help us be better prepared and hopefully better able to cope.

Collusion

Perhaps because of the extreme reactions of people like Stephen Fry or Pat Robertson, we are often nervous of talking about how we understand the problem of suffering. If you think the person you are going to open up to is going to launch into a diatribe ridiculing your beliefs, it might make you think twice about baring your soul. Equally, if you want to offer solace to someone who is suffering by offering prayer, there is the chance you may offend them. The other reason we are nervous to be honest about these things is that there never seems to be a good time to discuss them. Sometimes we are very aware of someone dealing with the pain of suffering, and we don't want to aggravate the problem by talking about that suffering in an offhand or callous or academic way. Sometimes we are totally unaware of those friends around us who are secretly suffering, and so we do not know of the need to address the subject.

In my son's A-Level year, many of his friends faced significant suffering. Between them they knew more than their fair share of issues – relating to bullying, family breakdown, disability, sickness, financial hardship, relationship break-ups, disappointment, work pressure, exam stress, false allegations and bereavement. And yet these boys rarely talked about their feelings and concerns. Perhaps they were afraid of losing what composure they had managed to pull together to make it into school each day. Perhaps school, or other previous experience, had taught them not to be vulnerable. Perhaps they found some relief in the inanity of boys' banter or in focusing on their schoolwork. Perhaps faithful friendship was the best medicine. Watching them, it was evident that suffering was indeed a taboo subject, even though it was one of the things they absolutely had in common. Some of them are Christians and some of them are not. I wonder if their awareness of difference when it comes to faith attitudes actually made it harder for them to open up about their struggles, knowing that they risked scorn in their bid for support.

Can you imagine coming across a major road traffic accident

involving multiple cars and victims, and being told that anyone with medical expertise should stand back and keep quiet? Would it help the victims to only be treated in the privacy of a hospital room, and not to be offered first aid at the scene of the accident? Surely the reassurance of a medical professional would bring some relief. What if a local GP and an Army surgeon both rushed forward to help, but had different opinions of how best to do so? Even then, in times of crises, the more help the better. But when my son's friends visited him in my home, I, despite knowing the issues they were facing, despite having personal experience of those same issues, despite having professional experience in helping people cope with grief and suffering, did not rush forward to offer specific help and support.

Perhaps I am just like most people, who often treat those experiencing suffering with a hands-off approach. Perhaps my faith, instead of helping me to bring comfort, actually made it harder for me to bring that comfort. After all, if I were to offer some encouragement, or a listening ear, or prayer, it might be seen as offensive, even an abuse of position, especially to a teenager.

There have been a number of recent court cases where people of faith appear to have been disciplined or even fired from their jobs because they have crossed a line between professional responsibilities and the expression of their faith. For example, much was made in the media of the case of the nurse who was fired for offering to pray with patients before surgery[5] – allegedly, she was more interested in talking about faith than in completing medical questionnaires – and for telling a cancer patient they had a better chance of survival if they prayed. Nurse Sarah Kuteh, who has fifteen years of experience, was sacked for gross misconduct from Darent Valley Hospital as a result of eight patient complaints about her and after the management had asked her to change her behaviour. These stories are often picked up by both sides of the Christian–Atheist debate and used as ammunition. Some Christians argue from them that they are being persecuted, while some Atheists argue that expressing Christian faith in this very public way is oppressive and exploitative.

As a foster carer I am aware that the children who come into my care are incredibly vulnerable, so I am very careful not to inappropriately impose my convictions about God on them. I try to imagine, if my own children were in care, how I would want their religious convictions to be treated. I would want dignity and respect to be given to them, and freedom to express their faith without hindrance or opposition. So I apply this principle of reciprocity to others, respecting whatever religious choices or heritage is required. Similarly, if an elderly relative was in hospital, I would want their faith to be respected and honoured by all the medical staff involved. If they wanted someone to pray with them, I would be very pleased if there was a nurse there with some experience in prayer. I do not know Ms Kuteh or the intricate details of her case, but her story and others like it serve to give the impression that no Christian should ever engage in talking about their faith.[6] It is entirely possible that Ms Kuteh was using her position as a nurse to inappropriately take advantage of patients at a very vulnerable moment in their lives. But while I would certainly agree that prayer should never be used as a means of manipulating somebody, giving them false hope, or creating inappropriately intimate situations, I do not believe that all spiritual help should be deemed improper all of the time.

When a fire ripped through the Grenfell Tower in South Kensington in 2017, leaving many dead and many more homeless, the council seemed to have neither the will nor the resources to respond adequately. St Clement's Church, which was next door to the tower block, became the locus of the community response because of its long history of working with the community. The Clement James Centre serves some 2,500 people annually, helping unemployed people find work, immigrants learn English, and children from deprived backgrounds make the most of their abilities.[7] Many celebrated the work of the church during this national crisis. While the impression is often given that faith and work should never be mixed, in this case, the fact that the church stepped in where the council had failed was celebrated. The discrepancy is difficult to grapple with. Prayer in a hospital by a nurse for a dying patient is frowned upon, but prayer for the survivors of a national tragedy is still widely appreciated. The Church may be ridiculed most of the time in the media, but during times of tragedy there is a social permission for the faith community to make a contribution – vigils, funerals, Bible readings – at least temporarily. The greater and more public the tragedy, the more religion is allowed to participate in the response.

This reminds me of the discrepancy I noticed when I was a child. I received plenty of racist abuse, but those same boys who bullied me did not have any problem with nationally respected black and Asian sportsmen who competed for our country in football and athletics. Today, as a Christian, I often feel the system is out to get me, but it is the same broken system that needs Christians to get involved, volunteer, pick up the pieces and bring the community together.

The challenge of suffering raises some uncomfortable questions regarding the potential for duplicity in our attitudes. Is it hypocritical to find comfort in prayers and spiritual language and ceremonies, when faith is off the agenda the rest of the time? Is it hypocritical to preach about a loving God, when he seems to rob us of our joy as things go wrong? Is it hypocritical to turn to God – either in desperation or in anger – if we claim not to believe in him?

Contention

As we have seen, the issue of suffering is the 'border crossing' for many Christians and Atheists, so it is appropriate and important to explore it, however briefly. Atheist philosopher Julian Baggini helpfully summarises the essential question at the heart of the problem of suffering.

> The existence of avoidable suffering in the world seems to be an undeniable fact. This must mean one of three things:
>
> - God can't stop it, which means he is not all-powerful;
> - he doesn't want to stop it, so he isn't all-loving;
> - or he doesn't know about it, which means he isn't all-knowing.[8]

This approach leads the Atheist to conclude that because suffering exists, we need to challenge the Christian view of God.

The Christian takes the opposite approach. Because God exists, and because he is all-powerful, all-loving and all-knowing, and still does not seem to intervene, then we need to challenge our view of suffering.

In order to work through these two approaches, we need to look more closely at four questions. Is God omnipotent? Is God all-loving? Is God all-knowing? And lastly, is suffering always bad?

First, let us look at the question of God's omnipotence. Of

course, this is a particularly hypothetical question for an Atheist, who has to suspend disbelief in the existence of God momentarily to ask if he could be all-powerful. This question has brought forth many a paradoxical conundrum from philosophers, along the lines of 'Could God make a stone too heavy for himself to lift?' If the answer is yes, then he is not all-powerful. If the answer is no, then, too, he is not all-powerful. Ironically, God himself is damned if he does and damned if he doesn't. But to ask these questions in the first place is to misunderstand the concept of power and of logic. It is like asking who would win in a fight between God and God. There is no answer that would ever be useful. If God, as described in the Bible, has the power to create and sustain the world, know the number of hairs on your head, care about the tiniest sparrow, control the galaxies, and raise men from the dead, then certainly the God of the Bible is all-powerful.

Does God have the power to stop suffering? The Bible teaches that he does have that power and that one day he will use his power to bring all suffering to an end – so the Christian will reply 'Yes.' Does God have to use his power to stop suffering now? That is a different question, to which the answer is 'No.' The Bible teaches that there may be good reason for God not to stop suffering yet.

For example, Jesus told a story explaining why he is able to stop suffering and yet doesn't . . . yet. The story involves a farmer who is cultivating a crop of wheat. Although he tends his wheat diligently, a spy has secretly entered his field and added weeds, which begin to take over the whole crop. The farmer wants to get rid of the weeds, but is worried that if he begins pulling them up, then his young wheat shoots may be damaged in the process. So he decides to let the whole field grow – weeds and wheat – and to separate them out in the harvest, when the weeds can be properly destroyed.

According to this parable of Jesus, if God ends suffering by uprooting all the bad things in the world, something good may be taken with it. Somehow, the removal of evil and injustice right now from our midst could mean the harming of human life, as our lives are inextricably interwoven with evil and injustice too. Aleksandr Solzhenitsyn, as noted earlier, put it like this: 'The line separating good and evil passes . . . right through every human heart.'[9] For God to remove the evil in the world, he would need to remove us. For God to remove the possibility of evil in the world, he would need to remove free will – an essential element of our humanity. Freedom of will is what distinguishes us from animals driven only by their instincts or from robotic automatons driven only by their programming.[10]

The second question has to do with whether or not God is all-loving. Sometimes my ten-year-old daughter thinks I do not love her. She thinks that because I won't let her go to the fair by herself, or let her chat to whoever she wants on the iPad, or only eat chocolate for dinner, that I am a cruel, vindictive father who obviously does not love her at all. Because I send her upstairs to calm down rather than allow her to rant, she then thinks I not only don't love her, but also don't want to be with her. However, it is precisely because I love her and her company that her 'pleasures' and movements are restricted. I have to put in place negative consequences to any attempt to break free of those restrictions in order, ultimately, to protect her and our ongoing relationship. I do not expect her to fully understand my reasoning as a parent, nor do I claim to be a perfect parent, but one day I hope she will come to realise that everything I did was out of love for her, and consideration for her long-term welfare. Just because we cannot always understand why God makes certain rules, or allows us to suffer painful consequences, does not mean that he is not all-loving. It may just mean that we cannot see the bigger picture.

My teenage children are more autonomous. They have to make an increasing number of decisions for themselves. I will not tell them what to wear to a party, or how much chocolate is too much. If one of them decides to start dating someone, and I can foresee heartbreak ahead with a degree of certainty, would it be unloving to allow them to go ahead with the relationship? Part of the agony of parenting is watching your children learn to be independent, even though that means they make mistakes. Some of those mistakes may result in temporary pain, but hopefully, too, their long-term gain. This helps me ask questions about God's care of us. Does our suffering really prove that God does not love us? Should he prevent all our suffering, at any cost? What if it is exactly because he loves us that he allows us to suffer, even though we can't always understand why? Could it be that it is because he has given us such a degree of free will and self-determination that he allows us to do things that will harm ourselves and others?

Third, is God really all-knowing? If God is all-knowing, then he would know how to minimise the damage done in this world, how to forewarn us of consequences, or how to stop suffering altogether. The Atheist may say that God does not do that and thus the existence of suffering negates the idea that God really does know what is going on. The Christian, on the other hand, would argue that God has indeed acted to address the problem. The Bible contains guidelines and boundaries and wisdom that, if followed, would have enabled us as the human race to avoid much of the suffering that naturally comes our way through the consequences of bad choices. This is not to say that now in a world that has in many ways rejected God's wisdom for living, an individual who followed the Bible to the letter would be guaranteed an easy life, free of suffering. Jesus clearly suffered even though, according to the Bible, he was morally perfect. Nevertheless the Bible does provide both wisdom for how to live well now and the hope of life beyond the grave.

Christianity also claims that God has made a way to stop suffering once and for all, but that, like the farmer waiting for the crop to fully grow, it is not yet time to extract the suffering from the world. This idea can give the impression that God is aloof and distant at present. He is just sitting back and waiting while the world struggles on, like someone who winds up a clockwork toy, setting it in motion and then leaving it to its own devices. Christians would challenge that idea. They believe that God does get involved in the world, and he does intervene. They may cite supernatural examples such as healings and miracles. Or they may point to other positive things that happen in the world, such as medical breakthroughs. Or they may paint the picture of a world that could be even more chaotic than it is if God hadn't invisibly intervened.

Christians therefore have reason to believe that even though God is all-powerful, all-loving and all-knowing, he does allow suffering to continue. So is there a different perspective on suffering we can take, apart from looking for somebody to blame and be angry at?

The Bible has a lot to say about suffering. It talks about God's empathy with his suffering people, his desire and promise to ultimately end suffering, and his mandate to his people to work hard to alleviate the suffering of others. The turning point of the Bible is God's choice to suffer alongside us and for us. Jesus knew what it meant to be bullied, be marginalised, lose his home, suffer bereavement, go hungry, suffer physical torture, be betrayed and abandoned by his friends, face injustice, pain, temptation and shame, and to be killed for no good reason. Christians find great solace in the fact that when we pray we speak to someone who can relate to our suffering.

Christians also believe that when Jesus died, the purpose of his doing so was ultimately to bring about the end of all human suffering. He was making possible the reconciliation of all things, the undoing of all that has gone wrong in our world. If God is all-knowing enough to see how messed up the world is, if he is nevertheless all-loving enough to allow his son to die on behalf of humanity, if he is all-powerful enough to raise Jesus from the dead – then nothing is too difficult for him to fix, heal and restore. Jesus' suffering proves that our suffering is just temporary and that one day we will see the rhyme and reason for it.

Christians also believe that Jesus' self-sacrifice is a way of life that we are called to emulate. No one else can (or needs to) die for the sins of the world, but we can all be willing to lay down our lives for others – to fight injustice, nurse the sick and the dying, feed the hungry, care for the suffering, and work to build institutions and social structures that will help to transform society for the common good. And when we suffer through no fault of our own, Jesus' attitude to suffering is one we are called to emulate: trusting God, hoping for a better future, and expressing our pain to God in prayer.

I don't know why there are parasitic worms in our world that burrow into children's eyes and cause them to go blind. I don't know why my mother got cancer, or why two of my children were born with chromosome disorders, or why I struggle with aches and pains that get worse the older I get. But as a Christian I believe that God did not intend the world to be like this, and that one day he will put it all right again.

I believe that in the meantime he calls us to alleviate suffering, even if we suffer in the process.

For someone who claims not to believe in God, Fry comes across as very angry with him. He seems to have a very emotional (dis-)connection with the God whose existence he denies. His outburst seems to demonstrate that a big part of him might not be in tune with his declared commitment to an atheistic view.

Dawkins writes:

> In a universe of blind physical forces and genetic replication, some people are going to get hurt, other people are going to get lucky, and you won't find any rhyme or reason in it, nor any justice. The universe we observe has precisely the properties we should expect if there is, at bottom, no design, no purpose, no evil and no good, nothing but blind, pitiless indifference.[11]

In other words, according to this line of thought at least, at bottom Atheists have only one good answer to the question: 'Why suffering?' Why does the natural world contain creatures that cause blindness? Just because it does. Is there really no reason for it and no purpose to it? Is the universe as indifferent as Dawkins declares? This is a fantastically difficult set of assumptions to live out consistently without courting despair.

My question to Dawkins is: if the world is indifferent to suffering and injustice, why are Atheists not indifferent to suffering and injustice too? Why are they, at least all the ones I know, compassionate, with a strong sense of justice, passionately engaged in issues of social change? Why, when we experience personal injustice or suffering, do we cry out *to God* or become outraged *at God*? Most of us live as if our life has some kind of purpose or meaning. Most of us believe that suffering and injustice should not happen, and if or when they do, most of us demand some accountability.

C.S. Lewis describes his own conversion from Atheism to Christianity. His starting point was not unlike that expressed by Stephen Fry.

> My argument against God was that the universe seemed so cruel and unjust. But how had I got this idea of *just* and *unjust*? A man does not call a line crooked unless he has some idea of a straight line. What was I comparing this universe with when I called it unjust? If the whole show was bad and senseless from A to Z, so to speak, why did I, who was supposed to be part of the show, find myself in such violent reaction against it? A man feels wet when he falls into water, because man is not a water animal: a fish would not feel wet. Of course I could have given up my idea of justice by saying it was nothing but a private idea of my own. But if I did that, then my argument against God collapsed too—for the argument depended on saying that the world was really unjust, not simply that it did not happen to please my fancies. Thus in the very act of trying to prove that God did not exist—in other words, that the whole of reality was senseless—I found I was forced to assume that one part of reality—namely my idea of justice—was full of sense. Consequently atheism turns out to be too simple.[12]

Some may say that the Christian view of suffering is too difficult to reconcile with our experience of suffering. However, others find that the Atheist view is difficult to reconcile with our experience. So where do we go from here?

Collaboration

I remember sitting in hospital with a mother whose son had been in for a routine operation, after which it became apparent that he had suffered massive brain damage. At that point we weren't sure if he was blind, deaf or both. We only knew that he was in terrible distress, unable to speak or move as he used to. In her broken English she asked why this had happened. The doctors explained that somehow the boy's brain had been starved of oxygen and so irreparable damage had taken place. That was the scientific answer to her question. That was not really what she meant, so she kept asking, 'Why?' The lawyers told her it was down to hospital negligence, as staff should have spotted his oxygen levels dropping sooner. But still she wanted to know why. She was a Hindu, and her relatives told her it was karma – that she must have done something terrible in a former life. But she simply couldn't accept that God would really punish her and her son for something she could not even remember doing. If Dawkins had been in the room that day I doubt that he would have been able to repeat to her face his brutal line that there simply was no rhyme or reason.

And to be honest, I couldn't tell her either that I believed that the world got messed up thousands of years ago and bad things will happen until God wraps up the universe as we know it. I couldn't tell her that one day it would all be put right, and expect her to be happy with that answer. I could, however, give her words to express her pain and frustration to God as she struggled with life and faith and the issues of justice and suffering during that critical time.

When people ask the question 'why?' in situations like these they find themselves standing at the border where their day-to-day understanding of life meets the reality of suffering, between the world as we know it and the world as we would want it to be. In my experience this is as true for Atheists as it is for Christians. It is an admission that our narrative of the universe does not fully make sense. 'Why?' is a metaphysical question – an existential question. Claiming ignorance and preaching indifference cannot calm our indignation. We need a bigger story, but a bigger story is hard to grasp.

As we have seen in previous chapters, in the middle of true crises Atheists and Christians are often able to work very effectively together. Side by side we can express our doubts and frustrations. We can have conversations that matter about the big questions in life. We can work together to alleviate suffering in all its forms. As I spent time with the Hindu family in hospital over the following weeks, all of us were able to express doubts about what we believed, to wonder about the validity of our different faiths. At the same time we were able to pray together, to comfort one another, to share intimacy that was meaningful and significant. In the middle of the darkest distress were moments of deepest love. We may not have agreed on the answers, but, critically, we could agree on the questions.

There is a real challenge in facing up to the question of suffering both for Christians and Atheists.

For Christians, the question means we must check whether our faith is truly robust enough to handle the realities of suffering in our lives and in our world. Some Christians live with an expectation that because of their belief in Jesus they will be protected from the troubles of this world. The Bible offers a very different picture. The Christ that Christians follow did not have a life immune from suffering. Becoming a Christian is not an escape from difficulties; in fact, allegiance to Jesus may lead to its own problems and suffering, especially as we draw alongside other people in need around the world.

For Atheists, the challenge of suffering is the same but from another direction – to check whether our worldview is robust enough to handle the realities of suffering in our lives and in our world. To what extent is our personal response to suffering consistent with Atheism? Does compassionate concern for others square with a universe that responds with 'cold pitiless indifference'? Do we end up asking the question, 'Why?' when suffering comes knocking in the lives of those we know and love?

Only recently two women came to my door battling the raw reality of these questions. They spoke in hushed tones as they explained they had come on behalf of their sister who had been my next-door neighbour for over ten years. It was clear they did not have good news to share, and were struggling to find the words to express what had happened just a few days earlier while I had been on holiday with my family. Their brother-in-law had contracted the flu, which had turned into a cough, then into pneumonia, then sepsis. Despite the huge amount of antibiotics the hospital pumped into him, all his vital organs shut down and he died. He was only forty-seven years old. His wife was in a state of shock and the whole family was facing the trauma of this unexpected bereavement.

There are no words to express how shocked, sorry and sad I was – not only for their loss of a loved family member, but also for my loss of a neighbour and the stark reminder that life is so very fragile. I tried my best to convey my genuine condolences and they invited me to the funeral. In fact, the two women also invited me to the traditional Hindu prayer ceremonies immediately preceding the funeral.

As they left, I had to think long and hard about how I could pay my respects. I had grown up with the challenge of that old song: 'When I needed a neighbour were you there?' and I knew I had to be there at the Hindu prayer ceremonies despite my very different beliefs. I wanted to do whatever it took to be sympathetic and practically helpful. But that song also asserts: 'The creed and the colour and the name don't matter.' That is wrong. Colour, creed and identity do matter. That is why my neighbours, in their suffering, had called a Hindu priest to help them express their grief at this most significant of occasions. And that is why as a Christian, I cannot with conscience pray to Vishnu. That is why my other immediate neighbours – Greek Orthodox and Atheist – would also be unable to join in the chanting. But we can join together to pay our respects, to pray or reflect in silence, to help practically in the days and months ahead. We have more in common than we think, and nowhere is that more obvious than when faced with our common suffering.

Questions

Why do you think the problem of suffering has been such a battle-ground for Christian and Atheist debate?

What are the main differences in the ways that Christians and Atheists understand suffering?

What are the positive and negative things that we can learn from the high-profile cases about people of faith in caring professions losing their jobs because of crossing professional boundaries?

What could the principle of reciprocity mean in your approach to people who have very different core beliefs to you?

How would you console someone who was going through tragedy?

Conclusion

It felt like trespassing on holy ground. I found myself standing on the steps of the Lincoln Memorial, looking out across the water of the reflecting pool towards the striking Washington monument. Apart from a couple of tourists with selfie sticks and the odd school group being shown around the sights, it was relatively empty on that crisp January afternoon. The only evidence that something world-changing had happened here were the four words etched into the stone steps: 'I have a dream'.

This is a beautiful, hushed part of Washington DC, close to the river and far away from the shops, hotels, museums and government buildings that otherwise crowd the centre of America's capital city. In the stillness, I tried to imagine that sunny day when Martin Luther King Junior addressed a crowd of a quarter of a million people gathered to hear what was to become arguably the most famous speech of the twentieth century. With television and radio coverage, King's dream echoed around the world, not only that day but over and again for the following five decades and beyond. And yet, as I stood at the steps of the Memorial, King's dream for a racially integrated America seemed paradoxically both closer and further away than when he shared it with the world. America had had its first black president, and yet racially motivated violence and discrimination were on the increase.

I would love to see Luther King's dream fully realised, but while we work together for a more racially integrated and diverse society I wonder whether there is another rift we need to seek to heal.

With apologies to Martin Luther King, I wonder if we might dream another dream together:

> I have a dream that we will believe the best about each other, even when we don't believe the same as each other.
>
> I have a dream that we will be able to talk honestly and openly about our beliefs, and listen attentively to the valid questions and struggles other people have with our beliefs.
>
> I have a dream that we will aspire above mere tolerance of one another, and towards a love that embraces the value, dignity and worth of each person, a love that is intolerant of abuse, denigration, exclusion and incitement to violence.
>
> I have a dream that whatever our moral framework, we will share virtues of hospitality, reciprocity, generosity and compassion, and that when it comes to doing good, we will all strive to be doing better.
>
> I have a dream that we will work together to create a society where freedom, independence and equality are enjoyed, where those who seek the common good discover happiness greater than their own.
>
> I have a dream that we will be both open-minded and discerning, where equality and free speech can flourish, where there is persuasion but never pressure, mission but never manipulation, conversation but never compulsion, disagreement but never disrespect.
>
> I have a dream that our sacred texts will be respected and

debated both by those who hold them to be true, and by those who do not, to mutual benefit.

I have a dream that we will work together to resolve conflicts and make peace, whether in our homes, communities, towns or nations.

I have a dream that, motivated by our common mortality, we will build a world safe for diversity, because although we may not all believe in life after death, we all believe in life before death.

I have a dream that the inequality of suffering will challenge us to equality in solidarity, working together to bring love, hope, freedom and justice.

I have a dream that together we will forge forwards on our exciting quest for truth and peace – for ourselves, in our relationships and for the sake of our communities.

Acknowledgements

This book is about having better conversations and this book is better because of conversations that I have had with friends and colleagues, Atheists and Christians, philosophers and theologians, believers and sceptics, scientists and artists, social workers and politicians, journalists and church leaders.

I am particularly grateful for conversation, collaboration and constructive criticism about this book from Arlen Anderson, Jonathan Brandt, Ed Brooks, Anthony David, Max Davie, Isabel Hardman, Katie Harrison, Steve Holmes, Andy Lyon, Ian Metcalfe, Theron Pummer, Prof. Michael Ruse, Nick Spencer, Tim Walker, Miriam Kandiah and the team at Home for Good.

Notes

Introduction

1. For the purpose of equality and respect, throughout this book I capitalise 'Atheism' just as I capitalise 'Christianity'. I also capitalise the noun 'Atheist' as I would 'Christian'. The only exceptions to this are when the terms are quoted from other sources, where I have not changed the syntax.
2. http://www.pewresearch.org/fact-tank/2015/06/22/what-is-each-countrys-second-largest-religious-group/.
3. Johnson, T.M. (2015), 'Christianity 2015: Religious Diversity and Personal Contact', *International Bulletin of Mission Research* 39(1) (January), pp. 28–29.
4. Ibid. According to the WIN/Gallup poll of 2015, just over one in ten (11 per cent) consider themselves 'convinced atheists'. The sample size for this study concerning religious beliefs was 63,898 people from 65 countries across the globe; www.gallup-international.bg/en/Publications/2015/223-Losing-Our-Religion-Two-Thirds-of-People-Still-Claim-to-Be-Religious. Finding reliable statistics for Atheism is notoriously difficult for a variety of reasons, including differing definitions of the God that Atheists don't believe in. See, for example, Zuckerman, P. (2006),

'Atheism: Contemporary Numbers and Patterns', in M. Martin (ed.), *The Cambridge Companion to Atheism* (Cambridge Companions to Philosophy), pp. 47–66.

5. http://www.pewresearch.org/fact-tank/2016/09/14/the-factors-driving-the-growth-of-religious-nones-in-the-u-s/.

6. Martin, M. (2006), 'General Introduction', in Martin (ed.), *The Cambridge Companion to Atheism*, p. 1. Although Gavin Hyman points out: '[A]theism defines itself in terms of that which it is denying. From this it follows that if definitions and understandings of God change and vary, so too our definitions and understandings of atheism will change and vary. This further means that there will be as many varieties of atheism as there are varieties of theism.' Hyman, G. (2006), 'Atheism in Modern History', in Martin (ed.), *The Cambridge Companion to Atheism*, pp. 28–29.

7. Religious trends commentator Molly Wall argues: 'generally speaking, the world is becoming more religious, and that is because the world's largest historical non-religious populations (former Communist countries, especially China) are becoming more religious. Non-religious populations are in decline there, and overall global figures reflect that change.' From a personal interview.

8. Note, I am not here equating humanism and Atheism. As Spencer and Ritchie have so convincingly argued, contemporary humanism owes much of its origins to Christian humanism and, indeed, Catholic humanism is still an important movement. See Spencer, N. and Ritchie, A. (2014), *The Case for Christian Humanism*, Theos Report.

Chapter 1

1. Justin Martyr (*c.* AD 100–165), *First Apology, the Second Apology, Dialogue with Trypho, Exhortation to the Greeks,*

Discourse to the Greeks, the Monarchy of the Rule of God, Catholic University of America Press, 2014, pp. 38–39.

2. See, for example, Plato's extensive discussion of the proper treatment of the impious in Book X of *The Laws*. Plato, *The Laws of Plato*, ed. Thomas L. Pangle, New York: Basic Books, 1980, pp. 280–311.

3. Stanley, R.F. (1983), *An Introduction to Plato's Laws*, Indianapolis: Hackett Publishing, p. 167.

4. Gey, S. (2006), 'Atheism and the Freedom of Religion', in Martin (ed.), *The Cambridge Companion to Atheism*, Cambridge University Press, p. 252.

5. Ibid. Denying the immortality of the soul 'has degraded the sublimity of his own soul to the base level of a beast's wretched body. Still less will they count him as one of their citizens, since he would openly despise all the laws and customs of society, if not prevented by fear.' Thomas More, *Utopia*, ed. George M. Logan and Robert M. Adams, Cambridge: Cambridge University Press, 1975, p. 95.

6. http://www.libdems.org.uk/liberal-democrat-leader-tim-farron-resigns (accessed 10 July 2017).

7. Kuo, M. (2017), 'Consciously Combating Unconscious Bias, *Science*, http://www.sciencemag.org/careers/2017/01/consciously-combating-unconscious-bias.

8. *Unconscious Bias and Higher Education*, Equality Challenge Unit, September 2013.

9. Equalities Act 2010. The eight protected categories are: age; disability; gender reassignment; pregnancy and maternity; race; religion or belief; sex; and sexual orientation.

10. See also Groeschel, C. (2010), *The Christian Atheist: Believing in God but living as if he doesn't exist*, Grand Rapids, MI: Zondervan.

11. Hobson, T. (2017), *God Created Humanism*, London: SPCK, pp. 2–7.

12. Lewis, C.S., 'They Asked for a Paper', in *Is Theology Poetry?*, London: Geoffrey Bles, 1962, pp. 164–165.

13. Matthew 7:24–27.

14. Nietzsche, F. (1882), *The Gay Science*, ed. Walter Kaufmann (1974), London: Vintage, pp. 181–182.

15. Ibid., p. 182.

16. https://www.simplypsychology.org/asch-conformity.html.

17. The Epistle to Diognetus is an anonymous letter from the second century. Cited in Lake, K. (ed.) (1912), *The Apostolic Fathers*, Vol. 2, Cambridge: Cambridge University Press, pp. 359–361.

18. Apple Computer, Inc.

19. Including the All-Party Parliamentary Group for International Freedom of Religion, the APPG on Religious Education and the APPG for Christians in Parliament.

20. All-Party Parliamentary Group for International Freedom of Religion or Belief and the Asylum Advocacy Group (2016), p. 5.

21. All-Party Parliamentary Group for Christians in Parliament (2012), 'Clearing the Ground', p. 6.

22. All-Party Parliamentary Group on Religious Education (2016), 'Improving Religious Literacy: A Contribution to the Debate', p. 32 (http://www.reonline). The All-Party Parliamentary Group on Religious Education noted that: 'Despite the training provided by the Civil Service and in other areas of the public sector, some respondents to our consultation perceived a lack of religious literacy among civil servants and public sector workers more widely, which is negatively affecting their ability to engage with faith groups and communities effectively. This may suggest that

the available religious literacy training is not sufficient in its design or depth (particularly if it is served within equality and diversity training); or that the uptake of such courses is not high enough to produce a significant improvement in the religious literacy of civil servants and others in the public sector.'

23. Harari, Y. (2015), *Sapiens: A brief history of humankind*, London: Vintage, p. 31.

24. Pascal, B. (1958), *Pensées*, with an introduction by T.S. Eliot, translated by Hegerson, J. and Sutherland, J., London: Dutton paperback edition, p. 68.

Chapter 2

1. This is a quote from an original article Richard Dawkins published on his personal website: https://richard-dawkins.net/2015/02/ dont-force-your-religious-opinions-on-your-children/.

2. Stedman, R. (2017), *31 Surprising Reasons to Believe in God*, Harvest House, p. 144.

3. *The Late Show with Stephen Colbert*, CBS, Wednesday 1 February 2017, Television.

4. Dawkins, R. (2006), *The God Delusion*, London: Black Swan Books, p. 74.

5. http://www.telegraph.co.uk/culture/tvan-dradio/8448250/ Christopher-Hitchens-most-provocative-quotes.html.

6. Dawkins, R. (1994), 'Lions 10, Christians Nil', *The Nullafidian* 1(8), quoted in McGrath, A. (2005), *Dawkins' God: Genes, memes, and the meaning of life*, Oxford: Wiley & Blackwell, p. 84.

7. Mencken, H. (1922), 'Types of Men', *Prejudices: Third series*, Volume 3, New York: A.A. Knopf, p. 267.

8. John 14:11.

9. For an account of the historical evidence for the Christian faith, see Strobel, L. (1994), *The Case for Christ*, Grand Rapids, Zondervan; Burridge, R. (2004), *What are the Gospels: A comparison with Graeco-Roman biography* (Biblical Resource), Grand Rapids, MI: Eerdmans.

10. This is what philosophers of science would describe as falsifiability.

11. John 20:30.

12. Hesselgrave, D.J. (1991), *Communicating Christ Cross-culturally: An introduction to missionary communication*, 2nd edition, Grand Rapids, MI: Zondervan, pp. 364–365.

13. 'Faith cannot move mountains (though generations of children are solemnly told the contrary and believe it). But it is capable of driving people to such dangerous folly that faith seems to me to qualify as a kind of mental illness. It leads people to believe in whatever it is so strongly that in extreme cases they are prepared to kill and to die for it without the need for further justification.' Dawkins, R. (1989), *The Selfish Gene*, Oxford: OUP, p. 198.

14. See Kristeva, J. (2009), *The Incredible Need to Believe*, New York: Columbia University Press, p. 3 cited in McGrath, A. (2016), *Mere Apologetics*, London: SPCK, p. 76.

15. McGrath, *Dawkins' God*, p. 77.

16. Newbigin, L. (1989), *The Gospel in a Pluralist Society*, London: SPCK, p. 48.

17. Dawkins, R. (2006), *The God Delusion*. London: Black Swan Books, p. 75.

18. Ibid., p. 77.

19. http://www.slate.com/articles/health_and_science/science/2017/04/here_s_why_people_saw_the_dress_differently.html.

20. 1 Peter 3:15.
21. Newbigin, L. (1991), *Proper Confidence*, Grand Rapids, MI: Eerdmans.
22. Interestingly, Richard Dawkins, Eddie Izzard and Christopher Hitchens point to childhood decisions they made to become Atheists, yet Dawkins, for example, is very critical of any form of religious education for children, which he sees as a form of abuse. He both elevates his own ability to make rational and informed decisions in childhood and dismisses children's discernment, which seems at least inconsistent and at worst the height of arrogance.
23. https://blogs.spectator.co.uk/2017/09/can-leading-politi-cians-get-away-with-opposing-abortion-and-gay-rights/.

Chapter 3

1. See http://www.secularism.org.uk/faith-schools.html.
2. http://www.dailymail.co.uk/debate/article-2609924/This-new-breed-militant-atheists-intolerant-religious-fundamentalists.html. Or, see also, Hedges, C. (2008), *I Don't Believe in Atheists: The dangerous rise of the secular fundamentalist*, Oxford: Continuum.
3. Kinnaman, D. and Lyons, G. (2007), *unChristian: What a new generation really thinks about Christianity . . . and why it matters*, Grand Rapids, MI: Baker Books, p. 28.
4. Based on a survey sample of 867 young people, from that total, researchers recorded responses from 440 non-Christians and 305 churchgoers. From those outside of the Church, their perceptions of the Church were as follows: anti-homosexual (91%), judgemental (87%) and hypocritical (85%).
5. McKitterick, A. (2003), 'Review of *Why the West Hates*

the Rest', *Third Way* (September), p. 31; see also Pearse, M. (2003), *Why the Rest Hate the West*, London: SPCK.

6. See also Buckle, J., Hurst, G., Parkinson, J., McAvoy, C. and Samuel, H. (2013), 'Dismissed Doctor Who Refused to Refrain from Using Christian References Was Not a Victim of Religious Discrimination', *Employers' Law* 7–9. I am not arguing that the cases were justified or otherwise, just that they incensed certain Christian groups, leading them to take further legal action.

7. Parliamentary Assembly of the Council of Europe debate on 29 January 2015 (8th Sitting) (see Doc. 13660, report of the Committee on Equality and Non-Discrimination, rapporteur: Mr Valeriu Ghiletchi). Text adopted by the Assembly on 29 January 2015 (8th Sitting).

8. The National Secular Society talk about putting 'an end to faith' in schools. See http://www.secularism.org.uk/faith-schools.html.

9. https://humanisthistory.blog/2014/01/06/getting-angry-with-bbcs-thought-for-the-day/. See also Ferguson, D. (2004), *Church, State and Civil Society*, Cambridge: Cambridge University Press, p. 2.

10. https://humanisthistory.blog/2014/01/06/getting-angry-with-bbcs-thought-for-the-day/

11. *Freedom of Thought 2014: A global report on discrimination against humanists, atheists, and the non-religious; their human rights and legal status*, was created by the International Humanist and Ethical Union (IHEU), pp. 452ff.

12. Ibid., p. 208.

13. Gey, S. (2006), 'Atheism and the Freedom of Religion', in M. Martin (ed.), *The Cambridge Companion to Atheism*, Cambridge: Cambridge University Press, p. 251.

14. Inazu, J.D. (2016), *Confident Pluralism: Surviving and*

thriving through deep difference, Chicago: University of Chicago Press (Kindle edition), location 1400.

15. George, R.P., posted on Facebook. Used with permission.

16. Twain, M. (1871), *The Innocents Abroad, Or, The New Pilgrims' Progress: Being some account of the steamship* Quaker City's *pleasure excursion to europe and the Holy Land: with descriptions of countries, nations, incidents and adventures, as they appeared to the author*, American Publishing Company, p. 650.

17. In the academic world this is why there was a prevalence of readings from different 'locations'. For example, you would hear about a feminist reading of a text or a non-Western reading of an issue. It was understood that the perspective that we come from shapes our approach to all that we see. For an exploration of this theme see Carroll, R. (1998), 'Poststructuralist Approaches: New Historicism and Postmodernism', in J. Barton (ed.), *The Cambridge Companion to Biblical Interpretation*, Cambridge: Cambridge University Press, p. 50.

18. https://www.theguardian.com/education/2016/may/05/ boris-tatchell-greer-were-they-actually-no-platformed; and see a fascinating discussion of the theme of 'no platforming' from a South African race context in Meyerson, Denise (1990), 'No Platform for Racists: What Should the View of Those on the Left Be', *South African Journal on Human Rights* 6(3), pp. 394–398.

19. Popper, K. (1945), *The Open Society and Its Enemies*, London: Routledge, p. 265.

20. Luke 11:46.

21. 1 Corinthians 13:4–7.

22. http://www.ohchr.org/EN/UDHR/Documents/UDHR_ Translations/eng.pdf.

23. Inazu, J.D. (2016), *Confident Pluralism: Surviving and thriving through deep difference*, Chicago: University of Chicago Press, (Kindle edition), location 1515.
24. http://www.latimes.com/la-op-flynt20may20-story.html.

Chapter 4

1. See Tomlins, S. and Bullivant, S. (2016), *The Atheist Bus Campaign: Global manifestations and responses*, Leiden: Brill, p. 379. But it must be noted that Gates's wife and cofounder of their foundation, Melinda, is a Catholic and recently Gates has started to make intimations that he may be agnostic. See Gates, B. (2014), 'Bill Gates: The Rolling Stone Interview', *Rolling Stone*, 27 March 2014.
2. Mother Teresa, cited in *Indian and Foreign Review* 21 (1983), p. 213.
3. Dostoyevsky, F. (1958), *The Brothers Karamazov*, translated with an introduction by David Magashack, London: Penguin Classics, p. 696.
4. http://www.independent.co.uk/news/world/americas/bill-gates-why-do-we-care-more-about-baldness-than-malaria-8536988.html.
5. http://library.fora.tv/2007/10/11/Christopher_Hitchens_Debates_Alister_McGrath (one hour and eight minutes in).
6. In its own internal report the BBC Trust challenged the 'see-saw approach' to balance as being inadequate. *From Seesaw to Wagon Wheel: Safeguarding impartiality in the 21st century*, The BBC Trust (2007), p. 36.
7. Matthew 22:37–39.
8. Cited in Maggay, M.P. (2011), *Transforming Society*, Eugene, Oregon: Wipf and Stock Publishers, p. iii.
9. There is also the tricky theological problem that if something is good independently of God then God is somehow

less, as he is under the authority of something called 'morality', which determines what he does.

10. This is a form of philosophical nihilism.

11. This is the way that Herbert Spencer's Social Darwinism came to be understood as 'an apology for some of the most vile social systems that humankind has ever known'. See Ruse, M. (2009), *Philosophy After Darwin: Classic and contemporary readings*, Princeton, NJ: Princeton University Press, p. 492.

12. Dawkins, R. (2006), *The God Delusion*, London: Black Swan, p. 247.

13. Dawkins, R. (1991), 'Growing Up in the Universe', The Royal Institute Christmas Lectures, London, BBC Television.

14. Dawkins, R. (1991), Royal Institute Christmas Lecture, 'The Ultraviolet Garden' (Lecture number 4). Cited in Ramachandra, V. (2008), *Subverting Global Myths: Theology and the public issues shaping our world*, London: SPCK, p. 187.

15. Dawkins, *The God Delusion*, p. 253.

16. That commentator described Harris's approach as 'reheated utilitarianism with wellbeing in place of pleasure'.

17. This is not an exhaustive list; for example, we have not mentioned deontological ethics. Kant's 'categorical imperative', for instance, argued that an action is moral if it can be universalised. But this idea is problematic, as if you are allowing Jewish people to find refuge in your basement and the Nazis are at the door, you could not lie because lying is not a universal social good.

18. Sandel, M.J. (2009), *Justice: What's the right thing to do?*, London: Penguin, pp. 35–36.

19. Ibid.

20. Harris, S. (2006), *The End of Faith*, p. 181, cited in Glass, D. (2012), *Atheism's New Clothes*, p. 212.
21. http://iheu.org/humanism/the-amsterdam-declaration/.
22. Ibid.
23. Pinker, S. (2012), *The Better Angels of Our Nature: Why violence has declined*, London: Penguin.
24. In Chapter 10 we will further explore some reasons for this common ground.
25. Parris, M. (2008), 'As an atheist, I truly believe Africa needs God', *The Times*, 27 December 2008.

Chapter 5

1. Cited in Fitzpatrick, V. (1989), *H.L. Mencken*, Mercer University Press, Macon: GA, p. 37. Mencken was specifically referring to the influence of the sixteenth-century Protestant group known as the Puritans, but sadly his comment has contemporary relevance.
2. Originally the poem 'Invictus' did not have a name; it was simply labelled 'To R.T.H.B'. See Henley, W.E. (1893), *A Book of Verses* (4th edition), New York: Charles Scribner and Sons, p. 56.
3. 'Religion is the sigh of the oppressed creature, the heart of a heartless world, just as it is the spirit of a spiritless situation. It is the opium of the people.' From an essay by Marx, 'A Contribution to the Critique of Hegel's Philosophy of Right' published in 1844. It was first published in *Deutsch-Französische Jahrbücher*.
4. http://www.huffingtonpost.co.uk/2016/02/02/office-for-national-statistics-well-being-data_n_9138076.html.
5. http://www.patheos.com/blogs/progressivesecularhumanist/2016/03/report-worlds-happiest-countries-are-also-least-religious/.

6. http://worldhappiness.report.

7. Ibid.

8. https://www.dailytrust.com.ng/news/columns/can-happiness-really-be-measured/139302.html.

9. US Declaration of Independence (1776).

10. See an article on the spiritual needs of looked-after children in Barratt, C. (2008), 'Supporting the Religious and Spiritual Needs of Looked-after and Accommodated Children in Scotland', *Scottish Journal of Residential Child Care* 8(1) (February/March 2009), pp. 38–50.

11. http://www.worldreligionnews.com/religion-news/atheism/richard-dawkins-still-says-religion-is-a-force-of-evil-even-after-stroke.

12. Matthew 13:44–46.

13. Frankl, V.E. (1992), *Man's Search for Meaning: An introduction to logo therapy* (4th edition), Boston: Beacon Press, p. 13.

14. Becker, B., cited in Keller, T. (2014), *Encounters with Jesus: Unexpected answers to life's biggest questions*, London: Hodder, p. 28.

15. Layard, R. (2011), *Happiness: Lessons from a new science* (2nd edition), London: Penguin.

16. US Declaration of Independence (1776).

17. Matthew 5:3–11 (author's paraphrase).

18. Unlike Marx's dismissal of religion as an opiate providing pain relief and illusory visions that prevented genuine transformational engagement in changing their circumstance. Marx, K. (1976), Introduction to *A Contribution to the Critique of Hegel's Philosophy of Right*, Collected Works, Vol. 3, New York. 'The abolition of religion as the illusory happiness of the people is the demand for their real happiness. To call on them to give up their illusions about their

condition is to call on them to give up a condition that requires illusions. The criticism of religion is, therefore, in embryo, the criticism of that vale of tears of which religion is the halo.'

19. Santi, J. (2015), The Secret to Happiness is Helping Others, *Time Magazine* (October); http://time.com/4070299/secret-to-happiness/.

20. See Gunderman, R.B. (2009), *We Make a Life by What We Give*, Bloomington: Indiana University Press.

21. Matthew 25:21 and 23.

22. For example, Layard's work has introduced happiness and well-being measures into the Organization for Economic Cooperation and Development (OECD) and the Office for National Statistics. See OECD well-being measures: http://www.oecdbetterlifeindex.org/ and 'Guidelines on Measuring Subjective Well-being', published in 2013: http://www.oecd.org/statistics/guidelines-on-measuring-subjective-well-being.htm.

23. See Layard, *Happiness*, pp. 133ff.

Chapter 6

1. Newbigin, L. (1989), *The Gospel in a Pluralist Society*, London: SPCK, p. 14.

2. Saxe, J.G., in Felleman, H. (1936), *The Best loved Poems of the American People*, New York: Doubleday, pp. 521–522.

3. Baggini, J. (2003), *Atheism: A very short introduction*, Oxford: OUP, p. 89.

4. According to Oxford University's own student-run newspaper, the *Cherwell*.

5. https://www.standard.co.uk/news/education/oxford-university-students-reprimanded-after-banning-christian-union-from-freshers-fair-a3654711.html.

6. See Yancey, G. (2015), *Hostile Environment: Understanding and responding to anti-Christian bias*, Downers Grove, IL: InterVarsity Press.

7. http://digitalcommons.georgefox.edu/cgi/viewcontent.cgi?article=1476&context=ree.

8. US library of congress; http://countrystudies.us/albania/57.htm.

9. As Atheist Julian Baggini laments: 'What happened in Soviet Russia is one of the reasons why I personally dislike militant atheism. When I heard someone recently say that they really thought religious belief was some kind of mental illness and they looked forward to a time when religious believers would be treated, I could see an example of how militant atheism can lead to totalitarian oppression.' Baggini, *Atheism*, p. 88.

10. 1 Timothy 2:2.

11. McGrath, A. (2007), *The Dawkins Delusion: Atheist fundamentalism and the denial of the divine*, London: SPCK, p. 23.

12. See Frisk, L. (2014), 'The Practice of Mindfulness: From Buddhism to Secular Mainstream in a Post-secular Society', *Scripta Instituti Donneriani Aboensis* 24(1) (January), pp. 48–61. Also Plank, K. (2011), *Insikt och närvaro. Akademiska kontemplationer kring buddhism, meditation och mindfulness*, Göteborg and Stockholm: Makadam förlag.

13. http://www.dailymail.co.uk/news/article-1237204/Christian-teacher-lost-job-told-praying-sick-girl-bullying.html.

14. It is possible that Voltaire himself never uttered this memorable phrase but rather that this is a statement crafted by Evelyn Beatrice Hall in her 1906 work titled *The Friends of Voltaire*. Hall's words memorably and gracefully

reflected her conception of Voltaire's viewpoint; https://quoteinvestigator.com/2015/06/01/defend-say/.

15. Rosenthal made this comment on the *New York Times* editorial blog: http://www.nytimes.com/2007/09/17/business/media/24askthetimes.html.

16. This is a quotation that Orwell wrote in 1944 but that remained unpublished until 1972. Orwell, G. (1972), 'The Freedom of the Press', *Times Literary Supplement*, 15 September.

17. UN General Assembly (1948), *Universal Declaration of Human Rights* (217 [III] A), Paris Article 19; Article 18.

18. https://www.youtube.com/watch?v=6md638smQd8.

19. http://www.independent.co.uk/voices/christianity-children-confirmation-schooling-atheist-parenting-a7627086.html.

Chapter 7

1. See Bragg, M. (2011), *The Book of Books: The radical impact of the King James Bible 1611–2011*, London: Sceptre.

2. https://www.gov.uk/government/news/prime-ministers-king-james-bible-speech.

3. Dawkins, R. (2006), *The God Delusion*, London: Black Swan, p. 385.

4. Eagleton, T. (2009), *Reason, Faith, and Revolution: Reflections on the God debate*, Newhaven, CT: Yale University Press, p. xi.

5. Dawkins, *The God Delusion*, p. 51.

6. John 3:16.

7. Exodus 21:20–21.

8. Dennett, D.C. (1995), *Darwin's Dangerous Idea*, London: Penguin Books, p. 17.

9. Sam Harris (2006), *Letter to a Christian Nation*, New York: Alfred A. Knopf, p. 14.

10. Philemon 1:16.

11. Galatians 3:28.

12. In historical context, it may help to know that Leviticus was written at a time when slavery was widely practised throughout the known world, and yet uniquely the intention of the Bible writers was to focus on preventing injustice and inequality. The Jewish form of slavery was therefore very different to that of both the surrounding nations and the indentured labour of the transatlantic slave trade in the fifteenth to the nineteenth centuries. Slavery in ancient Israel was a last resort to stave off destitution. It was a way to keep your land if you hit financial ruin, and a means to provide for your family. It was time-limited, as all debts were to be cancelled after seven years. In the New Testament there is clear teaching that slaves were in fact to be considered as equals before God – the social ordering that divided society was to be dissolved by the common faith.

13. See Bales, K. (2005), *Understanding Global Slavery: A reader*, Berkeley, CA: University of California Press, p. 103.

14. As Richard Dawkins puts it: 'People who do not know the Bible well have been gulled into thinking it is a good guide to morality . . . The surest way to disabuse yourself of this pernicious falsehood is to read the Bible itself'; https://www.theguardian.com/science/2012/may/19/richard-dawkins-king-james-bible.

15. See also Eckblad, B. (2005), *Reading the Bible with the Damned*, Louisville, KY: Westminster John Knox Press.

Chapter 8

1. http://www.independent.co.uk/news/world/middle-east/isis-fighters-throw-another-gay-man-off-a-tower-and-stone-him-to-death-when-he-survives-fall-10084618.html.

2. Dawkins, R. (2001), in http://www.theguardian.com/world/2001/oct/11/afghanistan.terrorism2.

3. This quotation is from a lecture Richard Dawkins gave at the Edinburgh International Science Festival in 1992. It is cited in Ruse, M. (2010), *Science and Spirituality: Making room for faith in the age of science*, Cambridge: Cambridge University Press, p. 3.

4. Isaiah 9:6.

5. Luke 2:14.

6. Matthew 5:9.

7. Rummel, R.J. (1994), *Death by Government*, New Brunswick, NJ: Transaction Publishers, pp. 8–9.

8. Pearse, M. (2007), *Gods of War: Is religion the primary cause of violent conflict?*, Downers Grove, IL: InterVarsity Press, p. 28.

9. Cole, Edward (1987), 'Book Review: *The Harvest of Sorrow: Soviet collectivization and the terror-famine*', *Grand Valley Review* 2(2), Article 19, p. 78.

10. Luke 6:46.

11. Matthew 25:31–46.

12. Matthew 7:16.

13. http://articles.latimes.com/1991-01-21/news/mn-477_1_holy-war.

14. Dawkins, R. (2004), *A Devil's Chaplain*, London: Phoenix, p. 187.

15. Solzhenitsyn, A. (2003), *The Gulag Archipelago, 1918–56*, London: Harvill Press, p. 132.

16. See Pearse, *Gods of War*, p. 30.

17. Pearse. M (2007) p. 30, quoting Keegan, J. (1999), *War and Our World: The Reith Lectures 1998*, London: Pimlico, p. 62.

18. Darwin, C. (1981), *The Descent of Man*, 2 vols, Princeton, NJ: Princeton University Press, 1981, Vol. 1, p. 201.

19. Pearse, M (2007), p. 32, citing Figes, O. (1997), *A People's Tragedy: The Russian Revolution 1891–1924*, London: Pimlico, pp. 524–525.

20. Ibid., p. 35.

21. 1 John 4:18.

22. Project Ploughshares keeps an annual update on global conflict. See http://ploughshares.ca.

23. Source: IISS, *The Military Balance 2015*. All figures in US dollars.

24. Matthew 5:9.

25. https://www.washingtonpost.com/opinions/how-to-take-christ-out-of-christianity/2015/05/01/a4e28430-eebc-11e4-8666-a1d756d0218e_story.html?utm_term=.d0915bf35d69.

26. http://www.reuters.com/article/us-pope-christmas-id USBRE9BN0MA20131225.

27. Reagan, R. (1982), Commencement Address, Eureka College on 9 May 1982.

Chapter 9

1. Cited in Merck, M. (1998), *After Diana: Irreverent elegies*, London: Verso, p. 59.

2. '[T]he mere existence of people with alternative cultural worldviews is fundamentally threatening in that accepting the validity of another conception of reality necessarily undermines confidence in the veracity of one's own cultural worldview.' Cook, C., Cohen, F. and Sheldon, S.

(2015), 'What If They're Right About the Afterlife? Evidence of the Role of Existential Threat on Anti-Atheist Prejudice', *Social Psychological and Personality Science* 6(7), pp. 840–846 (peer-reviewed journal).

3. Ibid.
4. Dawkins, R. (2006), *The God Delusion*, London: Black Swan, p. 360.
5. Ibid.
6. Incremental changes are made in line with cultural mores; for example, in 2014 'a 12A film has historically been allowed to include "infrequent" use of swearwords, but will now be allowed to use them frequently, if appropriate in context', Victoria Coren Mitchell in the *Guardian*. https://www.theguardian.com/commentisfree/2014/jan/19/bbfc-change-film-certs-here-are-mine
7. Dawkins, *The God Delusion*, p. 358.
8. Dawkins, R. (1991), Episode 5: 'The Genesis of Purpose: Growing Up in the Universe'. Available to watch at http://www.rigb.org/christmas-lectures/watch/1991/growing-up-in-the-universe.
9. Baggini, J (2003), *Atheism: A very short introduction*, Oxford: OUP, p. 31.
10. Gray argues: 'The larger problem is that a meme-based Darwinian account of religion is at odds with Dawkins's assault on religion as a type of intellectual error. If Darwinian evolution applies to religion, then religion must have some evolutionary value.' To put it another way, 'If the God gene exists although religion is an illusion it must be conducive to our survival.' https://newrepublic.com/article/119596/appetite-wonder-review-closed-mind-richard-dawkins.
11. Lewis, C.S. (1976), *Mere Christianity*, London: Fontana, p. 188.

12. Baggini, *Atheism*, p. 33.
13. Dawkins, *The God Delusion*, p. 73.
14. 1 Corinthians 15:3–8, 13–15, 17–19.
15. Strobel, L. (2016), *The Case for Christ: A journalist's personal investigation of the evidence for Jesus* (updated edition), Grand Rapids: MI: Zondervan.
16. http://www.christianitytoday.com/ct/2012/june/resurrection-bridge-between-two-worlds.html.
17. This is another example of genetic fallacy.
18. Isaacson, W. (2011), *Steve Jobs*, New York: Simon & Schuster, p. 570.
19. Ibid., p. 571.
20. Jong, J., Ross, R., Philip, T., Chang, S-H., Simons, N. and Halberstadt, J. (2018), 'The Religious Correlates of Death Anxiety: A systematic review and meta-analysis', *Religion, Brain and Behavior* 8(1), pp. 1–17; http://www.tandfonline.com/doi/abs/10.1080/2153599X.2016.1238844?journalCode=rrbb20.
21. Psalm 23:4.
22. http://www.npr.org/2011/12/23/144184623/mumbai-terror-attacks-the-heroes-of-the-taj-hotel.
23. Deshpande, R. and Raina, A. (2011), 'The Ordinary Heroes of the Taj', *Harvard Business Review* (December); https://hbr.org/2011/12/the-ordinary-heroes-of-the-taj.
24. President John F. Kennedy, Commencement Address, American University, June 1963.

Chapter 10

1. The name of the child has been changed to protect their family.
2. *The Meaning of Life with Stephen Fry*, RTÉ ONE, 1 February 2015.

3. https://www.theguardian.com/culture/2017/may/09/irish-police-halt-prosecution-of-stephen-fry-for-blasphemy.

4. The Psalms are full of questions to God asking why terrible things have happened. See, for example, Psalm 73. Also see the book of Job.

5. See http://www.telegraph.co.uk/news/2017/03/30/christian-nurse-sacked-offering-pray-patients-just-showing-compassion/.

6. http://www.telegraph.co.uk/news/religion/6850604/Christian-teacher-sacked-for-offering-to-pray-for-sick-pupil.html.

7. https://www.churchtimes.co.uk/articles/2017/30-june/comment/opinion/grenfell-tower-fire-why-the-parish-church-was-able-to-help-so-quickly.

8. Baggini, J. (2003), *Atheism: A very short introduction*, Oxford: Oxford University Press, p. 102.

9. Solzhenitsyn, A., *The Gulag Archipelago, 1918–56*, London: Harvill Press, p. 312.

10. Free will has become a hotly debated subject, with some Atheists arguing against its existence. See Harris, S. (2012), *Freewill*, New York: Free Press, p. 5, who argues that 'Free will is an illusion. Our wills are simply not of our own making.' It's not the place to debate the existence of free will here, but I did notice that Harris asserts that he is the author of the book and wants to be legally recognised as the author, which would suggest he had agency in writing.

11. Dawkins, R. (1995), *River Out of Eden*, London: Phoenix, pp. 131–132.

12. Lewis, C.S. (2012), *Mere Christianity* (Signature Classics edition), London: Collins, p. 38–39.

13. https://www.theguardian.com/commentisfree/2013/dec/
    24/atheism-richard-dawkins-challenge-beliefs-homeless.
14. Ibid.

HODDER &
STOUGHTON

Hodder & Stoughton is the UK's
leading Christian publisher,
with a wide range of books from
the bestselling authors in the UK
and around the world ranging from
Christian lifestyle and theology to
apologetics, testimony and fiction.
We also publish the world's
most popular Bible translation
in modern English, the New
International Version, renowned
for its accuracy and readability.

Hodderfaith.com   Hodderbibles.co.uk
@HodderFaith   /HodderFaith